Michelle
Remembers

Michelle Remembers

by Michelle Smith
and Lawrence Pazder, M.D.

CONGDON & LATTÈS, INC.
NEW YORK

Library of Congress Cataloguing in Publication Data
Smith, Michelle.
  Michelle remembers.

  1. Satanism—Case studies. 2. Smith, Michelle.
I. Pazder, Lawrence, joint author. II. Title.
BF1548.S65   1980   133.4′22′0926   80-67862
Distributor's ISBN: 0-312-92531-x
Publisher's ISBN: 0-86553-001-7

Published by Congdon & Lattès, Inc.
Empire State Building, New York, N.Y. 10001

Distributed by St. Martin's Press
175 Fifth Avenue, New York, N.Y. 10010

Published simultaneously in Canada by Thomas Nelson & Sons Limited
81 Curlew Drive, Don Mills, Ontario M3A 2R1

Printed in the United States of America by Haddon Craftsmen
Set in 11 pt Avanta
Designed by Bernard Schleifer

FIRST EDITION

*To all who have the heart to hear
the cries of children
and the courage to stand up for them.*

contents

Statement of Pope Paul VI, November 15, 1972   ix

COMMENT OF REMI DE ROO, BISHOP OF THE DIOCESE
  OF VICTORIA, BRITISH COLUMBIA, SEPTEMBER 28, 1977 ix

A NOTE FROM THE PUBLISHER   xi

Foreword   xv

Prologue   xvii

Part I   3

Part II   199

Epilogue   293

Appendices   299

Acknowledgements   309

[*vii*]

STATEMENT OF POPE PAUL VI, NOVEMBER 15, 1972:

Evil is an effective agent, a living spiritual being, perverted and perverting. A terrible reality. One of the greatest needs is defense from the evil which is called the Devil.

The question of the Devil and the influence he can exert on individual persons as well as on communities, whole societies, or events, is very important. It should be studied again.

COMMENT OF REMI DE ROO, BISHOP OF THE DIOCESE OF VICTORIA, BRITISH COLUMBIA, ON SEPTEMBER 28, 1977:

The Church is well aware of the existence of mysterious and evil forces in the world. Each person who has had an experience of evil imagines Satan in a slightly different way, but nobody knows precisely what this force of evil looks like.

I do not question that for Michelle this experience was real. In time we will know how much of it can be validated. It will require prolonged and careful study. In such mysterious matters, hasty conclusions could prove unwise.

It may well be that for people today, to hear this message coming from a five-year-old child is of particular significance.

a note from the publisher

*F*ROM my first meeting with Michelle Smith and Lawrence Pazder, I knew that their book would be not only important but also unusual. I felt that as readers began it they would want information about the authors and the writing of the book.

Dr. Pazder's credentials are impressive. He obtained his M.D. from the University of Alberta in 1961; his diploma in tropical medicine from the University of Liverpool in 1962; and, in 1968, his specialist certificate in psychiatry and his diploma in psychological medicine from McGill University. In 1971 he was made a fellow of Canada's Royal College of Physicians and Surgeons. He is a member of three Canadian professional associations and of the American Psychiatric Association as well. He practiced medicine in West Africa and has participated in medical task forces and health organizations. He has been chairman of the Mental Health Committee of the Health Planning Council for British Columbia. A member of the staff of two hospitals in Victoria, British Columbia—the Royal Jubilee and the Victoria General—he is in private practice with a group of five psychiatrists. His professional papers include a study of the long-term effects of stress upon concentration-camp victims.

Two experienced interviewers journeyed to Victoria and talked to Dr. Pazder's colleagues, to the priests and the bishop who became involved in the case, to doctors who treated Michelle Smith when she was a child, to relatives and friends. From local newspaper, clergy, and police sources they learned that reports of Satanism in Victoria are not infrequent and that Satanism has apparently existed there for many years.

The source material was scrutinized. The many thousands of pages of transcript of the tape recordings that Dr. Pazder and Mrs. Smith made of their psychiatric sessions were read and digested; they became the basis of this book. The tapes themselves were listened to in good measure, and the videotapes made of some of the sessions were viewed. Both the audio and the video are powerfully convincing. It is nearly unthinkable that the protracted agony they record could have been fabricated.

In the course of preparing the book, both doctor and patient were interviewed at great length—taken back over the story again and again. Their account varied only in small, occasional details. Michelle's distress during these retellings, the fresh pain they obviously inflicted on her, seemed to indicate that this was not some fantasy concocted for commercial gain. Indeed, the authors' relentless insistence on adherence to the transcript and on understatement, both in the text and in the presentation of the book (the jacket text, the advertising, and so forth), was hardly the mark of the charlatan.

I first met the authors two years ago and have had much contact with them. During the final stages of the editing of the manuscript, the authors came to New York and for nearly a month lived in my own home—shared meals with my family, sometimes talked long into the night with us. We came to know them well, in a way one does not come to know someone over the phone or in the office. Even my normally skeptical teen-agers found Michelle Smith and Larry Pazder the most decent and modest and genuine of people.

Along with Dr. Pazder and the Church officials who know her so well, I believe that Michelle is not a hysteric, not even a neurotic. She seems as clear as a glass of well water. She appears to be one of those rare people, like Joan of Arc and Bernadette, whose authority and authenticity are such that they can tell you things that would otherwise be laughable—yet you do not laugh, you do not dismiss or forget.

Though the names in the byline are those whose experience the book relates, the book is not written in the first person. It was decided that third person was the best way to convey this story—that since it was two persons' story, Dr. Pazder's as well as Michelle's, an "I" narrator would be awkward and limiting. Writing assistance was provided, but the book is principally the work of Mrs. Smith and Dr. Pazder. Their transcript, which consists purely of their own words, is the fundamental source material. Most important, the conceptualization of the book—its tone, its level, its structure, its emphases—is entirely theirs. Invariably they understood their own book better than any of us who were privileged to work with them.

THOMAS B. CONGDON, JR.

New York
April 22, 1980

foreword

To be with human beings during their struggles and discoveries is an experience that gives much to the psychotherapist. Both Michelle's struggles and her discoveries were of a magnitude far greater than that of most patients, and so were the rewards for me. It was my privilege to witness as she risked the abyss, venturing far beyond her normal memory pool, her imaginings, fantasies, and dreams, to somewhere at the very core of her being. Perhaps it was what Jungians call the "base of the psyche," the meeting ground of our ancestral past and our present, the source of myth and symbol, the juncture of mind and body, heart and soul. Most have touched it only for fleeting moments; Michelle visited it for hundreds of hours. There, acting with the courage that Rollo May says allows us to move in spite of despair, she grappled with the polarities of life and death, love and hate, light and dark, good and evil.

She unearthed and relived fourteen months of her past in astonishing detail. Her deeply buried memories, virtually untouched for twenty-two years, surfaced with a purity that is a phenomenon in itself. What she brought forth provides an understanding of how a child survives, one that seems more profound than modern psychology's emphasis on the effects of victimization. Her achievement—the psychological tenacity of a five-year-old child in the face of sheer madness—will confront and inform many generations.

—Lawrence Padzer, M.D., F.R.C.P.(C)

[*xv*]

prologue

THE tiny, two-passenger elevator lined with red velvet was slowly ascending, carrying Michelle Smith up to the residence of Sergio Cardinal Pignedoli. It was the fifth of February 1978, and she had been in Rome for two weeks, she and her friends, knocking on the door of every Vatican official who would listen, seeking an audience for the shocking yet inspiring story they had brought some ten thousand miles, from the far side of Canada. Crammed into the little elevator with her was Dr. Lawrence Pazder, the psychiatrist who had been the first to hear the story, which had poured forth during a long and agonizing year. Tall, blue-eyed, and tanned even in February, Dr. Pazder took Michelle's hand and squeezed it, as he had so many times before when reassurance was needed.

Two other companions were below, in the cardinal's anteroom, waiting for their turn in the elevator. One was Father Guy Merveille, the elegant, black-browed priest to whom Michelle and Dr. Pazder had turned when it became clear that her experience had ramifications far beyond the bounds of psychiatry. The other was his bishop, Remi De Roo, Roman Catholic bishop of the Diocese of Victoria, British Columbia. Skeptical at first, resistant to Michelle's story, De Roo had become sympathetic to her and impressed by her and had insisted that her experience required study. He had agreed that Father Merveille accompany Michelle to Rome, to bring her story to the attention of the highest Church officials, and he had given the priest a letter of introduction. "Father Merveille," he wrote, "has been entrusted with an important and confidential task, the nature of which I have carefully appraised and of which I hereby approve. I will personally appreciate every consideration afforded to Father Merveille in the pursuit of his task." Eventually, to deal with a matter of protocol, De Roo himself had flown to Rome.

As the elevator rose, Michelle thought back on the year of painful discovery she had gone through in Dr. Pazder's office—and beyond that, twenty-two years beyond that, to the extraordinary, nearly incredible events in her childhood. That was the trouble. Those events were, indeed, nearly incredible. Would the cardinal believe her? Or would he send her away?

The elevator doors rattled open and there, to greet his guests, was Sergio Cardinal Pignedoli, Pro-President of the Secretariat for Non-Christian Religions. He was a short, vigorous man, bald, with a fringe of white around his head, and with expressive features, like those of a veteran character actor. A prominent and powerful Vatican official, he was widely considered to have a good chance of becoming Pope someday. While they waited for Bishop De Roo and Father Guy, Michelle peered into the cardinal's private study. Gorgeous paintings in heavy gold frames. Cases and shelves full of dark-bound books. And photographs everywhere, of the cardinal with the various dignitaries he had dealt with in decades of official travel.

They had been invited for breakfast. Breakfast, it turned out, was tea and almond cookies—*amaretti*—served by nuns. The conversation began as the bishop introduced the case in brief and then asked Michelle to speak for herself. As she spoke she saw the cardinal's mobile face become grave and then angry. "Impossible!" he interrupted. "I know Canada. It is a civilized country. These things could not happen there."

Michelle, taken aback, began to cry. But she did not retreat. She kept talking, insistently conveying to the cardinal the personal odyssey that had first appalled and then persuaded, one by one, the three companions who had come with her from Canada. In time, and after many cups of tea, Cardinal Pignedoli became less irritable than concerned, less grave than absorbed—the change in attitude was clear in his expressions and in his tone of voice as he questioned her. At the end he turned to Bishop De Roo and said: "So this is what you meant. Now I see. You are right. This is serious. This is a matter that will require our most careful attention."

Michelle's heart leapt. She had become well versed in the basics of Vatican procedure, and she knew that when a cardinal expresses such a sentiment, it was as good as done. Three days later Archbishop Domenico Enrici, the papal appointee from the Vatican Secretary of State, called Bishop De Roo to his office adjacent to the Pope's chambers. He asked the bishop to undertake a study of Michelle Smith's testimony.

At last there would be ears to hear the remarkable things Michelle had remembered.

PART I

chapter 1

*V*ICTORIA, the capital of British Columbia, is a jewel of a city, a tidy metropolis on the edge of the Pacific that in its primness seems more English than Canadian. Baskets of flowers hang from its ornate lampposts. Its Parliament Building is outlined with thousands of tiny lights at night, a conceit that would have pleased the good Queen for whom the city was named. Oceangoing yachts tie up in front of the ivy-covered Empress Hotel downtown. Schools of whales frolic offshore. And the air blowing in from the sea is fresh and crisp. Many Canadians consider Victoria a modern Garden of Eden. Not so farfetched a notion—if one recalls that there was a serpent in the Garden of Eden.

On Fort Street in Victoria is the Fort Royal Medical Centre, a four-story building with shops on the first floor and, on the second floor, offices belonging to five psychiatrists. Ten years ago, finding themselves congenial professionally, the five had gotten together to share facilities and insights. A founding member of this group was Lawrence Pazder, who had studied psychiatry at McGill University and was a fellow of the Royal College of Physicians and Surgeons. A handsome man in his early forties, Dr. Pazder was warm, manly, soft-spoken—what people who live elsewhere consider the typical Westerner. He was lithe and athletic, a tennis player and skier, and had earned a brown belt in judo. His hair was brown, beginning to turn silver. On the midsummer day in 1976 when the receptionist of the Fort Royal Medical Centre

[3]

buzzed him to report a call from Dr. John McCracken, there was far less silver than there soon would be.

Dr. McCracken was a general practitioner in Victoria. "I'm calling about Michelle Smith," he told Dr. Pazder. "I've had to hospitalize her. She's having some trouble with bleeding. She had a miscarriage six weeks ago and despite repeated D&Cs and medication, she continues to hemorrhage. Not only that, but her grief over the miscarriage is extremely severe and persistent. I'm beginning to think the problem isn't just physiological but that there's some sort of psychogenic aspect. That's why I called you."

"It sounds pretty upsetting. Did you talk to her about my coming in to see her?" Dr. Pazder asked.

"Yes, I did. In fact, she encouraged me to call. I know about the work you did with her before and I'd be grateful for your opinion."

What neither doctor then knew was that Michelle, the night before, had been moved into the hospital ward in which her mother had died of cancer. Michelle had panicked and had felt she was dying too. The next morning she had asked Dr. McCracken to call Dr. Pazder.

The psychiatrist was shocked when he saw Michelle. A pretty young woman of twenty-seven, with a heart-shaped face, a delicate mouth, and bountiful brown curls, she had been vital and bright the last time he had seen her—four months before, when she and her husband, Doug, had brought some salmon he'd caught to Dr. Pazder and his wife. But now the face was as pale as the pillowcase, and the big brown eyes were full of tears.

She told him then about being in the ward where her mother had died—by now she had been moved again—and she confessed her apprehension about the bleeding. He allowed her to cry, to say what she felt, and at the end of the visit she smiled faintly and told him she supposed she'd survive. When he returned the next day, however, though her color was improved, she still seemed distressed, and after some gentle probing he encouraged her to tell him what was troubling her.

"I had a dream last week," she said, her lips beginning to tremble. It was clear to Dr. Pazder that this was no ordinary dream.

"A bad dream?

"Yes . . . a very bad dream."

"That can be pretty frightening—a really bad dream. Do you want to tell me about it?"

It was ten minutes before she could bring it forth.

"I dreamed that I had an itchy place on my hand . . ."

"Yes?"

"And when I scratched it, all these bugs came out of where I was scratching it! Little spiders, just pouring out of the skin on my hand. It was just—I can't even tell you how it was. It was so terrible."

As a psychiatrist Dr. Pazder had learned how to listen to dreams —to gauge the emotional tone, to pick up the reference points, to discern just how serious the dream was. This one was nightmarish, but it was more than that, it was blatantly symbolic. It connected subconsciously to something very important; he was sure of that. There was perhaps something wrong about the pregnancy and her acceptance of it—there had to be something on that order to produce a dream like this.

"It was really, really frightening," Michelle said earnestly, searching Dr. Pazder's face for any sign that he might think the dream too bizarre or consider her crazy.

"I can hear that it was," Dr. Pazder replied. "Dreams like that have a tremendous force, sometimes. They can be very hard to shake. If it's okay with you, I'd like you to come and see me when you leave the hospital, and we'll spend a little time talking about it. What we need to do is find out what the dream is revealing from the inside. I think that's important."

Michelle readily agreed, clearly relieved to see his concern. She well knew how helpful Dr. Pazder could be. She had first come to him in 1973, while a student at the University of Victoria, impelled by problems that were rooted in her family background and upbringing.

Her grandfather, Cyrus Gilbert,* had left England shortly after the turn of the century. No one knew exactly why. It may have been simply because there was more opportunity in Canada, and he was a younger son. He settled in British Columbia, where he prospered. When Mi-

*Cyrus Gilbert and Jessica and Eric Harding are not real names.

chelle was a schoolgirl, she was aware that her grandfather was a wealthy and important man.

Gilbert was over forty when his daughter Jessica, Michelle's mother, was born. Possessive, domineering, a tyrant, he stifled Jessica, and she rebelled, running off at eighteen to marry the first man who asked her. The marriage, a disaster, lasted only a few months.

Jessica married again after World War II and went to live in Victoria, on Vancouver Island, with her new husband, Eric Harding, a highly successful sales representative. Some ten years older than Jessica, Harding resembled her father in many ways. He had the same kind of virile good looks, and he was every bit as domineering as his father-in-law.

Jessica gave birth to a little girl. The Hardings had wanted a boy and had his name all picked out, Michael Donald Harding. Disappointed, they called the baby Michelle. They often spoke of how much they had hoped she would be a boy. The birth was apparently very disturbing for Jessica. She became emotionally exhausted, and developed medical complications. The child was taken away and lived with the grandparents for the first six months of her life. The strain on the maternal bonds was perhaps very great.

Michelle herself was an active, healthy child with a mind of her own. She had a fresh, natural beauty, a sunny, open nature, an easy smile, and trusting eyes.

Her parents' marriage was a stormy one. There were nights when her father erupted in drunken rages and beat her mother. Michelle used to cower in her bed, frightened that he might kill her mother, feeling that she had to stop him, knowing that she could not. There were long periods when he disappeared from the scene, and Michelle welcomed those times.

During those absences her mother was more loving, no longer sharply impatient. There might be a hug for a skinned knee, a goodnight kiss, perhaps even freshly pressed ribbons for Michelle's stubby braids. And stories. Jessica, when she was at her best, would spend hours telling Michelle about Sleeping Beauty and Cinderella and Hansel and Gretel. Michelle thought she had the best and prettiest mother in the world; as for Jessica, she sometimes seemed more disconcerted than pleased by her little daughter's open admiration.

Michelle attended school in Victoria where she did well, except for her multiplication tables. And there was one small problem: She ate erasers, the headmistress reported. One day Michelle was sent home from school when they discovered she had stolen a whole box of erasers from the supply closet. She could not explain why she had stolen them.

Her world fell apart when she was fourteen. Her mother died quite suddenly of cancer, and her father disappeared, relinquishing custody of Michelle to Jessica's parents. She never saw her father again. Her grandfather sent her away to a Roman Catholic boarding school. As one of the few non-Catholic students, she was not obliged to attend religious studies or chapel. This made her feel like an outsider. Although the nuns were consistently gentle and understanding with her, it was a time of great loneliness. A few months later, her grandmother died, and within the year her two remaining grandparents died. For all intents and purposes, Michelle was alone in the world. When the time came for university, she put herself through with the aid of a scholarship and a number of part-time jobs.

At the university she majored in psychology and, reflecting on her childhood, she began to realize that with a violent, alcoholic father in her past and a passive, somewhat distant mother, she ran the risk of falling into unwholesome patterns and repeating their problems. She wanted to avoid that, to break the cycle, and so she consulted a psychiatrist, Lawrence Pazder. She liked him immediately, partly because he looked nothing like her idea of a psychiatrist. His style was slacks and a sweater, his manner open and friendly, in contrast to the pinstripes and wingtips and careful reserve that characterized many in his profession. And Dr. Pazder liked Michelle. He was impressed by her ability to articulate her problems clearly and genuinely. Rarely had he seen a patient so motivated.

She told him she had a collection of minor problems—fear of airplanes; fear of spiders; fear of being alone. She sensed she had over-idealized her mother and that her grief over her mother's death was disproportionate and still largely unresolved. She wanted to marry and have children, she said, and she didn't want to pass problems on to them.

Doctor and patient set to work, one appointment a week. As they went deeper and deeper into Michelle's background, Dr. Pazder saw how truly horrific her early life had been. Deep psychotherapy was needed, and the endeavor extended over four years. Diligently they worked through the problems. At the end, both of them were pleased with the strides she had made. True, they had never been able to understand why she used to eat erasers, but that hardly seemed to call for further psychotherapy.

During this time Michelle became engaged to Doug Smith, a stalwart and bearded young Viking from Nova Scotia. Dr. Pazder went to their wedding. Later, they sometimes visited socially and talked about the young couple's progress in remodeling a house they had bought near Shawnigan Lake, some thirty miles from Victoria. It was going to be a cedar-and-glass dream house on the edge of the forest, with skylights to frame the moon and the stars. They all spoke of the time when there would be children romping through the house, filling it with laughter.

And now there had been the miscarriage. The bleeding had stopped soon after Dr. Pazder's hospital visits, but deeper wounds seemed to remain. Early in September Michelle once again climbed the steps to the second-floor offices of the Fort Royal Medical Centre. Once again she was greeted by Susan Austin, receptionist for the psychiatric group, and once again was waved toward the door of the familiar office. There it was—all just the same. The gold carpet, the turquoise-plaid sofa, the Danish sidechairs covered with black Naugahyde. At the far end of the room was a thick rubber mat, covered in green burlap, for body-release techniques; if a patient wanted to get angry, he could pound and kick as hard as he wanted without disturbing the customers in the beauty parlor downstairs. There was no desk, just two coffee tables, one of which bore the doctor's telephone and his various folders and papers.

In this visit and the half dozen that followed, Dr. Pazder saw that Michelle did not want to play up the terrible dream, and, taking the cue, he did not emphasize it either. He just let her talk. With her usual openness she described the growing pains of her new marriage. As she talked, he took the opportunity, when it arose, to treat her grief over the miscarriage. Most women who miscarry, he said, fear that it is somehow their own fault—that there is something wrong with them, whereas, he said, 25 percent of babies conceived are in fact lost. After several sessions Michelle seemed to be able to accept this reassurance but at the same time to be in great frustration.

"There's still something bothering me," she said. "I still feel blocked. We talk about the things I *think* are the problems, and then I go home and spend half the night . . . wishing I could. . . . I know there's something I want to tell you, but I don't know what it is!"

Dr. Pazder was surprised. In his previous work with her, Michelle had had the remarkable facility to open up, in an hour's session, to tell him what the problem was, deal with it, and gain ground. But here, something was really troubling her and she couldn't provide a clue.

"I sit up at night wishing I could write you a letter," she continued. "I actually try to write the letter . . . to put it down on paper. . . . I could write so hard that my pencil would rip the paper. But then I look at what I've written and there's nothing there, just slash marks with the pencil."

She suddenly took Dr. Pazder's hand in both of hers and squeezed it desperately hard. He was astounded. Dr. Pazder himself was quite at home with touching; he had been reared in a warm and tactile family, with plenty of hugging and kissing, and in his work he freely offered an arm around a shoulder, if someone seemed to need comforting, or his big warm hand if an anxious patient reached out to him. It was part of his personal and professional style and that of several other members of the group. But Michelle hadn't asked for that type of reassurance during the four years of sessions. Now she was clutching his hand and shaking it.

"I know there's something there," she said, beginning to cry. "And it's important—I know it's important!"

She reminded the doctor of a pressure cooker with a blocked valve. There was high heat underneath it. It was boiling hard. The steam had to burst out, or else the vessel would explode.

"I'm really worried," she said, sobbing now. "I keep wondering what's happening to me. I thought I had resolved things in my life, and now I'm feeling this pressure that is so much worse than any pressure I've ever felt before."

Over the next weeks Dr. Pazder tried everything, but all the normal ways they had worked together were of no value now. The pressure grew more and more intense. Whatever it was, though it was unidentifiable, it was real, he could "read" it, it was *there*. He was stymied. He considered himself a very thorough therapist, not the kind who pats the patient on the back and says, "You're fine," or "Take these pills and you'll feel better." He felt that in the earlier four-year analysis he had dealt with all the issues of any significance. During her therapy, he had been impressed with the unusual detail and consistency of her childhood memories. They had traced all the threads and unraveled all the knots. How could they have missed a matter of such apparent consequence?

There was nothing to do but look again—to review what they had previously covered, to take inventory, to see if they'd missed something. As they did, he listened very carefully to see if anything was triggered. Nothing was triggered. Nothing was of any help at all. And still the incredible, overwhelming pressure to divulge . . .

Then, in mid-October, came the rash—an angry red irritation that spread across Michelle's usually unblemished face. It was like none he had ever seen before, a very specific rash, sharply patterned. There was no explanation for it. But, thought Dr. Pazder, the rash was surely saying something, loud and clear.

"I'll tell you what," he said, realizing that he was about to go farther than he usually did with a patient. He firmly believed that problems should be solved during the office sessions, and that the psychiatrist who allowed a patient to break into his schedule or into his private life was risking the development of an unhealthy manipulation of doctor by patient. But Michelle was different, and her plight was alarming. He told her seriously, "I'll be available. If things get really bad, give me a call. I'll make time for you right away."

That day, three hours after she had left the medical center with tears in her eyes, Michelle found herself down at the waterfront; she was in her car, and it was parked. Across the Juan de Fuca Strait the snow-covered Olympic Range glowed rosily in the sunset.

"What's the matter with me?" She stared at the water without seeing it. "He's trying to help me. I know he is. Why can't I tell him? I want to tell him. It's important. My whole life depends on it. But I don't know what it is I have to tell him."

She put her head down on the steering wheel and cried until she had no more tears. It was dark and cold. Time to drive back to Shawnigan Lake. Doug would be worrying about her. She had better stop to telephone him before leaving Victoria.

Four days later, Dr. Pazder received a call from Michelle. "I was home this morning doing my usual things," she said, "watering my plants, and all of a sudden it was just like something 'fit' inside. The pressure went! And then I knew I was ready."

"That's a relief, Michelle. I want to hear about it."

"I don't know what I'm going to say," she went on, excitement in her voice, "but I know I'll be able to tell you."

Dr. Pazder gave her an appointment that same day. When she arrived, he received still another surprise: She was wearing black, all black—black blouse and black pants. He had never seen her wear black before. He quickly dismissed the thought of asking her about the clothing. That would be pushing it. But it seemed an unmistakable sign to him that something was up. So did her demeanor. She was somber —ready. Her eyes were right there, he thought, and her manner was serious. No small talk. She was like a high diver standing at the edge of the board on tiptoes, just at the moment when everything was in balance, the equipoise before a swift, sure motion. She had somehow gotten over the barrier.

"Do you mind if I lie on the sofa?" she asked.

She had never lain down on the sofa before. It was as if the mere act of sitting would be a distraction for her and that only by lying down could she concentrate.

But Michelle was not ready—not quite yet. She looked straight up at the ceiling, and after a few minutes she began to fidget, the way a child might. Then her eyes grew very wide, just staring. And in her eyes Dr. Pazder saw a look he could only describe as frozen terror. As though she had just seen fifty people murdered.

She said nothing, and neither did he. For twenty minutes she lay there, the look of terror never diminishing. Then her breathing became difficult, short and rasping. Her mouth began to tighten and her lips turned white. At last her eyes closed, and then she started to rub at her eyes and her mouth, as if trying to brush away cobwebs.

Through years of working with people Dr. Pazder had developed his sensitivities to the point where he could "hear" tears in a patient's voice several minutes before the tears started; where he could detect a scream coming long before it came; where he could distinguish the terror that was real—so real one could feel the chill. He was feeling the chill as he looked at Michelle. This was for real.

He guessed that she wasn't going to be able to say anything until she knew how he was going to react. She couldn't take the chance that he wasn't going to take it as seriously as she did. After almost an hour he decided she perhaps needed to come back up out of it, so that she could see his reactions.

"It's okay," he said soothingly. "I can see that something is really, really frightening. That's okay. You can tell me about it. I want to hear it. And I'm really happy that it's close enough so you can talk to me, because you're going to feel better when you do."

Michelle's eyes fluttered and then opened. Dr. Pazder waited until her expression softened, and then he went on gently. "I think it's important that we don't leave this for the next appointment. We can't just leave you like this. Let's see. Tomorrow's Saturday, but that's all right, I don't have much planned. If you can, I think it's very important that we work on this tomorrow."

"Thank God," Michelle whispered. "I was so afraid you wouldn't understand."

At home that evening, Dr. Pazder thought about the session with Michelle. It was unnerving to witness that degree of terror, and for so long. Not that he was afraid for Michelle. The only way people were really helped, he believed, was to allow them to go into their feelings. He welcomed the fact that Michelle was able at least to begin to touch the terror. Most people who are afraid just stay there, locked in fear. Michelle was not only touching it, she was also immersed in it—which in turn told him that there was an immense amount of fear there.

Why? What had caused it? Nothing that they knew from her past could explain it.

He had the strongest sense that he and Michelle were about to embark on something significant. He telephoned her and asked if she minded if he brought his tape recorder the next day. "I don't usually tape my sessions," he said, "but I think that if whatever there is inside you is strong enough to cause that much pressure, we should record it. If you don't feel comfortable with it, we can stop and erase what we've recorded. It's yours, so that would be okay."

"I don't mind the tape recorder," Michelle said.

"Another reason is that I don't think I should be taking notes by hand. I feel I should be totally there with you, completely available to you."

"I'm glad of that. I think I'm going to need you."

"But it's going to be all right, I want you to know that. I'll be with you all the time, hearing every word, every sound, every feeling. It's sort of like going back to a haunted house. You can't go back all alone—because it scared you before, too much, and all you'd have would be the same person you had before—yourself. If you're going back to a haunted house, you've got to have someone you trust go with you, someone you know it's safe with."

"It's safe with you. I feel very safe with you. But it's so horrible. . . ."

"Don't think of that tonight. What's important is that this time, you've got someone to go with. That's what the psychiatric journey is all about."

chapter 2

WHEN Michelle came back the next morning, she seemed very quiet and somewhat apprehensive. She and Dr. Pazder exchanged a few words and then she went over to the couch and lay down. She could not seem to get comfortable at first, but finally she propped one of the pillows behind her back. That seemed to be better. It was as if she needed to have her back protected.

Dr. Pazder moved his chair next to the couch and quietly turned on the tape recorder.

Michelle fidgeted with her fingers and then began talking about a subject familiar to both of them from the therapy years before.

"I was going to try to talk about my weight a bit," she began,* "because up until the last three weeks I'd been able to keep it under control. You know—normal. Just normal eating habits. But the last three weeks, it's compulsive . . . I was thinking last night, I was trying to think about when I first started, you know, gaining weight and things like that. I was thin at the start of Grade 1. Really thin. And by the time I was in Grade 2, I was a blimp. And my mother up until then had really a nice figure."

Dr. Pazder recognized the possibility that some family crisis at that time had triggered a sudden gain in weight. It was common that whole families would abruptly become obese when confronted by a problem

*This dialogue and similar dialogue in this book, as well as the indented material, are taken nearly verbatim from the transcript of the tape recordings made during the fourteen months of psychiatric sessions.

affecting them all. He asked Michelle if she was saying that her mother had become heavier then too.

"Yes, until then she never had a weight problem, ever. When I think about being overweight I just get in knots. It really makes me uptight. So, I thought, 'Well, maybe I'll figure it out sooner or later, right?' I don't know. . . . Somehow it's connected with being small. Like there's something back then that is really bugging me, something that's unresolved. . . . I don't know what to call it, a block or whatever. I don't know what to say about it, it bothers me so much. It makes me feel very nervous. I don't know what to talk about. So many things go through my mind that it's just scattered. . . ."

Michelle had been sighing frequently, Dr. Pazder noticed, and now the pace of her breathing was increasing.

"You see, I hoped . . . this is the most frustrating part of the whole business. See, it's so hard to put into words. It's so hard to tell you how I felt then." Michelle was beginning to cry. "You see, there's something in there to do with being ugly. I was ugly. I was! Oh, I got to put it into words. . . . I don't . . . it's all bits and pieces, like . . . it keeps, I . . . it seems dumb but I can't talk about it." She stopped, then continued.

"Can you come here, please? You don't have to touch me. Not too close. I just want you a little bit closer than you were. I can't talk to you about it. My arms . . . my arms . . . it's like they're moving by themselves . . . and I can't help it!"

"It's all right," Dr. Pazder said. "Let them go, let your arms do whatever they have to do. Don't hold anything back."

"Can you promise me something?" Michelle asked, eyes wide. "Can you promise me that when this is all over, we'll be able to put the pieces together? They feel so far apart. Promise?"

"Yes, I promise. That's why we're doing it."

"Okay," Michelle said, almost in a whisper. "Then I'll tell you as much as I can." She sighed deeply once again. "I have such a hard time to talk. . . ."

"Let it come, as much as you can. Don't judge it, if you can help it. Don't try to make it anything but what it was. Just let it be what it was. Just let yourself go."

"Are you sure I'm not going to die? Are you sure? . . ."

"You'll be okay. I'll be right here. Just try to let yourself go."

Michelle stared in silence at the ceiling for some time. Her eyes were full of fear. At last she closed them, hesitantly, and began to deepen her breathing. It was a very labored breathing, as if she were fighting strongly against something way down inside.

As Dr. Pazder watched, her hands flew up in front of her face, the fingers splayed wide and stiff. Her eyes squeezed almost painfully closed. Her mouth opened round, stretching her white lips thin. She drew a deep, deep breath. And then the terror broke. She screamed. It was a cry so violent that it drove her down into the couch.*

Dr. Pazder sat quietly as Michelle screamed, his hand on her head, waiting.

After twenty-five minutes, the screaming began to ebb. Michelle was shaking uncontrollably, almost convulsively. As the cries died away, he could see that she was struggling to speak. She was straining to get words out. He hoped the struggle would be a kind of birth. Perhaps the screaming had to come first before she could speak. Perhaps the screaming would release her.

> It's . . . it's . . . it's all black. Black. It's black! It's all *black.* No! Oh, please help me. Help me! Oh, help me! *Help me!* [More screaming, which eventually dissolved into agonizing tears.] *Oh, God help me! Oh, God help!* I don't know what to do. I feel so sick. I feel like my heart's going to stop. . . . Oh, I hate this. I'm on this bed. . . . I'm in the air. I'm in the air, and I'm upside down. . . . There's this man and he's turning me around and around!

"Who is the man?" Dr. Pazder asked softly.

"It's . . . Malachi."

*In the next office, Dr. Richards Arnot, one of the four psychiatrists who shared the suite of offices with Dr. Pazder, was moved when Michelle's shrieks came ripping through the walls, walls that had been double-insulated to make them virtually soundproof. "It was a piercing cry of genuine terror," Dr. Arnot told Dr. Pazder later.

What's happening to me? I don't know if it makes any sense.
. . . Oh! God, I hurt. . . . I'm hurting. . . . He's hurting me all
over, and something's really scaring me. His eyes are scaring me.
I can't stand them. They look crazy. No! Take them away. He's
hurting my arms. Ow. Ow. He's throwing me upside down fast.
It's hurting my arms. I want to run away. . . . He's grabbing me
tight. . . . I can't get away. No! I can't breathe. . . . [coughing,
gasping] He's got me by the throat with one hand. . . . Help!
Somebody's gotta help me. . . . He's *pointing* me. . . . He says
he's *pointing* me. . . . He says, "North . . . west . . ." and he points
me real hard. He turns me over and grabs my neck and points me.
I don't want to be all pointy. It hurts. Why is he hurting me?

It made me all sick. I hated it. I was so afraid. I thought I was
going to die . . . I thought he was going to kill me. No! No! No!
Help! *Mommy! Mommy!*

Where's my mommy? Why isn't she here? Mommy!
Mommy! I can't breathe. . . . I'm gonna die. I feel sick. I'm gonna
be sick. . . . I'm sick all over. I'm gonna die. I'm so scared. Oh,
God, I'm scared.

He's done it over and over. Then he . . . he . . . he . . . No!
No! No! He grabbed me by the face. . . . He's grabbed my fingers
. . . he's squeezing them. I hurt. He said if . . . if I . . . if I want
to stay alive . . . I better be a good girl. . . . I was so afraid! He
seemed so scary. He's bad. He told me . . . he said, "You listen,
Michelle." He said, "You have to cooperate." I don't know what
cooperate means. I don't know.

The strange man Malachi had the little girl stretched rigidly, like
a needle. He held one hand to her neck and the other to her groin as
he pointed her, again and again, north, west, south, east. Then he
began to flip her, head over heels, in front of himself, catching her
rudely by the arms as she completed each somersault.

I . . . when I found out I couldn't get away . . . and no one
was going to hear me . . . when they didn't care . . . I . . . I

. . . had to change. . . . I didn't want to get hit anymore. You see
. . . the first thing I had to do was not to hurt. . . . I didn't want
any more pain. . . . I had to put on a happy face. . . . I went all
numb. . . . I made it black. . . . I made a black wall all around
me . . . and my teddy was there. . . . Oh, I loved my teddy. I was
so glad I could see my teddy bear. . . .

Michelle's crying became agonized. Dr. Pazder noted the degrees
of her increasing fear and feelings of abandonment.

It was black and I could see my teddy bear. . . . First he was
really far away . . . down . . . he was in a tunnel. . . . I could see
him coming closer, and the closer the bear got . . . the more I
floated . . . I loved the bear so much I wanted to become the bear.
. . . I wanted to crawl inside with him and be safe. . . . Oh, my
arms hurt. . . . I feel numb . . . there was nothing left of me, just
my head . . . no body. . . . I was all gone except my eyes . . . and
my mouth was gone and my nose was gone and my eyes and my
ears were left . . . ahhh. . . . *All that was left of my insides was
a tiny warm spot. . . . That's all I was!*
But every once in a while Malachi would come through my
wall. . . . I 'd hurt . . . and then my bear would come back.
. . . I'd push him away so my bear would come back. *Get out of
my way! I can't see my bear!*

Dr. Pazder recognized suddenly that this was not twenty-seven-
year-old Michelle Smith speaking but . . . who? *A child?* Yes, of course!
In voice, in gesture, in language—there was no mistaking it: a girl of
perhaps no more than five lay on the couch before him. He was awed
and fascinated—and moved.

Oh, God! Something's happening! I don't understand. . . . I
. . . shut my eyes. . . . I got frightened again. . . . I opened my
eyes to try and find my bear and you see the door's open and there
was a li—li—light in the hallway. . . .

Michelle was struggling now, screaming.

> I don't *understand*. . . . There were people . . . standing there!
> They were looking in the door! They were laughing! *They were*
> *laughing!* Oh . . . why are they laughing? . . . I don't understand.
> . . . *It isn't funny!* Oh, I feel so sick! . . . I don't understand how
> that could have happened. . . . Where's my bear gone? . . . Oh,
> where's my bear? I want my bear. . . . I want my bear. . . . *I want*
> *my bear!*

Michelle's crying continued, but as Dr. Pazder watched, her color,
which until now had been ashen, almost blue, resumed a more healthy
tone. Her muscles became more relaxed. For fifteen minutes she lay
silent, her eyelids fluttering occasionally, as she ascended bit by bit from
wherever she had been. Finally she opened her eyes completely.

"Am I crazy?" she asked Dr. Pazder softly, her voice regaining its
usual timbre.

"No. You're not crazy, Michelle. I don't see you as crazy at all."

The tears began to flow again. "I'm so afraid that you're going to
tell me that I'm crazy. Do you believe me?"

"Yes, I do. You were obviously relating, almost re-experiencing,
some terrible memory, about a time when you were a little girl."

"I was worried I was making that up, because it didn't fit together.
But where did it come from? It didn't . . ." Michelle allowed the
sentence to remain incomplete. She sighed heavily.

"I don't know. I'm wondering that myself," Dr. Pazder said
thoughtfully.

Michelle thought for a moment. "I should have done something
back then. I shouldn't have just floated away."

"You had no choice. You had no choice in that."

Michelle sighed again. "I feel so guilty about that bear. You know
why? Because it wasn't real." She dropped her voice to a whisper. "I
never had a bear."

"You didn't?"

"No. But I still love it. When I shut my eyes I can still see it floating
there. . . . I feel so strange. . . ." Michelle's eyes were streaming once

again. "I never even knew about *any* of this before today. I just
. . . but now, when I think about it . . . about that time . . . I'm really
frightened. When I think back to that night and I still remember what
his face—what Malachi's face—looked like and everything . . ."

"Who was Malachi?" Dr. Pazder interrupted.

"I don't know. He doesn't seem like any person I knew. His eyes
. . . they were horrible!" Abruptly Michelle shifted gears. "I'm not
going crazy?"

"No," the doctor replied.

"Are you sure?"

"Yes."

"But I don't understand any of what was happening," Michelle
insisted.

"Don't try to, okay? You needed that teddy bear to hang onto. You
needed it, and it was the only safe thing you could have."

"I just wish I could make the scary parts go away. It wasn't just scary
like a nightmare, but a really serious scary. It was so serious—see? This
doesn't make any sense!"

"Stop trying to make sense of it, just let it come out," Dr. Pazder
said gently. "We have to work with this. After we work, you'll be able
to make sense out of it." He smiled at her. "Look, you're tired. Maybe
you should leave it behind for a few days."

"I am tired, it's true." But Michelle was not quite ready to end the
session. There were still a few things on her mind.

"That wasn't my own house I was in back there. And I know I was
very badly hurt. I know that. My body knows it. You know, for years
I wouldn't look up in the dictionary what 'cooperate' meant? I didn't
know for years. I got so angry whenever anybody said I wasn't cooperat-
ing. Do you think it will ever make sense?"

Michelle was repeating herself, but it was clear to Dr. Pazder that
his patient needed all the reassurance he could give.

"In time, it will all come together. We could guess some pieces, but
I don't want to do that. What happened there was very frightening.
But what you were doing to protect yourself from it seems to be just
as frightening to you. It's important to know that those are the normal
things children do—they don't make you crazy. There's no way you

could face that whole situation without having to cut your feelings off. This is what we can do. We dissociate, separate from our feelings. We build walls, we have fantasies. When you had your bear, you could get away from what was going on, you could keep yourself from feeling the pain.

"None of this," he went on, "is a crazy thing. Crazy would be if you believed you had turned into a bear and went around thinking other people were crazy because they didn't know you were a bear."

"Do you understand how I became very tiny inside?" She curled up her index finger and peeked at Dr. Pazder through the minute opening. "Like that! I just became a tiny, warm spot. That was the only place where I was really safe, where no one could touch me." Michelle went on, as if compelled. "And you see, my inside . . . my inside was safe and protected—no one knew it was there, but I did. My inside eyes could sometimes see what my outside was doing. You see, I had my inside . . . and then I had my outside."

Four and a half hours had gone by. It had been a debilitating, emotional experience for both doctor and patient. Nevertheless, Michelle looked far better now, at the end of the session, than she had at its outset. Beginning to get these horrible memories—or whatever they were—out into the open was obviously bringing her a measure of relief.

"You did well, Michelle," Dr. Pazder said. "You'll be free of it in time."

"That's what I believe," Michelle said, sitting up on the couch. "I honestly believe that."

chapter 3

MICHELLE returned to Dr. Pazder's office at the beginning of the following week. It was clear to both of them, even before Michelle lay down on the couch, that more was to come. What had been revealed in the Saturday session, although powerful and distressing, was not distressing enough to explain why these memories had been so thoroughly blocked. Indeed, Dr. Pazder thought, as his patient quietly prepared herself for the next phase of the psychic journey, the memories had not simply been blocked—they had been totally buried.

"My life seems so scattered these days . . . and these memories, they're so foreign," Michelle began, without prompting. "They're so out of step with the way I've always thought of my life, and I don't know how to make them part of me and still be whole. Do you know what I mean?"

Dr. Pazder nodded. "Yes, it doesn't fit with anything I know about you either. Right now, don't try to understand or make sense of it. We'll do that in time. First, you need to let yourself go wherever you have to. Just let yourself go back there. It's okay. You go wherever you have to go. I'll be with you."

"But you see, I'm afraid that when I start talking, it'll start me remembering things. I know some of the things that happened weren't normal, weren't things that normal people do. . . . Oh! My arms hurt." She began to weep softly.

The doctor could see that the process was starting already. "I don't know any way of bringing you and the memories back together," he said sympathetically, "without going back to them to where you think you came apart. See if you can let yourself go back. I'll be right here with you."

Her breathing deepened. Her eyes began to twitch beneath their lids as if she were watching something, just as they had on Saturday.

"The air's like this," Michelle murmured, holding out her hands and rubbing them together very hard. "Like this . . . *grating* . . ."

It became clear from her next few words that Michelle was back, alone in that room. Once again she spoke in the voice of a frightened little girl.

> I wanted to cover up . . . to cover myself up . . . I found something to put on. . . . You see, I don't know why, but I felt really ashamed, I don't know why. . . .

Michelle broke down into great, heaving sobs.

> I got a big shirt. . . . I was trying not to *be* there. You see, it doesn't make any sense, but I thought that if I didn't see my hands, I wouldn't be there. . . . I had this shirt pulled over my head. And I don't know why I thought I'd get away with it . . . except I was so busy trying to keep my hands up inside the sleeves, I didn't notice the people in the room!

Some women had entered the darkened space where the little girl was a prisoner. They walked in a single file, oblivious to the child's presence. Clad in the oversized shirt, she watched, in fear and awe, as they went about their bizarre tasks—methodical, coldly efficient, each of them doing a particular chore. One woman pushed the bed to the side of the room, another moved a bureau. Some of them went about tacking up large black sheets on all four walls. Then the women began to set up candles—perhaps twenty or thirty in all. Someone draped the bureau with a round black cloth embroidered in an intricate white design. On top of the cloth were placed two silver goblets and a knife. And more candles.

I thought . . . Mommies! I thought. . . . Oh, boy! There's going
to be a party. . . . Oh, boy! But . . . no! No! They're all looking
at me! They're staring at me! . . . All of them . . . all their eyes!

One of the women approached Michelle and picked her up. The
little girl's apprehension faded—she could not help but smile. The
woman was extraordinarily beautiful, with shining dark hair. Unlike the
others, who wore simple black dresses, this woman wore a black cape
with a hood. It set her apart. Michelle thought: *Ah! A princess!*
"How hurt you are," the woman cooed. "How sad! How sad I am
that you are hurt."

She's being like a mommy. And then she kisses me! She's
kissing me and sticking her tongue in my . . . *mouth!* It's stupid.
It's like a snake. She's not a mommy.
I thought she'd look after me. . . . But then they—they started
to talk about getting me ready . . . preparing me. . . . She started
rubbing me. . . . Some of the people grabbed my wrists.
I don't like them hanging onto my arms. I don't want them
to hurt me! I can't stand being pinned down! . . . Someone's
rubbing something on me, on my chest! It smells icky. It's mucky
. . . I looked and it had funny eyes and it . . . it's the funny eyes.
. . . It was like a mommy, but it had Malachi's eyes! Where's *my*
mommy? Those are other kids' moms! I don't want this mom.
You go away, I want my mom! . . . Please don't hurt me . . . and
she says, "I'm not going to hurt you." . . . They were all, like,
excited about something. . . . I'm all mixed up! I'd seen my mom
make a birthday cake and I thought maybe they're waiting for the
cake. I don't understand. . . .

Michelle was screaming, begging, her fingers bent like claws,
whether in a gesture of panic or attack, Dr. Pazder could not tell. He
was deeply moved by his patient's struggle, and at the same time
realized that the only way he could assist the child—and therefore the
woman whom the child had become—was to allow her to relive the
entire ghastly experience, wherever it came from, whatever it meant.

Help! . . . Help! . . . Help! . . . They were putting this stuff
. . . putting it in my eyes and my ears and my nose. Somehow it
was getting in me, every way.

Michelle wanted to close her legs, cross them, but the people held
them apart. She was unable to push away. The woman kept rubbing
the foul-smelling substance on the girl's body.

Several of them fetched a handful of colorful sticks—dark red and
brown, muddy yellow, dirty green, purple, and black. They handed
them to the woman in the cape. She held them in her hand for a
moment, pounded them roughly on the floor, then loosened her grip
and allowed them to spill to the ground. The other women had taken
up a chant. The woman in the cape studied the arrangement of the
sticks, selected one of them, dipped it in a silver goblet, and inserted
it in Michelle's rectum. Again and again she repeated this ugly performance, each time introducing the vile mixture from the goblet into
the little girl's body—her nostrils, her mouth, her ears.

They were poking me. It felt like *pins!* They stuck those sticks
not just in my mouth. They stuck them everywhere I had an
opening! They just kept poking and rubbing. . . . The inside of
me hates them, but my outside keeps pretending it's just a different kind of pick-up sticks. . . . They are putting *ugly* in me. I don't
want any more ugly in me. The lady is sealing it in now. She *says*
it's permanent. . . . She's making it permanent. Permanent!

Michelle was crying openly as she spoke, crying like a young child,
in uncontrollable, shuddering gasps.

I could hear them saying things. . . . "Try this . . . see if this
works." . . . The lady kept turning the sticks around and talking.
I didn't understand what the words meant. She kept changing all
the sticks and saying something about getting me ready for someone. I couldn't remember the name. . . . I never heard the name
before. . . . I didn't understand what they were saying. . . . They
say they're doing all these things to me so I'd be ready for the

other person. . . . Something about . . . they'd show God. . . . I
don't want Him to see me, not like this! . . . There was this dresser
and I saw them setting up more candles on it. . . . Everything was
black. . . . Then suddenly everything had to be clean. They all got
washed. And every time one of them touched me, they'd go and
clean themselves. . . . Then someone cleaned me off too. They
laid me on that dresser . . . it was all cold. . . . I'm cold. . . . I
thought I was lying on a birthday cake . . . afraid . . . afraid I
am the birthday cake! But I don't want to play their game anymore!

The child was lifted and placed on the bureau, made to lie down
inside a semicircle of candles. The dresser had a mirror attached, which
reflected the steady glow of the flames.

Michelle noticed that the room now also contained men, along with
the women who had been there all along. They too were in dark
clothing. Everyone was chanting as if in a strange, ancient language.

I didn't have anything on . . . and they unbraided my hair and
I don't like it. . . . There is a knife and cups . . . they are real shiny.
. . . It's like everyone has a stomach ache. They're moaning and
groaning. They have their eyes closed and they are making a
funny noise. I just kept saying inside, *I see with my eyes, I listen
with my ears, I talk with my mouth, but nobody hears.* I just keep
saying that over and over again. . . . All I hear is my words.
. . .

Suddenly Michelle started, as if struck. Dr. Pazder leaned forward,
alarmed, but did nothing to break the mood.

No! I don't want to be *cut!* . . . Help me! . . . They're making
lines on me with the knife. I'm afraid. It's like a line down the
middle of my face. Why are they putting that stuff on me?
. . . They're painting me with red stuff. . . . They're painting half
of me dark. I don't want to be a clown. . . . I'm going to have
half a red face and half a white face. They are putting red on half

of me and the stuff in my mouth on the other half! . . . They're all calling someone. They're all calling that guy and having stomach aches. They . . . they all started running around the room and screaming and yelling. I didn't move because I'm afraid the candles will burn me. . . .

The whole group gathered in a tight half circle around the dresser, gazing down at the little girl. Their eyes were wide, their faces expressionless. Abruptly, almost as one body, they turned their heads from her. And then they filed out, departing as coolly and noiselessly as they had come in.

They're all gone . . . all of them. . . . Everyone just left the room. . . . I blew out the candles. . . .

Michelle suddenly addressed Dr. Pazder directly. "Please," she said, she no longer spoke in the child's voice, "I've got to stop for a while. I've got to stop. . . . Help me. . . . I've got to come back again. . . . It's so dangerous. It's really dangerous. . . ."

Her breathing began to ease; it was no longer the heavy panting that characterized the deepest part of her remembering. Her eyes moved less quickly, though they remained closed for several more minutes. Dr. Pazder recognized these signals: The young woman was "ascending" and soon would be with him again.

"Do you understand now?" she said at last, opening her eyes, her face full of urgent concern.

"Understand what?"

"That I'm ugly! Don't you hate me?"

"Nothing in the world could make me feel you are hateful. How could I hate you?"

"I've done such awful things."

"No, you haven't," the doctor corrected her. "They clearly did awful things *to* you. You did nothing bad." He paused, looking for a response. "Do you hear me? You are not bad." Over and over again he repeated this assurance, attempting to explain to Michelle—to make her understand—that these people had wanted to make her feel as though she were to blame, as though she had committed some horrendous act. "There is no reason for you to feel this way," he finished, "no reason at all." Privately, Dr. Pazder was convinced that the group—whoever they were—had been using very sophisticated techniques of ego destruction.

He knew also, from his studies and from work he had done in Africa, that the Yoruba tribe of Nigeria (among others) used cola-bean pods in a fashion similar to the way these people appeared to use sticks: to predict. He sensed that this might have been what they were trying to do with Michelle. But how could she have known? And in such exact detail? Dr. Pazder admitted that he was amazed.

As Michelle began to grow calmer, Dr. Pazder asked for more details of the experience.

"How many people were there?"

Michelle thought, wrinkling her brow. She closed her eyes to visualize the scene. "There was the lady in the cape . . . and then one . . . two . . . three . . . I can't be certain, but possibly thirteen. . . . I don't know. I can't swear to it."

"That's all right," Dr. Pazder replied. "It may come clearer later on."

And then, almost in the same breath, they queried one another: Who were these people? Who were they?

The small office was filled with an almost unbearable tension, as if a live grenade had suddenly been placed between them, threatening to explode in their faces.

chapter 4

$\mathcal{D}$R. Pazder sat in his office, staring out the window and thinking of Michelle. She was due any minute, to resume the amazing testimony she had embarked upon the day before. Once again, as he had been so many times in the hours since he had last seen her, he was struck by the persistence of the child's innocence. No matter how bad things had got, no matter what they had done to her, she had been able to hold onto that pinprick of strength and selfhood. Spread a black cloth on a dresser and set out candles and the child would think "Birthday party!" Show her blank-faced women in dark clothes and she would respond with "Mommies!" Dr. Pazder felt sure, somehow, that in future sessions, that "warm spot" would always be there. She would always be able to hold onto it. It was critical for a therapist to have that when working with someone. If you could find that place and touch it, then everything else would melt away.

It was also critical, he knew, that he maintain his objectivity. Had he accepted her story unquestioningly, it would have been impossible for him to give her accurate help. Yes, it was important that he encourage her to divulge her memories, however bizarre; but he also must act as a measure of reality, a strong, knowledgeable presence who would be able to monitor Michelle and to tell when she might be veering off into psychosis. And so, in the three months he had heard her testimony —some 200 hours so far—he had pondered, taking each new piece of information and relating it to all the others, and to the whole. Constantly he had searched for contradictions, for signs that what she was telling him was not authentic, but was perhaps a fantasy, a neurotic flight into imagination. At every point he had stopped to ask: "Is this consistent with what has come out already? Is it logical, given the extraordinary dimensions of the experience? Could it be hallucination or invention? Do I see a sane and competent Michelle telling me this?" These had been his persistent silent questions, and they must continue to be, he knew, until the work was done.

When Michelle arrived, she was drawn and tense, but resolute. They talked a bit, before she descended into the past, about her fear of returning to that time.

"I wish I could have a sort of link to the present," she said, "something to connect with so that when I go down there, I won't get caught by it. Sometimes I'm afraid I'll get stuck and have to stay down there forever."

Her voice was quavering, and Dr. Pazder knew she spoke from real need.

"I could put my hand on your head again," he said, "the way I did yesterday. And look, here, I'll pull my chair all the way over to the sofa, next to you."

But that was not close enough. Still Michelle felt alone and endangered. He experimented with sitting beside her on the sofa, and for a while it seemed as if that would suffice. But then the terror thickened her voice again, and they shifted so that he could sit on the sofa with her head against his shoulder. This seemed to give her the closeness and security she needed. It made checking the tapes and coping with the telephone a bit awkward, but he could manage.

Again Michelle made her descent into the black pool of her past. As she neared the depths, she was weeping, and Dr. Pazder's tape recorder captured her words—the words of a frightened, five-year-old child—as they issued through the tears.

> I felt I'd go crazy in that room alone. . . . I curled up in a little ball in the corner and thought I was just a piece of fluff on the floor, but every time I opened my eyes, I wasn't a piece of fluff. . . . I had to get out of the room. . . . I couldn't hide in the room. I would have hid under the bed, but there was a bunch of stuff

under the bed, and I couldn't get under. . . . And I knew they'd look there anyway. I don't know. . . . I think I went down the hallway. I was going sneak-sneak-sneak, sneak-sneak-sneak, down the hallway. I had to hurry. I had to go quickly. Because if I got away downstairs, they'd forget I was in the house. I had to go quickly . . . but you see, I had to go around the doorway to the kitchen, and over there was the doorway into the other room. Oh, no! Something's wrong. They got knives! The men have got knives and they are *hurting* each other. I don't understand. I'm scared!

As Michelle, struggling for every sentence, pushed out her account, Dr. Pazder listened intently, trying to understand the horror so that he could help her deal with it later.* It was clear that after the men and women had abruptly turned and strode from the room in which the strange ceremony had taken place, Michelle was left alone and lying on the cloth-covered dresser. When she dared to move, she found herself looking into the mirror that rose from the back of the dresser, and for the first time she saw what they had done to her. Her body was painted in a ghastly manner—a thick red repulsive-smelling liquid down one side of her and a scummy, uncolored liquid on the other. It was terrifying for the child to see her body divided down the middle and made grotesque. In her distress, she tried to escape—into the mirror; she tried to climb through the glass into the world beyond it. But the mirror was unyielding, impenetrable. There was no escape.

As she struggled, she lost her balance and, grasping frantically for

*For the sake of clarity and brevity, only portions of Michelle's sessions with Dr. Pazder, which lasted over a year, have been chosen for detailed narration, and these have been compressed. Certain painful and deeply buried revelations, such as the ones in this chapter concerning the "lump" and Michelle's treatment by her mother, took many fragmented sessions to coalesce. Only after repeated journeys into her depths was Michelle able, in some cases, to supply crucial details that made events comprehensible. For this book, however, considerable portions of Michelle's testimony have been combined according to subject and theme and distilled into units called sessions, any one of which may contain material actually drawn from a number of sessions. But the atmosphere and procedure of the sessions were precisely as represented here; the general sequence of revelation is as it was; and the indented excerpts from the three-thousand-page transcript are faithfully reproduced.

something to hold onto, she fell to the floor. Again she tried to hide, under the bed—to no avail.

She looked for her bear, but he had disappeared. But that mental image she had of her external self—what she called her "outside"— turned into a friend. This pretend friend looked just like her, only she was clean and her hair was neatly parted and braided. She was wearing a dress with smocking, and she looked lovely. She was floating up near the ceiling.

"You'd better get out of here," her pretend friend advised. "Why don't you sneak down the hall and hide in the basement?" That sounded like a good idea. Michelle crawled over to the bed and pulled herself up to her feet. She was dizzy. She knew she was badly hurt. She was bleeding—from her mouth, her ears, her nose, between her legs. And she was so dirty she could not stand herself.

Outside the window, lights began flashing. She crept toward the open bedroom door, then stopped. Malachi was out in the hall, opening the front door just a crack. Through the opening, Michelle could see someone out on the porch. Black boots—a policeman! Surely he would save her. But Malachi, talking smoothly, persuaded the officer that there was nothing amiss, just a party that had become a little boisterous; he would have the guests quiet down. The door shut.

Soon after Malachi went away, Michelle moved slowly into the hall, now on tiptoes, as in a child's game: "sneak-sneak-sneak, sneak-sneak-sneak . . ." She was heading for the kitchen, hoping to find the stairs to the cellar. But as she passed the living room, she was stopped by a strange and dismaying sight: Men and women were participating in some sort of struggle, thrashing against each other as if they were animals. The men had "knives" protruding from their bodies and seemed to be using them on the others. Some wore pained expressions on their faces and were groaning.

I've got to find my mother. . . . *Where's my mother?* I don't understand. I don't understand! I want my mom. *I want my mom! I want my mom.* . . . Don't you see, that was my voice inside. You see, I knew by their eyes that I had to be good, I had to be my outside. Their eyes were scary. I couldn't let anyone see me crying. I don't understand. I don't understand anything I see anymore. Some of the people didn't have all their clothes on. What's happening? What's going on? I don't understand. So much is going on at once. I don't know where anything started and stopped anymore. I don't understand. Where's my mom? . . . You see, my inside always tried to find my mom. . . . My arms hurt! *Ow.* But my outside was going around laughing and twirling around. That was so everyone wouldn't know I was trying to find her. *Ow-w-w-w,* my arms hurt, my arms hurt. [Holding her arms and crying.] *Ow-w-w-w,* my arms hurt! But you see, I thought if I was going around and around and saying things, they'd just laugh . . . and they wouldn't know I was looking for my mom, you see. Because I knew . . . when I found my mom . . . it'd be okay.

Michelle reasoned that if they'd hurt her, they might also have hurt her mother and that perhaps her mother was in trouble too. Michelle reached the kitchen. More of the men and women were there.

I looked and there were two women by the table over there. And then I thought one of them was my mom, because she had hair like my mom . . . but she turned around and it *wasn't* my mom. Her eyes were funny. I hated them! I didn't know what to do.

The child ran to the woman she thought was her mother, calling out to her, "Mommy! Mommy!" When the woman turned around, Michelle froze. The woman's face was sick and demented, the features askew. She wore an awful smile, and her eyes—*crazy eyes.* The woman looked at Michelle as if she had known she were coming. She never made a noise. Michelle jumped back and ran out of the room.

I was turning around in circles, I was dancing. You see, I'd gone crazy too. I'm getting so mixed up. Where's my mom? What's . . . No! *No no no!* I don't understand any of it . . . and

I wish I didn't understand it now. Oh, how I wish I didn't understand. You see . . . it's not true! It . . . I don't understand. You see, I didn't understand those mommies. I don't understand. Something's hurting my mom. Mom! Mom!

Turning in circles, the child had fled the kitchen and stumbled her way to the living room. There was her mother, beautiful, her cheeks flushed, her red hair spread out against the back of the large green chair she was sitting in. She was wearing a skirt Michelle knew well—black and dressy, coming down to midcalf. Michelle tried to wave at her mother without attracting the attention of the others, to get her mother to see her. She couldn't. She tried and she tried, her heart breaking, desperate for her mother. But Michelle couldn't make her mother notice. Her mother's eyes were closed. She seemed to be in pain. There was something under the skirt.

It's a . . . a l-l-l-lump . . . a lump under her skirt. My mom looked like she was being hurt. I didn't understand. No! No! No! [She screams in extreme horror for some twenty minutes.]
I thought I was helping my mom. You see, I thought she felt like I did. I thought she wanted to get away too. Oh! I had to help her. You know . . . I had to help her. No one was helping her. They didn't even notice. My mother was my mom! I didn't mean to. I . . . I'm sorry! I'm sorry! *Dear God!* Oh, oh, oh! You see, I had to stop it, you see, I had to make those people quit. . . . I can't get me together. I can't. Ow-w-w, my arms hurt. My hands are numb, *they're all numb*. You see, the inside was scared for my mom, and the outside, it had to stop spinning around. And my eyes are just . . . I . . . they didn't want to look. And I had to get through that in the air. I had to *stop that in the air!*

The atmosphere in the living room was heavy, grating. As Dr. Pazder listened, he reflected that whoever these people were and whatever they were doing—ritual sex, apparently—they seemed to be moving toward some sort of controlled, deliberate frenzy, a kind of dissociative state in which any sort of action would be possible. He found himself petrified for the five-year-old child whose voice was calling to him so urgently now.

> You see, that's how . . . you see, I did pick that up. . . . Ow-w-w! My arms hurt. You see, this isn't going to make any sense to you at all, but it could have been a big spider or a snake. The lump could have been that, and it could have been hurting her. Oh! It was moving around! I didn't even think. I didn't even stop and think. I just grabbed the . . . *No! I didn't!* I didn't. I didn't even know . . . I didn't even know when I grabbed . . . except I know it was a bottle. . . . It was on the table . . . and it was just something to grab. And I had to. I just had to smash that thing under my mother's skirt. Oh! Oh! No! I smashed that lump! Everyone turned their eyes on me. I hate those eyes. No! No! They're all *smashing . . . smashing . . .* smashing . . . they're all smashing the lump! No! It got all bloody. It was just so awful bloody.

Now all the people in the room had those dreadful eyes—Michelle could see them changing. When they saw that the child who had been the centerpiece of their ceremony, just an hour before, had hit the "lump," they appeared to take it as a sign. Michelle recoiled, watching horrified as they began to beat the lump with their fists, attacking mercilessly, relentlessly.

> I've . . . I've got to stop it. Someone's got to. You see, my outside was really frantic. My outside hit it, but only once. It was really frantic, and its face was all like that. But my inside wasn't like that. I saw that blood. You're not going to want to know me. I did *awful* things! I put my . . . I put my . . . hand . . . on the lump. I did. It was all bloody.

As Michelle imparted this revelation, stuttering through her agony, Dr. Pazder saw an astounding thing. Though deep into the experience of reliving the incident, she was extending her arms and reaching out, as if to touch something in front of her, and as she did so, for just one fleeting moment she smiled.

It was all bloody, and I wiped it all over my face. I wiped it all over me. Then I ran around. That's why they didn't want me to touch them. I wanted to wash them off. I wanted to put blood on them. I was only trying to make everything okay. I ran all over and put blood on all of them. They stopped! Everything went quiet. They just stood there. You see, I had to make it stop. Do you understand that?

Dr. Pazder spoke to the child within the woman. "I do understand that," he said softly. "Very much."

It's okay if you don't want to touch me. It's all right. It'll be all right. You see, what I didn't tell you . . . Ow-w-w! My arms hurt! I was glad! I was glad! I felt happy inside. I smashed it and I was glad. That's why I was smiling, and when I turned around and I couldn't . . . ow, my arms hurt! I couldn't understand why the other people weren't happy too. I made everything stop! And I was glad! I could clean everything up then. And when they all stopped and everything went quiet, I thought they'd be pleased with me.

The frantic child began to twirl. Then she started to pipe out "Twinkle, twinkle, little star," spinning to the tune, hoping her mother would notice her, smile, hold her.

Michelle was crying now, so hard that she was almost choking. The sentences broke into phrases, the phrases shattered into single words. And then nothing. It was nearly an hour before she could resume:

I went to hug my mom. She . . . she . . . she yelled, *Don't touch me!* I couldn't understand. I went to touch someone else, and everybody backed away from me. *Don't touch me!* I looked at my hands, I looked at all of me. I was filthy. I knew why they didn't want to touch me. I just saw my mom. My mom was so upset. *Michelle, what have you done?* I was helping you, Mommy. I was helping you.

Michelle had dissolved into agonizing sobs. Dr. Pazder tried to comfort her, but her flailing arms and legs, her writhing body made it all but impossible. It was as if she were fighting against a memory that was too horrible to be borne yet that was inexorably forcing its way up and out.

What have you done? No! No! No! Please. Please, Mommy, hold me! Mommy, I'm scared! I'm scared! And that's when she hit me and yelled. *Look at your ugly face! Oooh, she's ugly! I wouldn't touch any of it! It's disgusting!* I couldn't help how I looked. I didn't know how I looked until then. *Get her out of my sight! Get her out of my sight!* I couldn't help it. She didn't want to help me. She just smashed me across the head and yelled, *Get rid of her! Ugh! Get her out of my sight!*

Once again, wild, desperate crying, a small child trying to deny the unthinkable: total, brutal rejection by her own mother. Dr. Pazder sat with her, saying nothing, while the sobs continued and began to ebb. When she spoke again, it was in a thin, fevered little voice.

Everyone's afraid of me. I'm afraid of me. I'm afraid of me. That's when Malachi threw me in the bathroom. He just picked me up by the skin and threw me in the bathroom. I tried to make myself clean. I scrubbed and scrubbed. My arms hurt. My legs hurt. My stomach hurt. I felt so sick. I just scrubbed and scrubbed. It felt like I would never be clean again. My hands are all numb. . . .
I'm afraid. I'm afraid! I crawled into the bedroom. I tried to crawl everywhere in the bedroom. I tried to crawl under the baseboard because there was a crack and I thought I might get under the baseboard like you see little mice do. Someone's got to help me. Someone's got to tell me what happened. I heard them

talking when I was in the bedroom. You see, there was so much noise they were worried the police was going to come because my mom was screaming so loud. All of a sudden the door was opening and closing, and all of the people were going away. And I could hear Malachi saying that they'd just cover it up. What are they covering up?

She peeked out the bedroom door. People were getting dressed and leaving. No one spoke. She watched them leave, and then she turned back to her mother. She was sitting there, slumped into the chair. Her skirt had lifted a little, and Michelle saw something that chilled her heart.

I looked. . . . I didn't want to see. . . . I could see, it was awful. The lump . . . oh, I feel sick inside. I feel sick, I feel so sick. What's the matter with me? Now I know I'm crazy. I shouldn't have told you. . . . I shouldn't have told anybody. I didn't want to tell anybody, ever. . . . The lump . . . the lump had shoes! Red shoes!

chapter 5

"*I* DIDN'T want to tell anybody, ever. . . ."

But Michelle had told, and now, as she began to surface, to rise back up from her place of reliving, Dr. Pazder was intensely aware of the crucial obligation he faced: to help her integrate the unspeakably horrible facts she had unearthed, to understand them, somehow, so that what had happened twenty-two years before would not destroy her sanity today.

She continued to cry for over half an hour, covering her face much of the time and avoiding Dr. Pazder's gaze. And then the crying eased, and her breathing was no longer quite so heavy and labored. At last she began to speak, tremulously, still in the throes of her experience in the depths, but very nearly now in her adult voice.

"I shouldn't have told you," she said. "I don't understand it. . . . Please tell me what happened. I feel just terrible. I feel like I did trying to crawl away. Do you think that *happened?*"

"We have to talk about it," the psychiatrist replied. "You're really wiped out, aren't you?"

"If I told you, would you believe me? I did it. But please, oh, please try to understand—I *had* to. I don't know what made me do it, exactly. . . . I didn't want my mom hurt. I couldn't stand the smiling. I couldn't stand the laughing. I couldn't stand the air. I couldn't stand my inside and my outside being separated, and I couldn't stand turning around. Oh, please, you've got to believe I had to do that. I didn't know what else to do. It just happened."

"I know it did."

"I'm *afraid*," she went on. To Dr. Pazder, she really did look afraid. "I'm afraid you're going to tell someone. Oh, please don't. You see, you understand about my inside and my outside, and no one else would. I *had* to smash that lump."

"Of course you did. You wanted to stop what was happening. You wanted to stop their craziness."

Michelle paused for a moment, making a great effort to collect herself. "I'm afraid of myself. Who can I be, after all that? It was all wrong there. I didn't want to hurt anybody. I just didn't know what else to do."

"You did what anybody else would have done."

"But . . . I'm pretty sure . . . something got hurt. They were all smashing and smashing."

"We'll find out," Dr. Pazder said gently, "and then we can work with it."

"Can you talk to me for a minute about my insides and outsides? I don't understand anything about it. I don't understand why I twirled around or anything."

"You had to. You couldn't face everything that was happening that night and survive. It was too much for your whole person to face. You'd have gone crazy. You had to pull away from the rest of you to survive. Perhaps twirling is some sort of spontaneous, innate behavior—a way of centering yourself and protecting yourself from being overwhelmed by what's happening around you. Then you could let your outside be what it had to so you could handle all that. It was just too much for anyone, let alone an abandoned five-year-old child."

Michelle looked up at the doctor. "Do you know that I didn't like doing that—hitting that lump?"

"Of course I do."

"That was the most horrible thing I've ever had to do in my life."

"I'm glad you were able to hold onto your insides."

"I'm afraid to put them back together."

"We'll bring them back . . . and it'll be okay. Your inside and your outside have to meet each other again. All the pieces have to meet to allow you to be one whole person again. You have to understand that those people were controlling your outside, so you had to give that up —and inside was the only safe place to go."

"I wanted my mom so badly." Michelle began to cry again. "I needed her to help me. I felt she would hug me and it would be okay. I felt so . . . so ugly when she wouldn't."

"I can imagine how you must have felt."

"There's just so much *confusion.* I know that maybe there isn't any connection between how good I felt when I stopped them—the air, and those mommies, and Malachi—but it's all mixed up together."

"Yes, it will be for a while."

"My hands are all numb. I wanted to hold onto your hand, but I knew I wasn't allowed."

"It's okay to touch me."

"But my mom made it sound like I should never touch anyone. I don't know what to do. That's what my mom didn't understand about me, that I needed someone to touch, even if I was ugly."

Michelle paused and looked away. Then she turned back suddenly. "I feel so scared inside. Oh, God, I feel so scared. I hate all those feelings. She kept confusing me so badly. I hate the confusion. Why don't you want to go away? Oh, I hurt."

"Michelle," Dr. Pazder said, "no part of me wants to go away from you. I understand what happened, I really do, and it will all be okay in time."

"I want to believe that."

"Please believe it."

"My hands, I know why they're all numb. I want to reach out to you and touch you, but I'm afraid to. I'm so afraid. That's why my hands are numb—they're afraid of being rejected too. That's why I had to hang onto myself all these years."

"Your hands and face now are both covered in that rash. You keep rubbing them like you're trying to get something off." He was alarmed at the way she was abrading her face with her knuckles and wringing her hands.

"You mean like the way I keep rubbing my face?"

"Uh-huh."

"I'm sorry. I'm sorry. The thing that's on them . . . the thing that's on them back there . . . is blood. I got to get it off."

"Leave it on! Leave it on. Don't run from it, back there. I want you to leave it on and tell me what it felt like."

Michelle gasped in fear. Dr. Pazder spoke more softly. "Look," he said, "can you let yourself feel a little good that it was on them? When you put your hand on the lump—when you told about that, for a slight moment there was a faint smile on your face. What did you feel then?"

Michelle lowered her eyes and was silent for a time. "It did feel a little okay," she said, finally. "It did feel a little good. Was it wrong to feel like that?"

"It was one of the most sane things you did all night. It was the most sane thing that happened there."

She looked at him urgently. "Oh, please, this is such a secret. You see, I thought the blood would . . . would wash the others. I wanted to sort of cover up what happened. I was so happy my hands were covered up. That's why I wiped it on all of them. I had to wash them and stop what was happening."

"When you were reliving it—do you know what your hands were doing while you were telling me about wiping the blood on them?"

"No, I don't understand what you mean."

Dr. Pazder took her hands and helped her to an erect sitting position. "Okay, now I want you to show me how you wiped it on them. Show me again, now."

Michelle balked at first and then hesitantly began to move her hands in the air in front of her, up and down, side to side. "I just . . . wiped it on them . . . like this . . . and this. . . ."

"What are you making on them?"

"Making on them? I don't know. You mean . . . I don't understand. Oh, I see. Crosses."

"Yes, crosses."

"I didn't realize I was making crosses on them."

"You were very clearly making crosses on all of them. I wondered at the time where it had come from."

"You mean why . . ."

"Did you know anything about crosses as a little child?" From his earlier years of work with Michelle, he knew that in her harsh, devastated family, there had been no religious observance whatsoever.

"Not much," she replied. "Just what every kid knows. We never went to church or anything like that."

"It seemed to have come from a very deep part of you. It is a very symbolic and powerful thing to do," he said.

"Do you suppose that was what made them all back away from me?" Michelle wondered.

"The crosses?"

"Putting crosses on them . . ."

"I don't know. What else did you feel? You were smiling. Was part of you happy?"

"I . . . think so."

"Can you let yourself smile about it now?"

"It feels crazy to smile about it now."

"It's not a bit crazy."

"It was crazy to feel happy."

"When were you happy?"

"When I was rubbing the blood all over everyone, I think."

"Yes. . . ."

"I was laughing. It wasn't even a crazy laugh. It wasn't that kind. I can't laugh right now, but I can let you know how I felt inside. My outside was really frantic. My outside hit the lump. But my inside wasn't like that. I saw the blood. . . . It's not . . . no, you'll put me away!"

Dr. Pazder waited until she looked up, and then he held her gaze. "You'll have to trust me here," he said gently. "It's important."

"My inside just went . . . I'll try to show you my inside. It was watching what my outside was doing. And it just went really quiet." She took several deep breaths. "I was really quiet . . . and then it felt warm."

"Warm?"

"Yes. And then the amazing thing was that I didn't need the bear. And it felt like a birthday party. This doesn't make any sense, you see."

"It makes a great deal of sense."

"And it just felt like it feels standing by a window with the sunshine coming in. It doesn't make any sense. But, you see, the blood was warm. The blood was warm . . . and it . . . it felt good." She was crying, but not bitterly; they were the tears of relief, of release. "And my inside smiled. It didn't laugh. It just felt warm, like sunshine. Not crazy laughing. I just wanted everyone to feel warm too."

"Of course. It was the only thing you could touch in that room that was normal and good."

"You think that was it?"

"Let me see your hands. I want to hold them."

"You don't mind?"

"Not a bit. They've changed a lot from the way they were earlier, haven't they?"

"Yes . . . yes, they have. They're better."

"The rash has gotten very much less, and they look fuller, and they feel warm."

"They haven't been warm for a long time, you know."

"Blood doesn't make them dirty."

"It doesn't make you ugly?"

"It doesn't make you ugly."

"Thank God you understand. Thank goodness."

chapter 6

*O*N the following Monday, Michelle told Dr. Pazder of a disturbing new thought that had come to her on the weekend.

"I was walking, just across the room," she said, "from one side of the room to the other, and all of a sudden, all of a sudden . . . all at once a really strange connection happened. I was thinking of my part in . . . feeling guilty . . . and all that blood . . . I'm afraid to say it. I can't say it because I don't know what I'll do." She sighed heavily, braced herself, and resumed. "The candles and the black, the color black, and people dressed in black—and those eyes, and you know, the stuff about that feeling in the air . . . ."

"Yes," Dr. Pazder said, "I know."

"Okay, all these things that I'm . . . these words . . . they're all connected, they all flashed together in my mind at the same time. And it sounds to me like witches."

"Yes, it does sound like that."

"I was thinking that if these people were witches, it somehow explains the things that happened to me, all the awful things. And then I thought—it doesn't make any sense—I thought I had to see a priest."

"A priest?"

"I don't know exactly why, but it's such a strong feeling. It's not that I think I have a devil in me, or anything like that. It's that, well, it's more than just my life that's threatened, it's my soul, too."

"They're very much the same."

"I know you're Catholic. I'm afraid I'll scare you away."

"How would my being a Catholic do that?"

"I don't know. Witches are against the Church, and maybe Catholics aren't supposed to have anything to do with them."

"Don't worry about that."

"Maybe they weren't witches or anything, but they were doing something funny that night. They all did everything for reasons. All the things they did to me—they did them for a reason. . . ." For a moment she seemed lost in the thought. "The reason why they hurt that lump, it wasn't like a frenzy or anything. It was all deliberate. I know I'm talking about it funny. I'm talking about it like I'm kind of detached from it, but that's all part of making sure it's safe."

"It's okay," Dr. Pazder said. "I know it's okay."

Michelle sighed again. "Do you have any idea of the confusion I have inside? I'm just torn by things that were so creepy and twisted. I'm trying to tell myself that those things aren't real and aren't true and aren't binding, and trying . . . not to feel so *threatened*. I don't know how to deal with it all."

"You'll be able to deal with it."

"This weekend I was thinking, how can this possibly have happened to me, in this day and age? I just couldn't figure out if it was just my fears, or if the things that happened to me got all distorted and pulled out of perspective. But every time I tell myself, 'Oh, Michelle, it just got distorted,' I just get this really, really heavy feeling like there's something really wrong here, something really wrong. It was more than people just hurting each other or doing weird things to me, and so far the only way I've been able to describe it is that like there was *something in the air.*"

"In the air?"

"Except I know it's got something to do with the time of the year. I can't tell you, the whole thing just scares me so terribly. The thing that scares me the most is all the connections that are there. All the pieces that don't fit in place any other way—they fit in place that way! And I just don't know what to do."

Dr. Pazder looked at the face of the young woman and once again saw the terror he had seen the day before the first descent.

"It's like," she went on, "as if I've got to go back and double-check everything to make sure that it's really safe. I've got to get safe."

"Is there something about letting yourself get into these feelings," he asked her, "that makes you think you may be in danger?"

"It's only that . . ." Michelle began to cry. "It's that I'm afraid you'll turn away from me. I know I shouldn't say that to you—you really care about me. But I just can't die."

"Now, wait a minute," Dr. Pazder exclaimed, speaking louder than he'd meant to, "you're not going to die."

"I'm afraid they'll take my soul away."

"No one can take your soul away. And they haven't taken it. That's the one thing they can never take away. They can take away your heart, and they can maim your body, destroy your mind, but only you can give up your soul."

"I want to believe that."

"Your fear about death and their twisting that around, that's the scariest thing they can do to a little girl. Part of you had to go along with them, to save yourself. But that part is not where your soul is. I've met your soul. I've looked into your eyes. And I know you're not a person who's had her soul taken away."

Michelle's expression lightened.

"About getting a priest," Dr. Pazder continued, wondering momentarily what he was saying. Psychiatrists in general tended to regard religion as something of a crutch, and as for bringing a priest into the psychiatric situation—there was almost a taboo against it. But the request for a priest had come from Michelle so intensely, and her concern for her soul was so strong, that he felt he could not ignore the entreaty. "Any time you want to see a priest, I can get one. I know a priest who may be able to relate to what we're doing."

"Really?"

"His name is Father Leo Robert. He's not what you might expect. He's young and he's got a beard and a great sense of humor—you'll like him. I'll give him a call."

That afternoon, after Michelle had left, the doctor telephoned Father Leo. "Father," he said, "I'm working with a young woman who apparently had some pretty terrible things happen to her when she was five—involving some kind of groups, they were into some sort of cult-type things, some kind of ceremonies going on. There seems to have been a lot of threat to her as a child, a lot of guilt for a number of things that happened. We've gotten to a serious place for her, and she is very frightened. Today she said she wanted to see a priest. She's sincere and I think it's genuine. I'd appreciate it if you could find a little time to talk to her."

Father Leo readily agreed, and an appointment was made for the following morning. On their way to it, Dr. Pazder gave Michelle something wrapped in tissue paper—a small cross he had bought in Rome along with others just like it for his wife and children. "If you're feeling frightened," he said, a little self-consciously, "you can hold onto this." She took the cross gratefully, too moved to speak.

When they arrived at Queenswood Chapel, she was surprised, despite what Dr. Pazder had told her, by Father Leo's appearance. He was tall and good-looking and wore a turtleneck instead of a clerical collar, and jeans and boots. Not at all her notion of a priest.

He talked with her earnestly and sympathetically, but doctor and patient both sensed a certain nervousness on Father Leo's part. After an hour, he took Dr. Pazder aside. "You're right," Father Leo said, "she's obviously completely sincere, and she obviously has been through something really horrible. I'll do whatever I can to help her. But there's one thing: The whole time she's been here, she's been holding something tightly in her hand. I wonder if I could see what it is."

Dr. Pazder burst into laughter. "Michelle," he called, crossing the room back to her chair, "would you show Father Leo what you have in your hand?"

Michelle opened her fingers, and there was the little cross Dr. Pazder had given her. Now it was the priest's turn to laugh.

"I'll tell you what," he said, when the mirth subsided. "I'd like to say Mass. Let me say it for you both."

Michelle looked at Dr. Pazder, who smiled yes, and she nodded. She was thrilled at the idea, and yet the tiniest bit apprehensive, as if she were having a premonition.

The three of them entered the chapel by the rear door. There was no one else there for Mass, so the priest invited them to stand with him at the altar. The Mass began, and Dr. Pazder soon noticed that Michelle was trembling.

After the Mass was over, Michelle and Dr. Pazder waited in a pew while Father Leo changed out of his vestments. When he rejoined them, Michelle started toward the door by which they had entered. "Oh, no," said Father Leo to Michelle. "You may have come in the back door, but you're going out the front door." And he unlocked the big oak door and let them out.

Later, back in the office at the Fort Royal Medical Centre, the tape recorder whirring, Michelle told Dr. Pazder what she had felt during Mass. By analogy, she had been taken back to that first horrific night. That time there had been a dresser covered by a black cloth; this time there was an altar covered with white. Again there were candles . . . and a chalice . . . with something red in it . . . and a man dressed in clothes with purple markings . . . who read from a book with droning solemnity. Rationally Michelle knew that Father Leo's Mass was as different from the ritual of that awful night as, literally, white was from black. Still, it was a ceremony, and the correspondences for Michelle afflicted her at first with deep visceral panic.

But, she also told Dr. Pazder, the Mass had brought her relief. "It was wonderful to know that there are forces stronger than the ones I'd experienced," she said. "When Father Leo first started talking, I thought, 'Oh, no, what do I do now?' But then I felt that God understood. I felt like I'd walked a million miles and then I was given a chance to rest. I finally could let God know how much I hurt.

"But I still have to face myself," she went on. "Father Leo blessed me, but he didn't say anything about protection, and I still feel I need it, and I think I'm going to need it a lot in the days to come."

When Michelle and Dr. Pazder began a session, they usually chatted for a while, and Michelle often would mention something that was on her mind, some topic or theme. Today, Christmas Eve, Michelle advanced one such topic. "I think I'm going to talk about hospitals," she said with a slightly confused smile. "I don't know why, but I can't stop thinking about hospitals. I wish I knew what it was.

Do you think I could have cut my hands with that bottle?"

Or, Dr. Pazder thought, perhaps the injuries inflicted on the child the night the lump was bludgeoned were severe enough to require hospitalization.

"As you well know," Michelle said, "I've always been afraid of hospitals. I've had the hardest time trusting doctors and nurses. I don't know what any of this means. I'm just going to have to believe it means something, right?"

"Right. Just let yourself talk about it now. Don't try to make sense out of it. We'll do that later."

Michelle then went on to talk about her various hospital experiences at length—her tonsillectomy, her emergency admission to a hospital for acute stomach pains, her mother's death, and so forth. As she talked, her breathing changed and she gradually began her descent.

"Oh, God . . . I hate going back there. Why is it so hard?"

Dr. Pazder took her hand and held it tightly. "You've spent your whole life holding all that down there in that dark place. Half of you is doing everything it can to keep it down, and the other half is letting it come and wants very much to get it all out so you can rest. It knows you have to face whatever it was. We can face it together. I just want to listen very carefully and hear everything as it comes out."

"Why don't you eat your breakfast?" Michelle's mother was saying.

It was the next morning. The night before, Malachi had angrily sent the child into the bathroom to clean herself up. She had tried, but she couldn't; she was so upset, so weak, so hurt. And the substances that had been painted on her had dried and were hard to get off, and they made the washcloth dirty and the water dirty, and she began to feel that she would never be clean again. She tried and tried . . . she desperately wanted to make everything clean and neat and normal again. Eventually she was told to go to bed, where she collapsed and somehow went to sleep.

And now here it was, the day after, and she was sitting in the kitchen, a bowl of cereal in front of her, with her mother. It was just like a pretend. Her mother was acting as if nothing had happened.

"I said to eat your breakfast!" But Michelle didn't want to eat, and she couldn't bear the pretense, so she threw her cereal bowl on the floor. Her mother was furious and sent her to her room. All day long she stayed there, but at dusk she ventured out.

> I'm not sure what happened or how it happened, but I was afraid of something in that house, and I went creeping out into the hall and opened the door of a bedroom. And do you know what was in that bedroom?

Michelle's voice was that of a scared five-year-old who has just seen something dreadful.

> Malachi was in there . . . and the lump was in there. Why was Malachi dressing it? I'm afraid. Somebody help me! *Help me!* And my mom came, and she's scary, her eyes look the same way they did when she told me to go away. She shut the door and she bent over and she had one hand on the door so that it was shut tight, and she had ahold of me. But she was being so quiet. And she said, *Don't . . . go . . . in . . . there!* And I knew I could never go in there. I didn't want to look in her eyes anymore. I just wanted to be a good girl. Yes . . . yes, Mom, I just want to be a good girl.

Michelle went back to her room. In what seemed to be the middle of the night she was awakened. Her mother and Malachi were dressed up and were getting ready to go somewhere.

> I was told to shut my eyes. . . . My pretend friend had come back, and she said I was silly to keep them shut, but I didn't dare open them. They said we were going in the car. My pretend friend kept doing things like, she'd turn and stick her tongue out at them. She made it a game. But I didn't think it was funny.

Michelle was led out of the house. She could hear foghorns—they must be near the ocean. She opened her eyes, just for a minute, and she saw the car: rounded nose, rounded back, and shiny black. She opened them once again. Malachi was dressed in a trenchcoat and a hat. Michelle was told to get into the back seat and stay on the floor.

He carried out a woman. At first she thought it was her mother—the clothes were her mother's—the fox collar, the pillbox hat with the veil. Hands held the woman up and placed her onto the front seat in front of the child. It was not Michelle's mother.

Malachi got behind the wheel and started the car. They drove for what seemed forever.

> It didn't have a back door! No, no! I'm getting all mixed up. My hands are all numb. I see crazy faces and . . . I can't do anything. I don't want to be in the car with a dead person. Help me! Help me!
>
> It wasn't funny. You see, he shouldn't have left me in there with somebody else. He's laughing. He looked at me and laughed and then he *got out of the car!*

The car was rolling down the mountain road as Malachi laughed his cruel laugh and jumped out. The car gained speed, and Michelle saw that it was heading for a rock embankment. The car smashed into the rock wall. The lifeless body in the front seat shot forward, then came violently back. Its head spun freely around, all the way around, as if the vertebrae were shattered, the face suddenly stopping inches from the child's. Its eyes were rolled up into the head.

> Make it go away. Make it go away! It's a mess. The head's a mess! Make those crazy eyes go away! Help! Help! Make them go away. I'm going crazy! I'm going crazy! That head just turned around. It was all wobbly. It was all covered in blood—it was all mashed up. The face was all mashed up. No one will ever know what that face looked like. It has a broken neck and the face is turned around backward!

The car had burst into flames. Michelle clawed at the metal till her hands bled. The car was full of smoke and she began to cough uncontrollably.

I remember lying on the ground. It was black and wet and hard . . . and there were black boots. There were ducks with black boots . . . I think they were firemen. I thought they were ducks because they had yellow coats on. All I could see were black boots. . . . I wanted them to be ducks. I kept pretending I wasn't there. Malachi! He was there! *Don't let him near me!* I knew I had to stop screaming, I knew I had to be quiet. I didn't want to be hit again. I had to *cooperate* or he'd kill me. I knew he would.

As she lay there she could hear Malachi talking. How could he say those things? She was in pain, but now he was hurting her even more by his words.

He told them . . . he told them I was playing in the back seat. I couldn't believe it. He told them it was because I put my hands over his eyes . . . that's why. I wouldn't have done that. I wouldn't have touched him. He was crying. He's so phony. He's only crying because I didn't die!

A white car came, an ambulance. Malachi said he wanted to ride in the ambulance with Michelle. But she began to thrash and kick and scream. He bent down to her and whispered, "Michelle, you keep your mouth shut!" She began to vomit, and he pulled away abruptly.

They put something on my face. I couldn't stand it. I couldn't stand them putting anything on my face. I thought they were trying to choke me. They kept saying how difficult I was. I thought I was difficult to kill! . . . Where are you?

The psychiatrist put his arm around the young woman's shoulders. "I'm right here, Michelle, I'm right here."

"I've got to rest."

"Yes."

"Is it okay if I stop here?"

"Of course, Michelle. You've done well. You must be exhausted. Try to leave it and come back up."

Slowly Michelle ascended, weeping most of the way, heartbreaking tears. It was an hour before she and the doctor were able to talk about what she had relived, so that he could help her understand it.

"Does any of this make sense to you?" she asked.

"It all makes sense."

"Oh, please help me. I feel so scared inside."

"It's a scary place."

"That's why I had my pretend friend."

"You couldn't cope with it any other way. I'm glad you had her."

"I can't cope with it now, either," Michelle stammered, and began to sob again. "I can't even let myself be as afraid as I feel. Do you know what that wobbly head looked like? It almost looked as if it were alive. I want it to go away. I didn't start all that. I was just helping my mom when I smacked that person on the head."

Dr. Pazder leaned forward. "Smacked what?"

"Smacked that person on the head."

"You know," he said, "that's the first time you've admitted that lump was a person—the first time with your eyes looking at me."

"I know," Michelle said. "I've always talked of it as a lump and things like that. It takes me a while."

"It's so important for you to face all of it."

"I know a person was hurt. It was someone who had feelings, like I had feelings. I didn't want her smashed by everybody there. I just wanted to protect my mother and stop that craziness. But it didn't work, and I guess I can't blame myself for what they did to her."

"That's right, Michelle. It's good to hear you say that. You've been too hard on yourself about it. You certainly were not in any way responsible for what those people did back there. But it's like you've said, that children always feel responsible for the wrongdoings of adults, especially mothers. I'm glad you were able to face that yourself, because that's how you free yourself from it. It's much more important than my saying it to you."

In time the conversation turned to the events themselves.

"Do you remember the accident at all now?" Dr. Pazder asked.

"Yes, but I can't think about it without crying."

"That's okay. Just let yourself cry."

"It seemed like the fire was all around me, and then it wasn't. . . . It was around that head. But then I don't know. . . . Then it's nothing . . . and then it's all these black boots and I hear sirens."

"How did you get out of the car?"

"I don't know. I don't remember that."

"What day was it? Do you have any idea?"

"I don't know." She remained silent for a few moments. "Although, before they made me go to the car, my mom and Malachi said something like, 'They won't pay much attention to it, they'll just think it's tragic this time of year.' I didn't know what tragic was. I thought it meant fire, because that was what one policeman did say—'What a tragic thing to happen at Christmas.' "

"So it was Christmastime. What year was it?"

"I don't know what year it was. It was before I was in Grade One, I think. I was in Grade One in 1956.

The psychiatrist stood and stretched and reached out his hand to help Michelle up. "Let's leave it for now. This has been a very long day. We've got a lot to talk about, don't we, a lot to go through?"

Michelle said nothing.

"We'll work it out."

"I know. . . ."

"You've got to drive over the Malahat, don't you? Those mountain roads are icy and treacherous. Be careful on the way home, won't you?"

"Yes."

"I know what you're thinking. . . ."

"I know."

"You're thinking that maybe the car crash happened up there on that road."

"Yes."

"I wish I could drive you home, but I can't."

"I know. And don't worry. I'll be fine. I'll be very careful, you can believe that." And Michelle smiled to ease Dr. Pazder's concern.

chapter 7

*I*T was the nicest Christmas that Michelle had ever had. She and Doug were in their beautiful new home together. He gave her an afghan and a pretty brass lamp—warmth and light, ideal gifts. Michelle and Doug had spent a whole day three weeks earlier preparing homemade mincemeat. They baked Christmas cake, shortbread, and a variety of cookies. On Christmas Day, friends came over bearing their own special treats. Everyone admired the big tree that they had all cut down together the week before. After gifts and music, Michelle called them all to dinner, a festive meal served on the best china and crystal, tall candles lighting the happy faces. The food was traditional—turkey, stuffing, potatoes, sweet potatoes, gravy, turnips, cranberry sauce. For dessert, hot plum pudding with rum sauce, trifle, and the mincemeat pie, aged in brandy.

The next day was Boxing Day, and more neighbors from around the lake trudged through the snow carrying presents, many of them homemade.

Later that evening, after all the celebrating was over and Michelle and Doug were sitting by the fire having eggnog, she began to tell him a bit about what she had discovered during her session with Dr. Pazder on Christmas Eve. There apparently had been a car accident, she said, and an ambulance had come to take the little girl to the hopsital. As she spoke, Michelle began to cough. She couldn't stop. She coughed all night, and the next day she went to her physician, who gave her some antibiotics. Still the cough persisted, and by the time she arrived for her appointment with Dr. Pazder, her throat was sore, and she ached all over.

Dr. Pazder listened to her severe cough—this wracking, whooping cough—and he examined her throat. He felt quite certain the cough had nothing to do with disease—pneumonia, for instance—and wondered if it was connected to the smoke and flames of the car accident. Again, perhaps, Michelle's body was remembering.

"We've got a lot to cover today," he said. "Tomorrow I'm leaving for Mexico, and at the end of our session we have to talk with Dr. Arnot about his being available to you while I'm gone." Michelle had known of Dr. Pazder's impending month's vacation with his wife, and Michelle was glad for Dr. Pazder to have a rest, for he clearly needed it, and glad too that she would have a rest from the agonies of unearthing the painful past. She looked forward to a quiet, simple time at home. Dr. Pazder, on his part, felt comfortable about leaving Michelle in Dr. Arnot's care. Richards Arnot, the colleague in his group to whom he felt closest, was experienced at treating children and dealing with terror, pain, and body memory. The one thing Dr. Pazder wanted to caution Dr. Arnot about: If Michelle's cough should get worse, he should not put her into a hospital except as a last resort. Hospitals for Michelle were unspeakably frightening.

Michelle then made her descent rather rapidly, and promptly began the process she would later compare to "watching a rerun of an old movie. That's how real it seems."

She was lying in a room draped with cloth—white cloth on all four walls. There were people around her, and they were wearing white. Muddled by pain killers and shock, her child's brain concluded with horror that these were merely a new and different group of people who were going to hurt her. Two of them undressed her—it was happening again. A man made her open her eyes, her mouth—and probed them. A woman inserted something into her bottom. When she resisted, she was told to cooperate.

Two men in black asked her questions. "What happened?" one inquired. Michelle thought he meant, "What happened to the lady?"

Remembering Malachi's admonition, she squeezed her lips tight shut and refused to talk.

The white cloth on one of the walls was pulled back, and out in the corridor she saw a table on wheels and, on the table, a long plastic bag. Instinctively she knew that the bag contained a body. And then the white-clad person who had been standing by the table moved away, and Michelle saw something that froze her heart: Resting on top of the plastic-clad corpse was a pair of red shoes.

Again she awoke. This time she was in a room with green walls; the upper half of one wall was glass, and through it, out in the hall, Michelle could see a clock. There was a crucifix on the wall; Michelle did not know what a cross was, let alone a crucifix, but she was struck by its form.

There were strings—tubes, really—stuck into her arms and running to upside-down bottles, one red, one white. In panic Michelle pulled the tubes from her arms. A woman in white came running over and scolded her, officiously putting the tubes back into her arms.

Once again she drifted up from unconsciousness. Everything looked funny, the clock looked fuzzy—it was as if she were underwater. And then she realized that she too was in a plastic bag. Am I dead? she wondered.

She pulled out the tubes and pushed back the covers and crawled out of the plastic bag. She wanted so much to sneak away—but she had no idea where to go. She inched her way into the hall. Almost immediately hands seized her from behind, and two persons in white carried her back to bed.

"She's a very difficult child," one of them said.

"We're going to have to tie your hands down," said the other. Soon her hands were tied to the bedposts.

"She just wants attention," the first person said.

"Good morning, Michelle." The child looked up and saw her mother. Several people in white stood by as pale, beautiful Jessica Harding came to the bedside and tried to show affection. But to

Michelle her caring was plainly artificial, done not for Michelle's comfort but for the benefit of the people in white. Michelle pretended to fall asleep.

"This must be terribly difficult for you," one of the people in white said to Jessica.

Malachi was standing just outside the room, looking in at Michelle. She recoiled in shock. He was talking to two policemen.

"She was one of my closest friends," he was saying to them, referring to the dead lady. He was pretending to cry. "I'll never forgive Michelle . . . no, that isn't right, she's just a child . . . but it seems so cruel that a wonderful woman like that could be killed just because of a child's misbehavior." The policemen listened, nodded gravely, and walked away.

Malachi turned and started for the door to the room. With all her heart Michelle knew that she must not allow him to enter, must not let him anywhere near her. Without thinking, acting on blind impulse, she yanked the red tube from her arm and let the liquid squirt freely. Blood covered her face. Through the crimson bath, she looked out at Malachi and then—out of pure detestation—made crazy eyes at him. It worked. Malachi took a step back, then another, then hurriedly left the room.

In Dr. Pazder's office in the Fort Royal Medical Centre—just a few miles in distance from the scene Michelle had been recounting, but precisely twenty-two years away in time—the doctor watched as his patient sat up, turned her head quickly to the side, and opened her eyes wide in horror.

"I looked at him like he looked at me that night," she said, almost screaming. "They were *his* eyes. I just wanted to give him his eyes back. I just didn't want him in that room. I thought to myself, 'I shouldn't have done that.' Oh, God help me. Help me! All of a sudden I didn't know who I was, and I was afraid to open my eyes again—I'd be crazy forever. Those eyes in the car, the woman's eyes, they were full of crazy. Are my eyes crazy? Am I crazy? Please . . ."

"No, Michelle," Dr. Pazder said, "I saw your eyes, and I saw you, and it was okay. They were scary, but they were your eyes, and I'm glad you had them. You weren't crazy. You were just terrified and fighting for your life."

"No child should feel as guilty," she said a short while later, "as they made me feel. It was wrong—you don't make a child feel like that. *I was just a child!*" Now she was openly screaming and pounding and kicking against the mat she was lying on. "They made me feel so awful. I was so mad at everyone!"

"Let it all out," Dr. Pazder said. "Let it go. It's okay to cry. It's really okay. You've got a lot of crying to do."

"I do, I do. . . ."

"You've got a lot of crying to do with that little girl, because you've had to protect her and be so brave about it. Here, Michelle, I want you to take hold of this doll. Do you remember it? You made it for me a long, long time ago, for my other patients to hold onto when they felt really bad. Here, you hold onto it now. Hold it close, just like you wanted someone to hold you, a long time ago."

Michelle took the big soft doll and pressed it to her, beginning to cry convulsively. As the tears came, she gave up the doll and hugged herself.

"You've got to go back there, Michelle, and *embrace that little girl* —that little girl who was so abandoned and wounded. The only thing she really has and needs now is *you.* She needs you to look after her. That's what you're going to have to learn how to do."

"What do you mean?"

"You've got to understand that there's a big difference between then and now. Now you have her, and she has you. The hard part is that no one can ever make up for what happened to you back there . . . but you can *love* her, you can love her as much as she needs. We all have to love ourselves again, all the time."

Michelle continued to cry, deeply sobbing, but now, more and more, it was with relief. "I don't feel numb anymore," she said.

"No, you don't. That's good."

"I've never wanted to cry so badly in my life."

"You must let your tears come out. You don't have to hold them back anymore."

"Thank you so much for listening to me and understanding. Today will make your going to Mexico a lot easier."

"I hope so."

"Could we talk about back there, if we have the time?"

"Yes, it's important. We do have a little time left."

"They put dead people in a plastic bag, don't they?"

"They can, especially if they are badly burned. Do you know why you were in an oxygen tent?"

"That's what it was? I thought it was a plastic bag and I was supposed to be dead. I wish doctors and nurses knew how important it is not to say anything that frightens children. If somebody had just taken the time to explain things to me it would have made such a difference. Do you see why I'm so afraid of hospitals?

"I certainly do."

"They put a black tube in my mouth and down my throat. Why did they do that?"

"Well, from everything you told me, I'd say you were likely bleeding from your mouth and throat, and the blood was draining down into your stomach. Were you throwing up anything black?"

"Yes."

"Well, they had that tube down there to drain the blood from your stomach so you wouldn't be nauseated and so they could keep a watch on how much you were bleeding. It was black because blood turns black in the stomach."

"Will my cough go away?"

"It does sound as if your body is remembering coughing from all that smoke. It will probably get better when your chest gets better back there. You know. . . ." He paused.

"Know what?"

"Well, it does seem that you are reliving everything that went on back there, day for day, almost hour by hour. It's absolutely amazing. It's almost too much to believe, but you're exactly on a cycle with this moment twenty-two years ago. I mean, every psychiatrist knows of anniversary reactions—for example, people who get sad and can't imagine why, and then it turns out that something terrible, a death or something, occurred exactly a year ago. But this is the most astounding anniversary reaction I've ever heard of."

"I know, like today I was really hot, for a change, really just pouring sweat, and I very seldom do that. I wondered if it was because I was in bed in the hospital."

"It's possible you got an infection back there, like you can get from burns. That might account for the heat. Or maybe you were about to get one. Do you know whether that's it? I'm just asking because I'd kind of want to know what to tell Dr. Arnot to expect while I'm away."

"I wish I knew. I don't know what's going to happen to me. I don't know how I got out of the hospital. It's absolutely blank."

"Well, maybe I'm wrong, but I feel relieved knowing you ended up in the hospital. Hospitals aren't great, but at least you're in safe hands and away from those people."

Michelle smiled. "I hope you're right."

"There are just a couple more things I want to say," Dr. Pazder added. "In many ways it was a very symbolic place you were in, where we were working today, and much of what was happening to you was colliding with what had happened earlier—like, for example, the lights and candles . . . the stretcher and dresser and bed . . . the white curtain and black uniforms . . . the colored tubes, needles, thermometers, like the colored sticks . . . the bags and cups of colored liquids . . . the strange talking . . . the smells . . . the way you were treated, it was all so overwhelmingly symbolic. And I couldn't help thinking about that dream you told me just before all this started. Do you remember it?"

"Yes. It's exactly what I was thinking about when I told you about those people sticking those things in my arms. I could feel little bugs crawling under my skin."

"Our time is just about up. I'm leaving you the tape recorder. You've been used to talking about your memories so much lately that they'll probably come up a little, at least for the first few days I'm gone. And it'll help you to talk—sort of like letting off steam. When I get back we'll go over it and work with it. If you feel more comfortable using my office, come on in, but check with Sue first to make sure it's available. I also want you to have my sheepskin coat to help you keep warm and know that it's okay."*

"Thank you. I'm going to try to get a holiday too, if my body will let me."

"Remember that Dr. Arnot will be there if you need him."

"All I need is a hand once in a while," Michelle said whimsically. "Tea and sympathy, as Janis Ian calls it."

---

*Michelle had been using the doctor's old coat as a blanket to warm her against the chill she often felt while in her depths.

chapter 8

"I'T'S December 28," Michelle said into the tape recorder. "I feel pretty silly, sitting here in bed with a hot-water bottle and with your sheepskin coat pulled up to my chin like a comforter. But a comforter is exactly what it is. I'm doing this because I've got to tell you some things. Some of it'll make sense, some of it won't. Some of it will just be words here and there. Reminders. Things I can't deal with right now. . . .

"I keep getting little flashes into the future but I don't know what they amount to yet. I think before you come back I'll probably know. It's about eleven-thirty at night and I was getting more and more scared and farther and farther away, so Doug suggested my trying to talk to the recorder.

"I get so frightened at night. I think it's just being alone, alone then, alone now; it hurts so much I hadn't thought I could get through today. It's not just because you've gone. Being alone has a lot to do with then, with awfully long nights alone in that hospital room knowing there was no one I could reach out to. I also think I was probably quite ill and wasn't entirely sure whether I was going to make it through the night—just me, physically, if I was going to make it. I feel that kind of fear tonight—like, am I going to make it till tomorrow morning?

"I had four or five friends call today. When I answered and I began to try to talk, you know like, 'How was your Christmas?' and all that, I couldn't do it. I just had to say I wasn't well and I would phone them back later. I've never been like that before. I've always been able to somehow bluff my way through better than that. I can't bluff at all, at least not today. It's too real. The pain I feel's too real, the loss—the loss back then.

"I feel like I'm going to pass out. I think I'd better stop for a minute. It's okay. I know what the problem is now. I got so paranoid in that hospital about people hurting me that every time anybody came near me I thought they were trying to kill me. It's so hard to be afraid for your life when someone's there and the minute they walk out the door you're even more afraid because you're alone. Oh, what do you do? What do you do? I think I spent a lot of those nights screaming silently or pretending.

"Well, it's getting late and Doug wants to go to bed so I guess I'm going to have to go. I wish I could hear your voice telling me it's going to be all right. The fact is I just don't know it's going to be all right. I don't know."

Thus began for Michelle the month that Lawrence Pazder would be in Mexico. Bits and pieces of memory continued to surface while her body began preparing for the new memories that lurked below. She felt herself getting cold—a familiar sign that something was happening back there; maybe she wasn't so safe in the hospital as she and Dr. Pazder had hoped. The remembering hadn't stopped—it couldn't be turned off for a vacation. Once the process was started, it had a movement of its own. But Michelle couldn't allow herself to remember fully without Dr. Pazder there to hear it and help her deal with what came out. She was reminded of something she had written soon after the remembering began:

> I tried not to have it happen, but this process, I am realizing more and more, is not consciously controllable. I kind of think it is "me" inside trying to come out and be whole.
>
> It's funny how it starts. It's the same every time. First of all I get really cold, nothing keeps me warm, my whole body is cold, I turn up the heat, put on an extra pair of socks, pull the afghan over me. Warmth helps. I need the warmth.

Then comes the wrenching in my stomach and chest, my insides just keep grinding away. That's what surprises me, this is such a physical thing, and if it weren't for the physical signs I wouldn't have a clue. There's the rash, so itchy I can't help wondering what it is trying to say. I used to put ointments on, cover it up, hide it, pretend it wasn't there, make excuses, or ignore it; but now I *want* to scratch! Now I know if I don't work through the rash it will always bother me. I'm so inflamed, swollen, incredibly itchy, I feel tormented, angry, guilty, unclean, and definitely like something is wrong with me. The other thing I've realized is there is no possible way my rashes could have been any other than the way they look, and here I just have to associate inflamed—anger—red—blood—ooze. Where they show up and their patterns all explain something to me. My body is my only clue. It's the one thing I couldn't compromise or rationalize. It was there. My mind and feelings could go away but my body was there and had to be there the whole time. I could shut my eyes but my body could see what was happening.

You see, my "inside me" could shut everything off but there was still my body and it had its own life "outside" of "me inside." It is my outside that really knows. It's my eyes that saw, my mouth that felt, spoke, and took in; my arms, they have memories too. Before I can let my inside "me" remember, my body's memories have to come out. The reason the connections don't always seem to fit together is because my arms don't have the same experience my mouth had, and my eyes didn't feel what my stomach felt. I have felt like I was fractured into so many pieces, but it was the different parts of me remembering. I had to fracture that way. You see, "me" could not look after it all at once!

And then it's so hard putting the body memories together. That's why they came out separately, so that when my eyes, ears, nose, mouth, arms have all told their versions, that is when "I" will understand "me"; that is when I will be whole again.

Remember all those times I've begged you to help me put it all together? Well, it's not just understanding it and putting things together that way. I am beginning to realize that it is a much more literal request—help put me, my body, the parts of my body, my memories, and my body memories (imprints) back together.

Still beset by the memories, Michelle again turned to the tape recorder.

"I've tried to do housework or work with my plants or do things that distract me today, but I'm never completely there. There's always such a large part of me that is trying somehow to work something out. I don't really know entirely what it is except that it's there and it can't be ignored. . . . I've had thoughts about New Year's . . . something about a funeral."

"I watch the clock on the hospital wall so much. If I could get inside the clock and be its hands, I could quit being myself for a while. . . ."

"There's a picture on the wall of a nice man and lots of little children, like me, around him."

"A few funny things are starting to happen. It's got something to do with the person that was there that night that was a nurse and things being in my room. I hope you don't mind that I have to take away some of the feelings in telling you about it now. That's the part I can't share and I won't be able to until you come back."

"My mom's come back to see me, but it's all different. She isn't even pretending to care. She just doesn't care anymore. I can't get any feeling from her. I can't reach her at all, and I'm afraid to. I just have to lie here and listen and watch very carefully . . . and just . . . be ready. . . .

"She's got something in her arms. She's brought me something in a box. . . . Things are starting to happen. . . . I'm screaming. . . . She's doing something funny . . . something funny behind me. I can't stop coughing. I'm choking! I can't breathe. I'm dying. I'm going to die."

On December 30, Michelle phoned Dr. Arnot to tell him that serious memories were beginning to surface. He asked her to come to the office, but he knew that for him to step in and attempt to work with Michelle, to try to substitute for Dr. Pazder, to allow her to descend all the way into these memories without his knowing precisely how to monitor her or to help her climb back out of them would not be wise. The effect might be to break all the bonds and allow the process to run amok. And her gasping coughs were in themselves truly alarming.

Dr. Arnot told her that under the circumstances it seemed best that she try to phone Dr. Pazder.

"I really don't want to do that," she replied. But she desperately did, and, the next day, New Year's Eve, after talking it over with her husband, she placed a call to Dr. Pazder in Mexico. "Something's wrong! It's not all over back there!" she cried across the thousands of miles. "The memories keep coming! I feel like I'm going to die!"

Dr. Pazder was shocked. He had been having a wonderful vacation, full of swimming and sun. He had thought about Michelle but only peripherally, as, for example, once when he had seen a pigtailed little girl playing on the beach. He had not been worried about Michelle, and he had been a psychiatrist too long to bring his patients' troubles along with him on holiday; that did no one any good. But as he listened to Michelle blurting out the fragments of memory through her coughing, he was grateful she had called. When she said, "I'm not going to make it," he believed her. There seemed every likelihood that something dreadful was happening to that child again, and this time in the hospital. If the adult Michelle should happen to unearth that experience and it should prove unbearable, it seemed possible that in some real way Michelle might not survive.

"Thank God you called me," he told her. "It was the right thing to do. I understand a little of what's happening. It must be very, very frightening for you, but you're not alone. We can talk. I want to talk. I want to know what you're going through."

"Just for you to know, that means everything."

"The important thing is to stay away from the memories as much as you can. Don't encourage them, but if they've got to come, tell the tape recorder. And we can talk on the phone every few days."

"That would be . . . that's so good of you. I won't call unless I really have to."

"We can't handle too much over the phone. You can't go into all that with you up there and me down here. But it's important for me to hear anything really scary. Maybe even at this distance I can put it to the side enough so that it won't hurt too much."

Michelle was greatly relieved that Dr. Pazder had heard and understood. The contact between them made it possible for her to keep the memories under better control, and she was able to enjoy the rest of the month. She and Doug went to the movies. She set about repotting her large collection of tropical plants, some two hundred of them. She went out to the university, where she had taught a course in fiber sculpture, and, choosing tones of white and gray and brown from the stores of coarse, handspun wool, she wove a tea cozy. She was pleased with it, if she did say so herself. Some of her fiber sculptures had sold for more than a thousand dollars, and this little tea cozy was as good as any of them. She took it to the Fort Royal Medical Centre, along with an assortment of her best plants. Some years ago she had nursed a number of neglected plants back to health, and she had a very special feeling about her "greenhouse." Each plant had a personality of its own, this one liking sunny, open spaces, that one happier in a small, shadowed nook. She learned how to care for all of them, she watched them grow and respond to her attention. And she was rewarded—her plants were thriving, lush, and beautiful. Now she wanted to bring the joy of these natural, growing things into Dr. Pazder's admittedly drab office.

But the memories returned.

"She's back. That lady is back. The one who was there that night in the black cloak. Only . . . now she's all dressed in white. She's smiling, but she scares me!"

"My mom . . . she keeps saying she's really sorry. She's doing something. I can't breathe!"

On the phone, Michelle would say again and again that she felt she was going to die. Dr. Pazder suspected that this was still another body memory—like the coughing and the rashes, but far more extreme . . . a memory of the process of dying. Asking few questions, merely letting her know he had heard her and understood it was important, he helped her allay the distress as best he could. And then, during the call just before his return, she forced out a revelation that she obviously had been holding firmly back.

"There is something really scary that happens with my mom," she said, "when she comes to visit me. I don't know what it is, but I know it has something to do with why I feel as if I'm dying." Then came tears that were so achingly genuine that Dr. Pazder, despite the distance and his wife's obvious confusion as to why he was sitting with the phone to his ear for a quarter of an hour without saying anything, allowed them to go freely on and on.

chapter 9

*W*HEN Dr. Pazder and his wife returned from Mexico, they found themselves the guests of honor at a surprise party. The hosts were their four children—three sons and a daughter, Theresa. Theresa had baked the cake. Dr. Pazder had set aside four days to be with the children and to work with Michelle before resuming the rest of his practice. He had promised Michelle over the phone that if she could hold off until his return, he would see her right away. And so the following afternoon, January 26, he found himself back in his office.

Michelle was in the waiting room when he arrived, talking with Dr. Arnot: "Boy, are we ever glad to see you!" Dr. Arnot exclaimed when Dr. Pazder walked in. In the office was another surprise—the touches of beauty Michelle had added—the plants, the unique tea cozy, and also a macramé wall-hanging she had made. They livened up the place.

There was a lot of catching up to do.

"It's good to see you," Dr. Pazder said, shutting the office door.

"It's really good to see you," Michelle replied. "I can't believe I'm talking to the real you instead of to a machine."

"Just go ahead and talk."

"I'm not very sure about anything I've been remembering. I've got to talk really fast and jump around, okay?"

"Okay."

"There's something that really has to be said today. I'm not sure what it is. It's something to do with time—I had this really panicky feeling that time was important to my mother and her friends. I don't know if it was because I was being a clock, or what. But something clued me into the fact that they were doing everything in some sort of definite order."

"You knew that?"

"I knew the dates were . . . that's why New Year's Eve scared me so much, the night I first called you. I had the strongest feeling that it was more the end than the beginning. It felt like the *end*—the end of me. I can't explain."

"Keep going."

"I felt I was going to die. Really *die.*"

"I know you did."

"It was something that happened. . . ."

"Something to do with . . ."

"Something to do with"—Michelle turned and twisted on the couch—"something to do with . . . my . . . mother. . . ."

"You said that on the phone, I think, the last phone call."

"I don't want to think about that."

"I wouldn't blame you."

"I remember the clock. . . ."

"You said you actually became the clock."

"It was out in the hall. I looked at it all day long. And then I found myself turning into the clock. That made me feel good. If you're a clock, you matter, people are always looking at you to see what you're doing. I was sort of running their day. They'd walk by and think, 'Gee, I'm late,' and they'd hurry, and I'd think, 'Well, I'm making them hurry! Or they'd worry about not having enough of me —enough time. I was afraid *I* didn't have enough time. I liked being a clock."

"It sounds like fun."

"It was fun. I was really pleased with that one. Clocks are never sad. Plus the fact that clock *moved;* I was lying on the bed and couldn't move. It had a face that people liked and hands and a heart, because it ticks . . . and it knew its numbers, it was really smart. That matters to little kids. And clocks never run out of time. I mean, I actually remember thinking that I wasn't going to die because I could hang on with my hands and because I literally 'had time.' "

"It's wonderful how a child finds ways to hold onto its sanity."

"It helped a lot."

"I'm sure it did."

"No matter how bad things got . . ."

Michelle fell into a troubled silence, and Dr. Pazder wondered if she was about to begin a descent. But when she spoke again, her voice, though strained, was still her adult voice.

"On the tape, I told you about . . ."

"Yes?"

"I told you about something that was so bad, so frightening . . . it scares me. . . . Do you want to hear it on the tape?"

"I could hear it from you now, if you want me to."

"Well, I was in my bed. I must have been asleep. Or half a-sleep . . ."

She was under sedation, Dr. Pazder speculated, groggy, perhaps running a fever. "I was just lying there, and I heard this voice. 'Michelle . . . Michelle . . . Michelle . . .' I woke up, but I didn't open my eyes, and this voice said, 'Michelle, *I'm* your special nurse.' And I was so happy and opened my eyes, and I saw this pretty lady all dressed in white, and I started to smile—and then . . . it's *horrible!* . . . I recognized her. . . .

"It was . . . she was that lady! You know, the *lady,* the one who'd been at the house the night the lump was killed . . . the lady in the black cloak who did those things to me with the colored sticks. And I got the feeling that she really *was* a nurse—she was so . . . efficient. She just went around the room, tidying up. She went over to the wall and said, 'You won't be needing this crucifix anymore.' And she took the wooden thing down from the wall."

Dr. Pazder went pale. Whoever these people were, Michelle's tormentors, they were not ordinary cultists.

Michelle misread his pained expression. "Do you want me to stop? I can't stop . . . but I don't want to upset you."

"No, no, no. I don't want you to stop."

"I'll stop and go home, if you want me to." Michelle's voice was tremulous, her face drawn with tension and then, suddenly, panic. "But . . . what if I go home and she comes with me?"

"Where do you have to get to, in this experience, to feel safe?"

"I don't know," Michelle said, whimpering.

"Well, let's just begin."

"Are you sure? Please, I can't . . . I can't do anything, I'm so weak now." She was crying. "I can't see you. I don't know what to do." The crying was mixed with coughing and great gasps for air. She quickly drifted into her depths and began the reliving.

Something's wrong. Why do I see my mom all dressed up? She's in that really nice green plaid suit—dark green with yellow stripes, mostly green with yellow and blue. It has a pleated skirt and a tailored jacket, and a great big hat with flowers on it. . . . She looks real nice in it.

One of the nurses is saying, "She's got to *want* to pull out of it." . . . I don't know where I'm going and I'm afraid. Oh, please don't. . . . I hate it. Oh, please don't. I'm afraid!

Maybe my mom has come to save me. She comes over and sits down by my bed and she looks so pretty. . . . Oh, my chest hurts! My chest hurts! I couldn't say anything to her. It was the other me looking at her, I had my eyes shut.

Michelle paused for a moment, her body motionless, her face blank. Then her alertness slowly returned.

"Do I have to tell you everything that's happening to see if it's not true?"

"Yes, everything."

"I don't think it's true, but I don't know where it came from."

"It seems quite important to you."

She's leaning over saying something to me. I wanted her to hug me. I could have hugged her back, I could've. And then she said, "Here, I brought you something." And I opened this box and I . . . there was a doll. . . . I took it out of the box . . . and underneath it . . . there was a dead bird! It was my bird, my budgie, all *dead!*

Michelle's sobs shook her body, and Dr. Pazder drew her to him and held her while the agony played itself out.

> Then she said, "Oh, Michelle, I'm sorry, I'm so sorry this had to happen. And I'm sorry about . . ." But that's all she said. And when she said that, something in her face just went away. I don't think I ever saw my mom come back again. She was fiddling with something beside my bed . . . and she . . . Oh, my chest hurts, I feel faint, I feel faint. . . . I can't breathe. . . . She's just sitting there looking at me. . . . I can't breathe!

As he listened, caught up in the terrible story, Dr. Pazder realized that whatever had happened long ago was having a physical effect in the present. Michelle had turned white and was on the verge of fainting. She was gasping for air, struggling to breathe. Her pulse was slow, but it was within safe limits, and he refrained from speaking to her, afraid a voice might shock her. For ten minutes she lay like that on the couch. Then, mightily to his relief, her color began to return, her face came alive, and her eyes opened. And then she began to surface, crying as she rose.

"I can't take any more," she said. "I didn't want to try anymore. I just gave up. I was going to die anyway. What did it matter? It didn't matter to anybody. That's what the truth was—I didn't matter to anybody." And then, after a few minutes, she said: "But I must have mattered if they wanted me dead."

"You matter," Dr. Pazder said, "a very great deal."

"I had to stop—I know you want to go see your kids. I made myself stop because everything was beginning to make sense."

"I'm very glad you can go back there and start picking it up again. I thought it would take longer."

"There's too much of it to take longer," Michelle whispered.

"For what?"

"It'd take longer."

"Really? But you didn't get left behind today, did you?"

"Hmm?"

"You didn't get left behind. You've allowed it to come up."

"Well, yes, but now I've made this connection and everything. . . . But I know you've got to get home."

"Tell me about it."

"Tell you about it? Well, okay. You know I wanted to get out of the hospital. Well, it all makes sense now. It was like I had to get out of the hospital New Year's Eve . . . because the nurse was there. She had a lot more power than the other people did. I think she had more than my mom. She was sort of like the female counterpart to Malachi. I'm not sure if it was Malachi who told my mom to bring those things in or if it was her. But I can tell you something very definitely. I'd never seen that doll before. It wasn't mine!"

Michelle stopped and put her hand to her chest. "I keep feeling like I'm having a heart attack."

"A lot of pain there?"

"No, my heart just feels like it's moving around. I'm just scared. Now you see"—she began to cough again—"I feel so dumb doing that, the coughing."

"Talking about what happened in the hospital still gives you a lot of trouble in your chest."

"The doll's eyes were poked out," Michelle continued, very distressed. "And I went to pick it up and its head fell off . . . and the underneath part of the bird was all rotten! Aaggh, all bugs!"

"Bugs on the bird?"

Michelle was moaning. "And they crawled out from inside the bird's head. I just smashed it away. But I couldn't say anything, because my mom, she was such a blank . . . but the nurse, she was looking at me with those crazy eyes." Michelle gasped. "I couldn't yell at any of them. I could just throw things. Then the room got wiggly, and I began to vomit."

After a time Michelle forced herself to resume.

"She wasn't ugly either, the nurse. That's what's deceiving. She was really pretty. But then she did that . . . thing to me. It was New Year's Eve. Of course I wasn't asleep. I was being a clock. I'd heard them say it was New Year's Eve,* and time is important on New Year's Eve, so I was spending a lot of time being a clock that night. She said she had to give me a bath." Michelle was panting, groaning, partially descending.

She started talking to me like she did that night—you know, that she was being all like . . . a mommy. And she was saying she was there to look after me and make me better. She pulled my clothes off. The other nurses didn't care, they just thought she was giving me a bath. Eleven-thirty . . . she had this silver thing . . . she knew . . . it wasn't like those cups that night, it was much bigger. And I just shut my mouth very tight, I wasn't going to open it. And she thought that was funny . . . oooh . . . she told me I had to put my legs like that, like when she was washing me. She went and got that silver thing, and this long tube. She said the doctor had ordered an enema. I didn't understand. You see, I hadn't gone to the bathroom for days—I wouldn't let myself. I didn't know what an enema was; I didn't know for years after that.

As soon as she put the tube in my bottom . . . it was so much like that other night, with her and those sticks and that stuff. She told me I wasn't allowed to move. . . . It's such a terrible pain down there, it's like hot and cold. I couldn't go to the bathroom, I wasn't allowed to do that. It's ten to twelve. . . . Oh, I hurt, I really hurt. But I wasn't allowed to say anything, I had to be really quiet. She said I couldn't go to the bathroom until midnight. I felt like I'd lost control down there. . . . I can't stand hurting like this. Oh, what am I going to do? What am I going to do?

At midnight she said, "You have to go to the bathroom right now!" I could see the shiny thing, it looked like a toilet seat. She was bringing it to me. I couldn't get out of bed. And just when

*The dates during the hospital experience are uncertain. It later became clear that Malachi, the nurse, and the others were using a calendar year that differed from the ordinary. It appears possible that their New Year's Day was the thirteenth day of the thirteenth month—that is, January 13.

she told me I could go, she pulled the pan away. I went all over the bed. She tricked me. And she smiled.

I had to get out of the hospital. I had to get out. But they put bars up that night. I woke up and there were bars around the bed. I knew I had to pretend I was better, go along with everything, that's the way I could get out of there. When I left, I wasn't very well, but I pretended I was. I still don't know exactly when I got out of the hospital.

In the second session after Dr. Pazder's return, Michelle dealt with what would prove to be one of the harshest realizations she would have to confront. In the session before, when Michelle was relating her mother's dreadful visit to the hospital and then broke off into some semblance of death, Dr. Pazder had been stunned by the mention of the mother's "fiddling" with something behind or beside the bed. He had two dire thoughts. Either the woman was trying to put air into one of the intravenous tubes or she was shutting off the valve on the tank that supplied oxygen to the plastic tent and the child's smoke-scorched lungs. The latter seemed the likelier, in view of Michelle's desperate complaints that she could not breathe, and her lapse into a comatose state.

In her depths and later during the period of integration, Michelle went back over the experience, trying to add details. It was extremely painful for her to face the growing knowledge that her own mother had tried to kill her. But what astounded the doctor was that Michelle revealed very little bitterness. Indeed, she experienced real grief for her mother, never relinquishing the hope that when her mother had said, "Oh, Michelle . . . I'm so sorry," she really had meant it—sorry not only for what had already happened to her little girl but also for what she knew was about to happen.

Michelle, however, was never able to explore sufficiently her experiences in the hospital. The memories had come up haphazardly, most of the time without Dr. Pazder there to assist or to integrate. And there was no time to go back over these memories, because time past was moving relentlessly forward. The child was having new experiences that were propelling her on.

chapter 10

"*D*ID you listen to CFAX this morning?" Michelle asked Dr. Pazder, wide-eyed, as she was taking off her coat. He said he hadn't. "Well, they were talking about *The Victorian* and the different things that are written in *The Victorian,* and the guy, the announcer, said, 'Black magic is being practiced in Victoria and has been for years, and if you want to read about it, get a copy of *The Victorian.*' And he was talking about how it really shocked him, this cultism, and about a woman who'd been their victim. Poor woman— I wonder if she still lives here."

"Did you go buy a copy?" Dr. Pazder asked.*

"No way!"

The nurse said, "Get out of bed. You're leaving the hospital." The child was terribly torn—between relief at escaping the place where so many awful things had happened, and fear of the nurse and of what might lie in store. But there was no choice. The nurse wrapped her cloak around Michelle and walked her right out the front doors. They got in a car and the nurse drove it away. They drove until they reached a dirt driveway with tire tracks leading off through overgrown shrubbery and lawns gone to high grass and weeds. The car drew up to a large, rambling, turn-of-the-century house in poor repair.

They entered. The windows were boarded shut, but Michelle could

*This article is reproduced in Appendix 1.

see in the dim light that there were no furniture, no carpets. And no people. She was all alone with the nurse.

"In here," said the nurse, indicating an open closet door. Michelle went in, trembling. "North," the nurse said solemnly to no one, and shut the closet door. Michelle stayed in the closet for some time—she did not know how long—and then the door opened. "This way," the nurse said, leading her into another closet, across the room.

"West."

After a time in the dark, Michelle was moved again—"south." And then "east."

And then she was shown to still another door opening into blackness. But beyond this threshold were stairs, going down. Michelle went down two steps and then turned back to plead to the nurse. The door closed in Michelle's face. She heard the lock click and footsteps recede, then the front door slam shut, then the car start, then the sound of its motor fade away.

The child stood motionless on the steps, in total darkness. She was silently frightened, but she was not hysterical. She stayed on her step for a long time. Eventually she moved just enough to determine with her bare feet that the staircase was narrow and made of rough wood. The air was musty, the smell of a dirt floor somewhere below.

I'll take a step, she thought, but didn't. And then she did, slowly extending her foot, trying to move her toe down the vertical board to get to the horizontal one. But there was no vertical board. The stairway had no risers, only treads, and her toe met nothing. For a moment she thought she might lurch off balance and crash down the stairs into the unknown awfulness at the bottom. But she steadied herself and summoned her courage and bent her knee until the lower foot touched the next tread. Then another, and another. She had no idea where the bottom was, no idea when she might step off into . . . she didn't dare think what.

Her eyes at last grew accustomed to the dark. There was the slightest bit of light coming from somewhere. She could see the floor. She crept down step by step and then, when she reached the floor, she stopped. She peered off toward the dark corners.

Are there monsters? she wondered. Quickly she felt her way down and around and under the stairway. She huddled there.

If I don't move, she thought, *I'll be all right. I'll just be part of the dust on the floor. If I move, it's so quiet here I'll just scare myself.*

She became very hungry and then went past hunger.

She heard footsteps, somewhere up in the house. Hopefully, she came out from under the stairs and crept halfway up. The footsteps went away. She went back and crouched under the stairs again. She had the strongest sense of needing her back to be protected.

Some time later—a long time? a short time?—she heard footsteps again. *Someone is going to come to save me,* she thought. *Oh, maybe I'm going to get out of here.* And then something inside her said: *"Don't get caught by it, don't let yourself hope too much."*

The footsteps drew closer and stopped. A key turned in the door lock. The door creaked open.

"Michelllle . . ." It was the nurse, calling in a long, drawn-out voice in an eerie minor key. "Michelllle . . ."

The voice didn't scare her. It made her feel very alone.

The hunger was back. She was lying on the steps. They were her world now; she had come to know them very well. Her head was on a tread, and she found herself gnawing it, breaking off splinters with her teeth and chewing them. The taste wasn't nearly as bad as she'd thought it would be, and it was good to be chewing. More than that, she was *doing* something. Taking care of herself. It eased her fear.

"Michelllle . . ." The voice would return from time to time. Once Michelle thought she might answer, but just then the voice went away. Again Michelle's hopes had been raised and dashed, leaving her in a deeper desolation.†

She was desperately thirsty now. She had to go to the bathroom. She squatted and began to urinate. On impulse she put her hands down

---

†As Michelle relived this scene with Dr. Pazder, her voice grew flat, monotonous, uncaring, and he realized that she was moving into a kind of death of the spirit. They were isolating her from everything familiar and disconnecting her emotions from all normal references.

and received the warm liquid into them, then raised it to her lips. It was bitter but not impossibly bitter. She repeated the process until there was no more.

The door opened wide and a shaft of light lanced down into Michelle's prison. It was dull but seemed dazzling. From her hiding place under the stairs she could see big, booted feet going clunk-clunk-clunk down the steps. Through the treads she made out the form of a large man in a heavy coat, his collar up. The man was reaching toward the ceiling. He was hanging ducks from the rafters. They were bleeding onto the floor. And on the floor, was that a *spider?* She was dreadfully afraid of spiders.

The man hung the last bird, then turned. It was Malachi. He left without glancing around. It was as if he didn't even know she was there.

She awoke with a shriek. She'd been dreaming of spiders! In panic she leaped to her feet and scrambled up the steps. She seized the doorknob, and to her amazement she found the door was unlocked. She imagined suddenly that there was someone just on the other side of the door. That terrified her, and she ran back down the stairs.

After a time, she inched her way back up. She touched the knob. The door was still unlocked. She pushed the door the tiniest bit. She saw nothing but a dim, empty room. But the room was the world again —it rushed back in upon her and, deprived of all visual stimuli for so long, she was nearly overwhelmed.

She entered the room. No one. No noises. She began to feel strangely exhilarated. This was an adventure.

A stairway led up—a broad, curling stairway—and she followed it. At the top there was a door. She went through it into another empty room. Coming from a window, where the boards that covered it had worked loose, was a sliver of . . . sunshine! Rich, brilliant, wonderful sunshine. She forgot her caution and ran to it and pushed her face into its path. After the endless damp of the cellar, it felt unbelievably warm and nourishing.

She took one of the boards in her hands and tugged. It came free easily and fell into the room. And sun poured in. She could see her arms, her dirty bare toes peeking from beneath her tattered nightgown —she could see *herself.* She was a person again. It felt so good. The sun was so comforting. They had told her the sun was gone. *Now I will never believe them again,* she thought. *I'm a little cat, and I'm going to curl up and go to sleep right here in the sun.*

"Michelle!"

A hand seized her shoulder and yanked her away from the window. It was a woman. It was her mother, and her mother was enraged. She began hitting the child and at the same time trying to block off the light. "That's *wrong,* Michelle!" her mother cried out. "You're a bad girl." And she led the child back downstairs.

They entered a large room with hardwood floors and shiny paneling and a big stone fireplace. There were twisted, two-colored candles on the mantel. The nurse was there, and so was Malachi, both in black. Standing off in the corner were two wizened old people, watching, never speaking. They made Michelle shiver.

"Poor Michelle," said the nurse sweetly. "You must be very hungry. We have something for you." Malachi handed her a bowl, and the nurse held it for Michelle to eat from. Michelle wrenched her head away. The contents of the bowl smelled putrid. They said there were ashes in it.

"If you eat this, you'll be allowed to go home," the nurse said. Michelle would not budge; her jaws were tightly clamped.

The nurse was unperturbed; nothing could fluster her. "I know," she said. "You'd like a nice bath, wouldn't you? Eat this and you can have a wonderful hot soapy bath."

Michelle was adamant. Malachi had told her before to keep her mouth shut, and now, to spite him, she would do just that. She clamped her hands over her mouth.

The nurse addressed Michelle's mother. "Give it to me," she said, and Michelle's mother handed the nurse a doll.

Oh, no, not again, Michelle cautioned herself, *there's probably a bird under it. I'm not going to be fooled again.*

Suddenly the nurse flung the doll to the floor, smashing its head, and a seething glob of little bugs came out. Michelle screamed. The moment she screamed, Malachi shot the horrible stuff in the bowl into her mouth. It was like ooze, like garbage, asphyxiatingly pungent. Michelle gagged but she would not swallow. The people in the room, however, seemed not to notice that. They were obviously very pleased with themselves. They thought they had won. The ritualistic task accomplished, they gathered up their things and immediately left the room and the house, the nurse dragging Michelle along with them.

They drove through the dark to a graveyard. Michelle was made to stay in the car while the others went off. After a while they returned and, without saying a word, got back in the car and returned to the old house. Michelle was put back in the cellar for the night.

The next night and for the two following nights, there were identical expeditions, except that, each time, the graveyard seemed to be in the opposite part of the city from the location of the graveyard the night before.

The fourth night was different. As they drove, Michelle recognized a street—Stannard Avenue. It ran along the lower border of Ross Bay Cemetery.

The nurse had a cat with her. It was a really cold night, and it seemed like I had only a nightie on. It wasn't even a nightie —it was like a piece of sheet. I didn't have anything on my feet. It was wet, it was raining. . . . Oh, I'm getting the shivers.

The nurse, she had that black robe on again, the one with the red thing on the back of it. We stopped inside the graveyard, and someone got out and then I heard the trunk shut and I heard the cat start to cry. I didn't know why the cat was crying. It sounded like a baby. Why doesn't someone help? Please someone help!

She made me get out of the car. It was all wet and soppy. Over in a corner there were some really old graves. I kept thinking that ghosts were there. Or that people were dead, or that they weren't really dead. . . . Over in the corner there was this old grave, and she pulled me over to it. It was cracked on top, and she seemed to be able to move a piece of it away. There's an empty hole there! I thought graves were supposed to be *filled in!* I was sure there was a person down there. She had me by the arm and I couldn't get away. I looked back to where the car was. I couldn't hear the cat crying anymore.

Michelle, frantically worried, was now crying herself.

Oh, God! I'm gonna die tonight. I'm sure I'm gonna die!
She grabbed me, and . . . she put me down inside it and then she pushed the pieces back together over the top of me. It was worse than the closet. It was worse than the cellar. It was . . . ah . . . all *mucky* on my feet. I thought it was somebody! And it smelled. I thought it was somebody all rotten down there and that I was—standing on them!

For some time, lying on Dr. Pazder's sofa, Michelle wept, often screaming, "Get me out of here!" and "I'm going to die!" And then, painfully, she resumed.

Seems like I was down there forever. I was so cold. I was afraid to cry; all those dead people were sleeping and I might wake them up. I didn't want to breathe. . . . I didn't want to smell anything. If I moved my feet, my toes, I could feel that stuff. Aggh! I just stood still. I kept thinking toadstools would grow on my feet.
I could hear the nurse outside. She was talking funny, saying all those funny words. I couldn't understand what she said. And she was moaning and groaning. I thought, *Oh, no, what if she gets sick and I'm left down here and no one ever finds me?* I thought maybe I could dig a tunnel. 'Cept I probably couldn't do that— I might dig into someone else's grave. . . .
Please, I'm not . . . please . . . I think I'm standing on someone dead. . . . I can't move. . . . Help me!
I think I must have stood there forever. And then the stones started to move. And I thought, *Oh, thank God!* And the nurse grabbed both my hands and pulled me out of it. She said, "Don't bend your legs, come straight up." And so I came up straight, just like a ghost. Just like Casper . . .

The scene abruptly changed to another part of the graveyard, a mausoleum. Around it were people dressed in black.

It was a big, dark old house and it had bars across it. And all I could see behind it was rows and rows of white crosses.‡ All in rows; they were all tidy. She said to go into that house. All those ladies are outside making a circle around the door. They have two candles, a red one and a black one. They're doing a funny dance. The nurse started talking funny again. She took off her cape and put it on the floor and . . . it was inside out, and it looked just like the one they had on the dresser that night. Oh, no, I'm not going back there on that thing! . . .

She was all black. She was talking funny. . . . I wanted to keep my nightie, the sheet thing, on, but she made me take it off. I felt awful. I felt so ashamed. I'm not supposed to be with nothing on. . . .

She was turning all funny ways and standing up and kneeling down. And then she turned around. And she was talking like that funny talk. I didn't want . . . I didn't want to step on the black thing. What'll I do? I can't think of what to do. She made me step on that black thing [gasping]. Do I have to tell you about it? What is it you want to hear? . . .

She was dressed all in black . . . it was like her skin was painted black, but maybe it wasn't. Everything was black except her face.

I'm not a baby. I'm not a baby. She picked me up like a baby! I didn't want her to. She kept mumbling in that funny language and was sort of hissing and meowing, like a cat. I was really scared! And I couldn't yell for anybody. There's nobody in a graveyard. . . .

I thought, *Maybe she's sorry for me. Maybe she wishes I were a baby.* But then she turned me upside down. She made me keep my knees on my chest. And she hung onto me and moved me down really slowly. And all those ladies in black were hissing and meowing and dancing funny, like cats. I was all wrapped up in this

‡Ross Bay Cemetery in Victoria has an area where nuns are buried, each grave marked by a simple white cross.

funny position. And she started *licking* me! I hated her! I hate her!

And then she laid down on that black thing with my head stuck between her legs . . . and she made me crawl out. Then I had to stand up. And she held out her arms and I had to come back to her. And she breathed into my mouth and my nose. What can I do? The door was shut. What could I do? She said, "You're mine, Michelle. You're mine." She told me my new life was just beginning. I thought, *Oh, God, I hope I die!*

And then she came up and said, "You must eat this last bit of this," and she shoved it in my mouth. It was the stuff with the ashes on it. And I suddenly got the feeling—maybe it was just a feeling, and maybe I heard somebody say something . . . now, this is terrible—I had the feeling that the ashes were the lump, that lady who got killed, the lady with the red shoes. It was the strongest feeling. It made me sick, I had to be sick. I couldn't swallow it.

And then she took me to the car. She made me walk in a funny way, right up next to her, squeezed right against her side, and our legs were supposed to go together; it was like we had three legs. And she had her cloak wrapped around me. When we got to the car, she made me pick up the kitty. It was dead. Poor kitty. She made me put it in the same grave I'd been in. I had to be sick . . . and it just ended up all over me. I didn't care if it was on me. I was just really glad it wasn't on the kitty.

Michelle surfaced, extremely upset. The graveyard experiences were nearly impossible to accept.

"I don't know how I've lived with that for all this time," she said through her tears. "I don't know. . . . I don't know."

"I know," Dr. Pazder said, his voice choked. "It's terrible to hear it."

"I don't know why, but I can't help it. It hurts! It hurts!"

Several sessions later, tormented and impelled, Michelle returned to these same memories.

We weren't alone that night. It's just pieces. . . . When we went to the graveyard, my mom was there too. I've been trying to stay away from a little girl, because she's really unhappy. I'm just . . . I'm really worried about my heart. . . . It was an important time—my mom said it was our special time. She said she had a lot of things to tell me. . . . If that's what special times are, I never want special times! Just like I don't want a special nurse. . . .

I don't like her anymore. I don't think I'll ever like her anymore. . . . She told me she was . . . going to . . . *give me away!* That she wanted to . . . and it was really important that I be happy about it. That if I cared for her at all, I'd be really happy about it.

I begged her and begged her, I pleaded with her! I didn't want to be given away. I told her she couldn't give her baby away. . . . She said I wasn't her baby anymore. I promised her I'd be really good. I'd clean house, I'd do anything if she didn't get rid of me. She told me I wasn't hers. . . . I didn't know what she meant. And she told me . . . she told me like she was telling me the weather. . . . She told me she never wanted me. She said she never *wanted* me . . . and how I had to be happy about the way things were. . . .

Then Malachi came and said, "Did your mother tell you?" And I said, "Yes." And he said, "Listen to your mother, what she tells you is right." And he went away. . . .

I was standing there, and my mom came and grabbed me by the shoulders, and she said, "Look at me! Did you hear what I've been saying to you?" She said, "I don't want you!"

I didn't like her. She wasn't a mother anymore. She said she didn't love me, that there wasn't any part of me that was part of her . . . and I was to go be that other lady's. . . . I couldn't stand how much my heart hurt. . . . I kept trying to think about the toadstools, but it's really hard when somebody's talking to you like that.

I knew that Malachi and the nurse were listening. I said to her, I said, "No . . . please don't hurt me like this." I said, "No . . . please don't do this to me. Please! Please!" It wasn't gonna do any good. I was clinging to her. I said, "Please, *don't do that!* Please keep me. Please keep me. I don't care if you don't love me. Just keep me. You can't do this to me! Why don't you just kill me? Why don't you just kill me?"

And she smacked me across the face. She said, "You listen to me, I don't want to hear any more out of you!" She grabbed me by the wrist. . . . *She's* the one who grabbed me by the wrist! The nurse, she was in back of the car hurting the kitty. My mom grabbed me and pulled me away, and . . . oh, no! No! No-no-no! *She* was the one. It was my mom who put me in the grave! *She* put me down in that mucky stuff. . . .

But the other lady pulled me up—the nurse. My mother put me down there, and the nurse pulled me out. I can't stand it. . . . I can't stand how much my heart hurts. I can't stand it. I wanted to kill them. I wanted to hurt them as bad as they hurt me! And all those people with the candles . . . they knew my mom had given me away. I . . . I must be . . . a really rotten child.

It was the end of the session, and both psychiatrist and patient were numb. *What can I say now?* Dr. Pazder thought. *What could anyone say?*

chapter 11

*T*HESE things do exist in the world. Dr. Pazder knew that from his own experience. In Africa he had encountered beliefs and practices that, had he not observed them directly, he would not have believed could exist within humanity—sacrifices, cannibalism, rituals of every sort that responded to inconceivably complex psychological or mystical requirements. And in his own work as a psychiatrist he occasionally had patients with dark drives and fears and desires that, if encouraged by persons similarly afflicted, could surely have been manifested in bizarreness and cruelty on this order.

It was difficult to think that horrors like these could occur in beautiful and staid Victoria; the city, after all, was Canada's retirement center, for "the newly wed and the nearly dead," as the popular quip had it. But human beings were human beings in Victoria, too, one could be certain, with attributes both glorious and despicable and all shades in between. Indeed, the very prosperity, perhaps even the tranquillity, of a place like Victoria, it sometimes seemed to Dr. Pazder, appeared to nourish neuroses in some. He often thought of Victoria as a hothouse for discontent among the comfortable and the bored.

Still, for months now, part of his mind had been searching very hard for some other explanation for what Michelle had described. As his professional integrity demanded, he had been asking questions at every twist and bend of this remarkable story. Was it a hoax, or an elaborate fantasy? But he reached the same conclusion he had come to before —Michelle's reliving was relentlessly genuine. It maintained its remarkable intensity. It was too consistent to be false, had too much information, was too sophisticated from the psychological point of view to have been made up. There was nothing about it that whispered "crazy." It simply wasn't the kind of thing you fabricated if you were crazy or hysterical. It was being *relived.* That still seemed very clear to him.

Dr. Pazder reflected once again that he already knew Michelle very well, after four years of psychotherapy. Hoax or fantasy made no sense in terms of what he knew—and he knew a very great deal—about her personality, the kind of woman she was. Lots of people had a preoccupation with the occult, with death, with the weird—but not Michelle. She was one of the most down-to-earth people he'd ever met. Nor could he imagine that she was feeding his own predispositions. They'd never discussed his sojourns in Africa; he'd never told her of the strange things he'd seen. They never discussed his religious beliefs. She'd even had to ask, last fall, when the subject came up, if he were in fact a Catholic.

Beyond all that, he felt he could recognize well-known patterns in the actions of Michelle's molesters. For example, if the ashes they tried to make her eat before and after the graveyard experience were really the ashes of the woman who had been killed—the lump—they may have been trying to pass on, symbolically, the spirit of that person. In West Africa, in a number of regions, it was considered important to eat the flesh of another person. In the Christian Holy Communion, there was great emphasis on consuming the body and blood of Christ. Perhaps this business of the ashes had some relation to that, in a contrary sort of way.

These people seemed to have been very concerned about Michelle's eating the substance on her own volition. Obviously they could have forced open the child's jaws. But they did not. They tricked her to open them. Was it that the child must be made to believe she opened her mouth willingly? They seemed to be striving to create guilt. And they had succeeded. Dr. Pazder thought with sadness of Michelle's self-indictment: "I must be . . . a really rotten child." It was so typical of a child to assume the guilt.

There was also the business of walking away—abruptly leaving the child, ignoring her, once they'd achieved their ends—as when, once the child had been given the ashes, they swiftly turned and prepared to leave for the graveyard. It was a subtle manipulation, he speculated. To make a child feel she had done something bad, and then, instead of scolding it as a parent would do, walking away from it, leaving the guilt bottled up, unvented. How better to make a child understand that no one cares than to turn one's back and walk away as if she were merely an object. They seemed to know what they were doing.

The endless period in the cellar in the dark? It sounded like an attempt to inflict psychological death—isolation, loss of sense of self, total rejection. The placing of the child in the grave? Her first mother gave her to death, and through her new mother, the nurse, Michelle was reborn . . . forced down between the nurse's legs and then out. And then "life" was breathed into the re-created child.

But why? Why all this? What possible reason could these people have for using a child in this way? What kind of hell were they dwelling in?

He had been spending more and more time with Michelle, often as much as six hours a day, and each day made him see anew how much pain she truly was in. He realized that her pain was affecting him deeply. It was not just her pain now, it was also in some measure his pain too. He was suffering with her. And he felt instinctively, like Michelle, that he too must cry, must give vent to his own feelings. He was a professional, yet he was also a person, and he was being touched by what he was hearing, profoundly touched. There was, however, a professional consideration as well: If he didn't deal with his feelings about this, he might unconsciously defend himself against Michelle. He might unknowingly seek to avoid the pain of hearing her revelations, might not encourage her to tell him as much, might direct her away from sensitive topics, might deflect her testimony because it was too difficult for him.

He dropped by the office of his colleague Dr. Richards Arnot and discussed it with him. Even talking to Dr. Arnot, telling him how moved he was by Michelle's experience, and her plight, and her courage, he felt the tears begin. Dr. Arnot urged him to explain it all to

Michelle and to ask her, in effect, to let him have his own feelings.

Michelle listened, not quite understanding, but willing to grant any request from this kind, extraordinary man. When he began to weep, she at first wanted to stop him.

"No, don't," Michelle said, and tried to wipe his tears away. But then, after a time, she began to get the implicit point: Yes, her mother had rejected her—but here was someone who cared for her, who cared enough to cry. Not in sympathy—she sensed that he was not crying because he felt sorry for her. It was empathy. He had entered her pain and was there inside it with her.

By the end of the day—nearly six hours later—both doctor and patient were crying together. It was a very different thing than crying separately. It was a coming together of the pain. Later, looking back on that day, Dr. Pazder would conclude that it was this sharing of the pain—this manifest evidence of her being cared for—that enabled Michelle to go on from there, to accept his help in facing the horror of what her mother had done, and all the rest.

She was still very upset about the time in the basement, especially distressed about having drunk her own urine. "I can understand your feeling," he told her, "but what else did you have to drink? People who are lost at sea in a boat, people who are in concentration camps, sometimes must drink their own urine to survive. You weren't crazy for drinking it. It was the right thing to do."

Most of all she was distressed about the ashes. "Those are the kinds of things you don't get forgiven for," she said. "God doesn't forgive you for those kinds of things."

"Which kind?"

"For eating . . . especially for eating people who've been murdered!"

"What sin did you commit?"

"I ate a dead person."

"Did you? Well, to a child having something in its mouth and eating it are the same thing. Did you swallow it?

"No, I spit it out."

"Then you didn't eat it."

"I know that now."

"But I think it's still important to ask if it is a sin to eat a dead person."

"It's not funny."

"No, I'm asking you a question. Is it?"

"Yes."

"Really? How do you know that?"

"I don't know. What about cannibals?"

"Cannibals aren't bad for eating dead people. Cannibals are bad for killing them to eat them."

"Same thing, isn't it?"

"No, it's very different. Don't confuse their doing evil things with your being evil. That's what they wanted to confuse you about."

"I am confused."

"You can go through a whole ritual, and if you don't commit your soul to it and your heart to it and embrace it and take it on with every part of you, you're just not there, you're just not doing it. Do you understand what I mean?"

"Yes."

"That's very important. To be guilty you have to choose. You have to be free to choose, but you weren't free at all. I don't accept that you're guilty in any way. In any way at all. More than that, I want to talk about whether you became committed to or taken over by any of them . . . possessed. That's what you're afraid about—that they could do that. But the fact is, you didn't commit yourself to any of them.

"They wanted to give you warped ideas about where life comes from and where it goes—and for you to carry on with those crazy ideas. That was wrong of them, unforgivably wrong. But you fought off those ideas. You kept your sanity, your sense of the truth. And now, all these years later, you must keep fighting off those wrong ideas of theirs. You have nothing whatsoever to be ashamed of, Michelle. You have everything to be proud of."

There was a difference now, a different air of seriousness about the endeavor in which they were involved. They were aware that it might go on for some time, that it could not be cut short, that it was something that would have to be lived through, right to the end. They had developed a commitment to deal with it, to try not to judge it, just to go ahead. And now there was an even closer trust between them. Michelle knew that Dr. Pazder understood, that he would not think her crazy—that he was listening.

They also had learned more about the process of Michelle's remembering. There were two modes. The first was the deep level. She'd go down and never leave that place, though she still would be capable of speaking to him, when she was frightened and needed to have her "anchor line." As she spoke to him then, her voice would alter slightly, changing back when she resumed.

The second mode was this: After she had relived an experience, she could continue with it during the integration period, going on from there. The initial remembering made all the memories available to her, and she could bring forth more of them, more and more and more, filling in details. In this second mode, she would speak as an adult and have the language of an adult available to her.

Their working postures had evolved too. They seldom used the sofa —it was not stable enough for the shaking and trembling that Michelle went through as she relived. They had moved to the mat. Sometimes Dr. Pazder would sit on the floor beside it. At other times he would lie back, a pillow under his head. It was the only way to work, considering that the sessions often went on now for five or six hours. No one could sit in a chair that long.

In her depths, Michelle was like a child, and like a child she needed contact. Dr. Pazder did not look upon her then as an attractive twenty-eight-year-old woman. He knew that when she was reliving, she really did need human contact if she were to get out a story like that. Sometimes she would have her head on his shoulder. But he was careful about the way he touched her. Her depths were even deeper now, and he feared that touching her might severely distract her. As long as he was close, in some kind of contact, that seemed to be enough.

The nurse was driving the car—it was long and black with running boards and a silver statue of a springing cat mounted on its hood. She insisted that Michelle cleave closely to her side, as if attached to her.

And this insistence went on when they reached the house—the house where the lady had been killed. Wherever the nurse went, Michelle was forced to go too, her leg moving with the nurse's, as if they were joined for a three-legged race. It was difficult and silly and then irritating for Michelle. It made her muscles stiff.

The nurse read to her frequently, but in a language she didn't understand, reciting passages over and over again, as if it were a classroom and she were trying to teach Michelle something important. "Here," she said, handing the child a pair of scissors and a photograph of a man. "Now, do what I'm doing." Then the nurse took another photo of a person and poked her own scissors carefully into one eye. Snipping very slowly, she cut a little vertical slit through the iris, and then another through the other iris. She stood over Michelle while the child tried to follow her instructions. Michelle was not an apt student. The nurse often had to correct her.

"Denounce God," the nurse said to her. But Michelle did not know what "denounce" meant.

"I don't know how," she told the nurse with a trace of defiance.

"Well, you'd better learn," the nurse told her. "If you don't learn now, you'll be in big trouble later."

Michelle was put to bed at sundown and awakened in the middle of the night. The sleepy child saw the nurse's cloak spread on the floor. On the cloak was a bedpan—like the one in the hospital. The nurse gave Michelle an enema, and when the child could wait no longer, the nurse led her over, forced her to squat down—and then yanked the bedpan away and flipped aside part of the cloak. The child found herself helplessly defecating on the floor. But on the floor where the cloak and bedpan had been were a crucifix and a Bible. When Michelle saw that she had soiled them, she was horrified.

But her dismay meant nothing to the nurse. Once the two objects had been defiled, she had flown into action, pulling a sheet from the bed and gathering up into it various objects from the room. Unseen, Michelle took her nightie and wiped off the book and the cross. She felt she had to. And when she did, suddenly it was not so hard to keep from falling apart from the guilt.

chapter 12

I'M trying to tell you where I am. It's so awful. I've never felt so strange in all the time I've been talking to you about things and remembering things. Some of what's happening there just about scared me to death.

Dr. Pazder spoke softly. "Just let yourself tell me about it as you can." Michelle was breathing heavily.

I'm cold. When I wake up, we're not in the car anymore. We're coming into this room, but it's not at the house. There isn't any door . . . I just remember an opening into this room. Wherever it is, there aren't any windows. At least I can't see any. And there weren't any corners. It was round. It wasn't dark; maybe the windows were just high. I don't know. I can see stones like churches are made of. It's got a dirt floor, and the walls are all dark, brownish, and it's like spiders would drop from the ceiling. I didn't like that building. I don't like it at all.

It looked like a church, except I never saw a church with a great big bed. There's nothing there except that silly round bed. I never saw a church before, except in pictures. You know, with churches and fields and cows and stuff, and families go inside— that's the kind of churches I've seen in pictures. They don't have any stupid white things standing at the front.

I don't like this. I don't like the bed. It's cold. I like flannelette

sheets. These are shiny sheets with those stupid marks all over
them. Those marks really make me mad, you know?

The sheets on the round bed were satin, marked with the same
thirteen-pointed symbol as the cloth that had covered the dresser that
first night. As Michelle looked around the room, the nurse ignored her
and went on making preparations of some kind.

The nurse is very busy. She takes her sheet full of stuff from
the house and throws it into the corner. When she wasn't looking
I stole two things from it and hid them under the mattress. You
see, I wasn't very nice. I wanted to get even with them all. I stole
that cross and the white book. That's what I had under the
mattress. I knew how much it would bother them. Especially
since I had cleaned it all off.*

I don't like that funny-looking white thing at the front. It's
ugly, with those little knobs on top of its head. That nurse is
always looking at it and mumbling.

Michelle later described the white thing as a hideous white statue,
considerably bigger than Malachi. It had the form of a man, with
openings for eyes and a mouth, but with horns protruding from the top
of its head. It stood on a stagelike area at the front of the round room.

The nurse lights some candles, and then she starts this funny
kind of moaning, like she's got a stomach ache. She's got her arms
folded across her front and she's bending down, moving her body
in circles.

Then she's got a finger. This is awful, but first I tried to

*By this time Dr. Pazder realized that Michelle had ample reason to know that
the cross was a significant symbol for these people. First, the nurse had dramatically
removed the crucifix from the hospital wall. Then, only a short while later, Michelle
had been tricked into defecating on the cross. The nurse had underlined the impor-
tance to her of this dirtying of the cross by abruptly turning and leaving the moment
it had been done. These acts were quite possibly a sign to Michelle that to the nurse
the cross was powerful and dangerous, and therefore that for Michelle it must be
powerful and helpful.

imagine it belonged to a cat or a guinea pig or something. But it didn't. She had it wrapped up with something. Whatever it was, it was pretty messy, but she made it all go in this pan. It was like blood.

I started to get nervous of the white thing. You see, she took the finger. She did this stupid moaning and groaning and lighting candles and . . . oh, I got so tired of it. I can't be upset by it, though. She takes the finger and rubs it on the white thing and makes red marks. You see, she told me they were going to bring the white thing to life.

One by one, a number of people came to the round room. First the men came.

Every night was the same way, but a different man came each night. It was always at bedtime. The nurse has her cloak on, the one with the mark on the back like a spider, with a tail like an arrow at the bottom. The man comes in with a white kitten. Those poor kittens. They're always white kittens, and different fingers and pieces like that to make the white thing red.

Michelle began to cry.

Kittens don't hurt anybody. I wanted to play with one. I said I wanted it. It was crawling away. You know how kittens play. It found a piece of dust and was chasing it and I said, "Kitty, kitty." It was my fault. If I didn't say anything they might not have hurt it. Why do they *cut* things? I thought it was still alive because its paw moved, and I thought I could put its head back where it belonged. They thought it was funny. It had something to do with . . . I don't understand. The man had to have blood on him. He used blood from the kitty . . . he put some on the nurse! I don't see how she could stand it. Not me! Not me!

After dismembering the cat, the nurse and the man picked Michelle up and brought her to the round bed.

They start like ring-around-the-rosy, where you join hands. Then they take me and hold me up in the air and turn me around. They're making me a pointy thing again. I'm frightened. They're saying things to each other that I don't understand. They do it over and over again, and all of a sudden, when they're finished, they just throw me on the ground.

I hurt when I hit the ground. And then they do more stupid stuff. I don't pay any attention. I just do my own little stuff. I don't watch. I don't like it. I hated that bed. That ugly white thing could see the bed.

This happened during the night. In the daytime, Michelle was alone with the nurse. The nurse would read aloud from books and sometimes speak, not to Michelle, but to the air, to nobody. At other times the nurse acted the same way she had back at the house where the lady was killed—as if she were trying to teach Michelle something. Again she showed Michelle how to slit the eyes in photographs, only this time she used what looked like a razor blade instead of a scissors. Once she demonstrated on a small animal. Michelle couldn't see what it was, exactly, but she could see that it was alive. The nurse didn't kill it, but when she was finished it was bleeding.

But mostly she used pictures. When Michelle refused to learn, it made her angry, so Michelle eventually obeyed. But as a protest against having to hurt the eyes in the pictures, she would also make little cuts in her own arm. It didn't hurt her to do that. The thing that was like a razor blade was so sharp that she couldn't feel it when it cut her arm.

She obeyed the nurse, but Michelle didn't understand what she was doing. The nurse showed her many kinds of photographs—"pictures of dead people and people, like at parties, and men and women together and stuff like that," all with their eyes slit. But Michelle did not understand what the nurse was trying to teach her. The main thing she remembered was the little book the nurse kept reading from, which contained a picture of a man with red hair and a red beard. He seemed to be someone the nurse knew well, but Michelle didn't think she liked him.

Whenever the nurse got up to go anywhere, she made Michelle

walk that funny way, up under her cloak beside her, their two legs moving together. The nurse thought it was funny that Michelle kept bumping into things, but Michelle hated it. She kept thinking that if her mother could only see her, if she knew what the others were doing, she would come back and help. Somehow Michelle kept believing that her mother would come back and get her, and everything would be okay.

Her mother did not come back. Day after day it was the same: She was alone with the nurse during the day, and at night one of the others would come, kill a white kitten, use Michelle as a pointy thing, and throw her to the ground. This happened for thirteen days. Michelle noticed because thirteen seemed to be their favorite number—all the cloths and all the sheets had the design with thirteen points. Then it came to be a Saturday night, and Michelle's mother came back.

The place is all funny. There's all kinds of candles and someone's playing the organ. You see, there's no door, just a place that's dark . . . a round hole. That's where the music is coming from. I don't like the music. It bothers me. It sounds like grating on a chalkboard. It just goes MMMMMMMNNNNNNNN. . . . It's all creepy.

That nurse has her black thing on. I was told I had to stay by her. She gets me all dressed up in this red thing, just like a ghost. That's the first time in ages I have anything clean on.

All these people are walking into the room in a long line, slow like a funeral march. They're coming through that dark hole and they all have black things on but you can't see their faces because they have these big hoods. Everyone's carrying a kitten. I don't like it. Then they get in a circle and start mumbling and moaning like they all have stomach aches.

Then I see my mom, all in white. She acts like she doesn't see me, so I stick my head out and yell, "Hi, Mom." The nurse smacked me and told me not to be stupid. I wasn't being stupid. That was my mom! I know everything that had gone on. . . . I know from the hospital I'm never gonna trust her again. I know that. But when I saw her walk in the room I thought, *My mom!*

My mom! Oh, she's come to get me. I can go home now. But Malachi was right behind her.

All the others were wearing black, but Malachi was painted red, like the ugly white thing. The organ music sounded hollow and metallic. Forced to stay under the nurse's cloak, stuck to her leg, Michelle felt stifled, hot, as if she were going to faint. Her mother would not look at her. The others started to moan and they all joined hands and said funny words. Michelle wanted to go and hold her mother's hand, but the nurse kept her by her side. The ugly white thing was up front and it frightened Michelle. There was smoke around it that smelled funny, and in the candlelight it looked as if it might be moving, wiggling, but Michelle couldn't tell.

Finally the nurse released Michelle and told her to do the dance she had been taught. The dance was funny, but she didn't mind doing it because at least she got to come unstuck from the nurse's leg. She just moved around in a circle, with her arms out and her legs together. It was just like the way a top moved, and that was what Michelle felt like: a spinning top.

Then all of a sudden, everybody's looking at me and my mom's coming over. I knew it! I knew if I was a good enough top she'd come and get me! The closer she got, I knew she was coming over to get me. I hugged her legs; I hugged them really tight and I looked up to see if she was smiling but she wasn't. She wasn't even looking at me. She just looked kind of blank. She took me by the hand, but I realized we weren't going anywhere. We weren't going because the circle had all closed up again. Malachi was standing up at the front of the room by that ugly thing, and my mother was taking me up there, even though she knew I was afraid of Malachi and the ugly thing with the red on it.

I knew I was supposed to keep quiet, but I couldn't. I said I didn't want to be up there. She said, "You're not mine, Michelle." "Yes, I am! I'm Michelle Harding!" Then she said really loud and clear so everyone could hear, she said, "You're not mine anymore, Michelle. You belong to the Devil." And she said she was glad. Then she left me standing there with Malachi and the nurse.

I'm not crying. I'm not gonna let anybody know it bothers me. But you see, I hated them. I hated how I felt. That's what I hate. Don't you understand? That's what's wrong! I don't care about the things they did, but the way they made me feel, *that's* what's wrong. I . . . I . . . I'm not just a nothing anybody can push around. Anybody can come in that room and do anything they'd want to! I'm not just a big joke everybody laughs at every time I get hurt. It's not a joke! I'm not a joke. God, it's not funny. It's just not funny, and if that wasn't bad enough I had to go and take that red thing off and there I am standing in front of all those people. I guess they're gonna kill me now. I don't care. I don't care.

Malachi was not looking at Michelle. The others started doing this funny dance, and the nurse was doing it with them. She would bend down and walk in a slinky way, as if she were a cat, and then she would jump up and turn around, and then she would walk like a cat again, holding her kitten in her arms. Then Michelle got very scared, because they bent and took the kittens in their teeth, holding the cats by the napes of their necks. And then Michelle started screaming, because now they were biting the kittens, and the cats were howling, and they were pulling the kittens apart with their teeth, chewing at their paws to make them come free, stopping only to spit out the hair. Then they rubbed themselves with the cats' blood, slowly, as they continued their catlike dance. Malachi picked up Michelle, who was screaming and crying bitterly, and laid her on a stone slab. On a table behind Malachi was the body of a baby, but so small Michelle couldn't believe it was really born.

Why am I lying on this cold thing? How did I get lying down? One minute I'm standing up thinking about how I could get those things I hid under the mattress, then I'm lying on something cold and it hurts my back. I guess this is it. I guess this is where I get cut up like the cats. Nooo! Malachi is coming over by me and then he's saying some funny words and smoky stuff's going up in the air. He's all crouched over me. He's cutting that baby over me! It's all over me. He's rubbing it all over me! Oh, God, there's stuff all over me.

Michelle, nearly overwhelmed, was screaming, recoiling frantically as her whole body trembled.

Now he's rubbing it on the white thing. I keep yelling, "It's a baby! It's a baby! It's a baby!" I don't know. I . . . I was . . . I was dying. I don't know what I was saying. Malachi keeps saying something about . . . something about a something coming to life. I don't know. Malachi was hurting me. I couldn't scream. Ahhh, he was choking me. His fingers were shoved down my throat and he was choking me. I bit him. I bit his fingers. I'm glad I did. But then I threw up. I threw all their timing off by throwing up. Malachi jumped away and started to jump around. He was mad. I just went crazy. I started running around trying to get away. All those people were just standing around like it didn't matter what I did anymore. You see, I really thought they were going to kill me anyway. I didn't care. I didn't have anything to lose. I couldn't reach the white book, because all the people were in the way. I didn't even know what I was doing. I was making crazy eyes at them, running around and screaming.

My mom got treated special. She didn't have to do what everyone else had to do. *She* wasn't allowed to get dirty! The rest of them got all mucky and would kill kittens and put blood on their hands, but for some reason my mom was different. So I was all crazy. I don't know why I did it. I went over to my mom and I grabbed her robe. I guess I must have yanked awful hard because she fell down. I wouldn't let her get up. You see, I was trying to make her hug me. She was getting upset and everyone else was getting upset because I was awful messy and I was getting her messy.

I shouldn't have done what I did because I only got in trouble for it later. Malachi just got angrier. The last time I'd seen him angry like that he was hitting the lady over the head. He stooped down and grabbed me and everybody else had to . . . everything is going on. That place is like a beehive. All the men are going over to clean my mom up . . . all the *men* are. Does that seem funny? Malachi is so mad. He sure hit me. I didn't feel it, though. I didn't feel anything.

The women are all angry. It's like the men are losing power. Things aren't going to happen like they're supposed to. There's not going to be candles every night and kittens getting killed. You see, they've got to take away my games. The nurse said that. When I heard her say that, I started to turn around and around like a top. I was laughing. It wasn't funny. I don't know why I did that. The nurse said, "I'm going to *teach* you!"

chapter 13

$\mathcal{M}$ICHELLE was so shocked by what she had remembered that for a moment she wanted to believe she was insane. As she returned to the present, she could do nothing but sob and cry out, "What am I going to do? I'm crazy. I must be crazy. They must be crazy. Things like that don't happen. I never heard of anything like that."

For a while Dr. Pazder only comforted her, without trying to direct her. He understood that what she needed was a refuge from the pain inflicted years before, alive again in her now. Claiming to be "crazy" was one refuge. Then, as she became calmer, she thought of another.

"I must have just made it up," she said firmly.

This was a possibility that Dr. Pazder had seriously considered, and had ruled out, but he knew she had to face her own question. "Did you make it up?" he asked her directly.

"What if I made it up and my mother wasn't like that and she loved me?" Michelle went on defiantly, not answering his question. More than anything, Dr. Pazder thought, she had been wounded by her mother, by Mrs. Harding's public repudiation of the child. Even with Dr. Pazder himself, whom she had grown so close to, it was hard for her to admit that that scene had really taken place, so she was asking him to help her deny it.

"Why would you make that up, if she had loved you?" he asked.

"I don't know," said Michelle. "If I tell you something, will you tell me whether or not you believe me?"

"Yes, of course."

"I didn't make it up," she said fiercely.

"I believe you," Dr. Pazder answered. "Do you believe it?"

"I don't want to," Michelle cried, suddenly losing control again. "I don't know how to cope with it. I can't stand it. I can't. I can't stand it if it's true. Please, somebody, where does it come from? I never read about any of that kind of stuff. That's not the way the world's supposed to be."

Dr. Pazder understood her need for denial. The scene in the round room had violated every sense Michelle had of the natural order of things—how mothers and daughters felt and acted toward each other; what human beings were capable of. As hard as it was for her to accept her mother's betrayal, it was even more important to Michelle that Dr. Pazder understand she had been the victim, not an accomplice.

"I don't want to be part of it," she sobbed. "Please, will you believe that? I'd rather be in a concentration camp for fifty years. This makes me feel so sick and ugly and scared. I hate it. I didn't want my mom to be like that. *I did not want it!* I wanted my hair in pigtails. I wanted to be clean."

Again Dr. Pazder was struck by the innocence of the child Michelle. As much as they had tried to reduce her to an instrument in their rituals, eradicating her identity as a person, she had remained the innocent child who only wanted her mother to love her. He wished she could see that, but they could not work any longer that day. Michelle was too exhausted. They agreed to talk more the next day, when she had rested.

That night Michelle's recollections haunted her, running endlessly across her mind. The next day she told Dr. Pazder that although there was still a great deal she did not understand, she now had a sense of pieces coming together. Certain elements of what she had experienced stood out: the death-and-rebirth ritual in the graveyard, the white statue in the round room, the nighttime visit of each member to the nurse.

A pattern had been apparent to Dr. Pazder for some time, and he was pleased that Michelle was beginning to recognize it. He asked what she thought the white statue symbolized.

"The Devil," said Michelle. "But they didn't call him that. They called him Lucifer and they called him the Prince of Darkness." Then she remembered a detail that had not come out in the previous day's session. In the middle of the rituals of dancing and chanting, smoke would surround the white statue and suddenly, mysteriously, Malachi would appear on the platform next to the statue. It was an impressive effect, one that added greatly to the atmosphere of the ritual.

One afternoon while the nurse was busy elsewhere, Michelle was playing under the stage when she discovered a hole in the floor. She crawled up and found herself inside the white statue, which frightened her because she felt she was inside the Devil. Looking back, now, she realized it was a gimmick Malachi had used to impress the others, Malachi and the nurse believed in the Devil, but they needed the others to believe as well. Each of the others had to believe, then to signify their belief. That was why each of them had had to come to the nurse, each on a different night.

"It's like Malachi started it," said Michelle, "but the more people that got in on the act, the worse it made it."

It was like a terrible synergy, Dr. Pazder thought, a combination of forces that created a greater force. The same principle was applied to the blood ritual that would bring the white statue to life.

"They couldn't just kill one person and pour all the blood on that thing in the round room," said Michelle, following her idea through. "Somehow that wouldn't be evil enough. Does it make any sense to you when I say he had different fingers and a different arm?"

"Yes, it does. Where would they get them?"

"I'm not sure, but I think from the pictures they showed me that they got them from accidents and hospitals. It seemed better for them if the person who died had been bad—like a drunk driver or something."

One thing was becoming clear to both Michelle and Dr. Pazder. However bizarre and helter-skelter the rituals might have seemed as Michelle relived them, they were in fact carefully orchestrated, with each one built on the one that had come before. All their actions seemed calculated to break Michelle's innocence, her belief in love, her good feelings. By desecrating what was sacred, they would make room for evil to take hold.

Dr. Pazder said, "They were trying to make you part of it by all the silly rituals they were doing."

Michelle shivered and shook her head. "They weren't being silly. They were serious. They do everything for a reason and they are very organized. That first night, with Malachi pointing me, and that nurse with those sticks, and the silver cups, and the candles, and their killing that lady . . . it was all deliberate. They knew what they were doing. They were trying to prepare me for something, and I don't like it. Do you know what I mean?"

"Yes. I agree with everything you've said. They are carrying out a calculated assault against all that is good in you. Their methods are sophisticated and seem to be based on a thorough understanding of the workings of evil, of basic symbolism and human nature. It's a psychology of evil."

For Michelle, it was a great relief to begin to see the pattern. She thought of the enema, of defecating on the cross and Bible, of slitting the eyes in the photographs, of seeing the kittens cruelly killed, of her mother's betrayal and, worst of all, of the baby.* Though each had seemed separate and distinct, each had celebrated hatred and death, and all of them had produced the same emotion in Michelle, guilt. She always felt it had somehow been her fault, and over and over she had pleaded with Dr. Pazder to believe that she hadn't wanted any of it to happen. Now she saw that her guilt—her feeling responsible—was exactly what they had wanted. Once they had destroyed all her good feelings about herself, she would be totally their instrument.

Dr. Pazder sensed that Michelle was now ready for one question he had been wanting to ask. "Michelle, did they ever call themselves a name?"

"No, not that I remember. Who could they be?"

*After much discussion, it became clear to Dr. Pazder and Michelle that live babies were not used in these ceremonies; they were most likely premature fetuses or stillborn babies, possibly stolen from hospitals.

"I've been thinking about it for some time. They seem more complex than ordinary cults or secret societies. Their rituals are very formal and established. When you stepped out of line and got your mother's dress dirty, they were furious. Nothing really spontaneous is allowed to happen, you know? All that makes me think this group has a long history."

"You mean you think they've been together for a while? But who could they be? It's hard to believe that people could carry on like that right here in Victoria."

"The only group I know about that fits your description is the Church of Satan."

"My God. You mean, like Satanists?"

"Yes, exactly."

"You know, I never quite believed they really existed."

"Well, they do. There's a lot in the psychiatric literature about them. Most people think they're strictly Dark Ages, but the fact is, the Church of Satan is a worldwide organization. It's actually older than the Christian Church. And one of the areas where they're known to be active is the Pacific Northwest."

"That's really frightening."

"You know what I find hard to understand?" asked Dr. Pazder. "How they carry out these rituals and still lead a normal life."

Michelle laughed. "Yes, me too. This morning, as the bits and pieces were coming together, I had the same thought: How can they do that all night and then get up and go to work the next day?" She thought for a moment. "Of course, they don't do it every day. Their timing is very important, you know. I've been looking at the calendar a lot lately and I realized that Sunday is very important to them. They have their big meetings every second Sunday, starting at 11 P.M. Saturday night. It all has something to do with certain special days in the Christian Church, I think."

"I've sensed that, too," said Dr. Pazder. "We're going to have to find a Church calendar for 1955 and compare it to 1977. You may be reliving all this on the same days that you lived it then. It really does seem to be something like an anniversary reaction, but not the same as anything I've heard of before."

As she left that day, Michelle touched Dr. Pazder's arm. "Thank you so much for understanding," she said.

"Thank you for what you're giving me," he answered.

"What do you mean?"

"You give me a great deal. For one thing, you're teaching me a lot about innocence and survival. In psychiatry we often focus on what parents and situations do to children, and not on how children survive them. We often ignore all the resources children have. But look at you: When it seems you have nothing left, I'm always moved at how your innocence has been your only ally . . . and God knows it has been a powerful one."

"I don't know," said Michelle. "When I'm in that crazy place, I always feel so helpless."

"From the outside, you are," said Dr. Pazder. "But inside, you're winning. You're keeping them from reaching the little spot inside you. You mustn't focus on the terrible things that were done to you. Think about some of the things you did. In the middle of everything they were doing to you, you cleaned off the cross and the Bible and figured out a hiding place."

"I stole them."

"You didn't steal them. You rescued them. You cried over the kitten, and tried to put it back together when they killed it. You liked the red dress the nurse put on you because it was clean; you wanted something clean. Just when the nurse thought she had you trained, you dirtied your mother's dress and ruined their whole ceremony. You made your mother share the mess, even though Malachi hit you for it and you knew the nurse would punish you. You're beautiful, Michelle. You always reach out and find the goodness. No one loved you. No one. That was part of their plan. But your goodness was still powerful, and whenever you could you reinforced it with some little bit of goodness from that crazy world around you. How can I tell you how good that makes me feel?"

chapter 14

*T*HE nurse had underestimated Michelle's resis-
tance for the last time. She would be sure not to let that happen again.

In the days following the ceremony in the round room, she never
left the tiny girl alone. Her training was unremitting. Sometimes they
would sit together and look at photographs—but they were all pictures
of corpses, and all the people had died violent deaths. One that Michelle remembered especially vividly was a photograph of two women,
dead in a car accident. The nurse said they were twins, but Michelle
couldn't tell because one of the bodies had no head. The nurse never
said, but Michelle had the feeling that it was these dead people who
had provided them with blood for their ceremonies with the white
thing.

Every day the nurse would take Michelle out in the car. The first
time it happened, Michelle was happy and excited to escape the round
room, even if only for a little while. But it was all part of the nurse's
plan. They drove directly to a street where Mrs. Harding lived, and the
nurse parked and let Michelle watch. She saw her mother leave the
house and walk down the street, but the nurse kept Michelle from
jumping out of the car and running after her mother. Michelle could
see her mother, but only at a distance. After a few days, Michelle began
to wonder whether maybe her mother knew that she was there.

One day, after they had been parked for a little while, she saw her
mother coming down the street, walking with another little girl. The
girl was holding Mrs. Harding's hand. Michelle wanted to chase after

[*119*]

them, to take her mother back from the other little girl, but the nurse smacked Michelle and forbade it. Michelle was not allowed to cry or complain; she had to behave. She did not belong to her mother anymore, the nurse told her, and they drove in silence back to the house with the round room.

The next time she was taken to observe her mother and the girl, Michelle didn't cry or misbehave; she didn't try to bolt out of the car and run to them. She just sat frozen. All she wanted was to go home. She just wanted to go home to her clean bed.

Eventually Michelle came to understand that nothing was the way it appeared. No time or activity was safe. She would be taken for a nice drive, then tortured with the sight of her mother. The nurse would give her a bowl of soup for lunch, but the bowl would have a mass of bugs or worms at the bottom. Michelle would eat a few mouthfuls before she saw them, then vomit up what she had already swallowed. Eventually she just refused to eat at all.

Sleeping was no better than eating. She was exhausted, but there seemed to be no regular time when everyone would sleep. At odd times of the day, the nurse would say, "Go to sleep now. Go to sleep." But if she did, someone would soon shake her awake again—then tell her to go back to sleep. She never dozed off on her own; she was too afraid that if she let her guard down she might be caught or tricked. She had to "stand watch," constantly alert for any move they might make against her. After a time, she became not only cautious, but also wise —she understood their ways and was always prepared to defend herself.

The nurse tormented her all day, but the nights were even more frightening. Every night the women came to the round room, and every night they would "point" with Michelle. They seemed to know how much that frightened her, how helpless it made her feel, but they did it anyway, very slowly and dramatically. When they first arrived they would ignore her and she would stay very still, hoping they had forgotten her. But sooner or later she would look up and see them forming a circle around her, and her heart would sink and her stomach would knot. Then the first two would reach for her, but they looked at her as if they didn't really see her. Numb with fear, she let herself be lifted quietly, and they would turn her body in one direction, then pause, then lift her above their heads as if in offering, then lower her again, and the next two would take her. They, in turn, would point her to a new direction, slowly lift and lower her, then relinquish her to the next pair. It seemed endless to Michelle. She especially hated the lifting part, which made her feel somehow vulnerable and in danger. As she was lifted, she would shut her eyes tight, afraid each time that something would reach down and grab her and she would disappear.

One night, after the pointing, they took her back to the graveyard. She had not been there since the night Malachi and the nurse brought her to the round room. The nurse told Michelle that this was part of teaching her.

Once again they bundled Michelle into the black car trimmed in silver. As much as she hated being driven to her mother's house, getting into the car at night was worse. As it hurtled through the quiet streets, she always felt it was taking her down into a darkness she would never be able to climb out of. That was what the graveyard was like—all blackness except for the slanting moonlight.

They brought her to an open grave again. Michelle couldn't tell if it was the same one, but she was terrified of what might be at the bottom of the pit. Slowly they lowered her, and she would have screamed out, but her throat was so tight with fear she could only make sounds as if she were choking. When she finally touched bottom, they let her go and she almost collapsed, because her knees were too weak to hold her. But there was nothing under her bare feet but solid wood —probably a coffin, but at least there was no mucky dirt, no creepy stuff. For a moment she thought they might bury her alive, but she could still see the sky. Except for a few stars, there was no light above her; the women with the candles had stepped back from the mouth of the grave.

She stood quietly for a few moments, shaking violently, trying to curl herself into the little spot inside her that she knew was safe. She was concentrating so hard on that, she barely heard the first muffled *thunk*. Then she heard another, and another. They seemed to be dropping things into the grave, but she didn't know what, and she was too frightened to reach down and pick one up. Then something hit her on its way down. It didn't hurt; in fact, it was soft. Now two of them came down and hit her at the same time. As she threw up her hands to brush them away, it suddenly came to her—they were dead kittens. All around her in the grave were dead animals. The women up above were throwing them down into the grave with her. This time Michelle did scream, high, uncontrolled shrieks that in her terror she hardly heard. She screamed for a long time, with only the graveyard and the women to hear.

Michelle knew that the nurse and the other women were getting her ready for something. The nurse read to her every day from the black book, trying to teach her to repeat sayings and rhymes. They also tried all the time to teach her to say the white thing's name. It gave Michelle the shivers. She called it Malachi, but wouldn't call it anything else. They seemed to accept that, but only for the moment. On Sunday, they told her, she would have to call it by its real name. On Sunday, they said, she would have to want the white thing or want Malachi; they seemed to be talking about them interchangeably.

Michelle had no idea how soon it would be Sunday—she had lost all sense of time in the round room—but she knew the day had to be close, and she was frightened. As far as she knew, any day might be Sunday, and every time she woke up she tried to get ready for the worst. Then one night she knew it was time. They took her from the round room back to the house where the lump had been. Then everyone left but the nurse, who stayed to get her ready. The nurse dressed her in a red dress.

> I think I was just pretending I was getting dressed up to go to a party. The only thing was, you put more clothes on to go to a party. I'm glad I was finally allowed to be covered up by something. They came and got me when it was dark. What do you do when you don't want to go somewhere and you feel like nailing your feet to the floor so they can't take you out the door? But at the same time you gotta smile and go along with it. It wouldn't have done any good. They would have just ripped my feet off.

They took Michelle back to the round room, but it looked very different from when she'd left it. In the weeks she had lived there, she had come to know the round room. She never felt safe or comfortable there, but she knew what it was like. Now it felt very strange. There were shiny sheets on the bed, black velvet draping the rough walls. It got very quiet when Michelle came in, and she knew it was because they had been waiting for her. Flickering candles stood on the floor, or in candlesticks. The dark, hooded figures also held small candles. The flames lit up their faces, but their eyes were hollow and so frightening that it was better for Michelle not to look at them.

> I'd been told over and over again about what I had to do. They tried to tell me it was like going and knocking on a friend's door and asking if he could come out to play. But that wasn't it at all. They wanted me to ask the same person to come back . . . the one that had gotten in the air when that woman was killed. I didn't want to ask. I didn't want to play with him but, boy, I'd sure been told all week that that was what I was supposed to do.

With Michelle there, everything was ready. Dressed in their black robes, they formed a circle around the child in the red dress and began to "point" her. To keep her mind from what was happening, Michelle played the game she had played in the hospital—she was a clock, and she was telling them what time it was. She held her arms and legs very rigid, the way the hands of a clock should be, and they seemed to like that; it made their own game better. The pointing went on for a long time, with each one taking his turn, and Michelle went on pretending. They were all chanting somebody's name, but Michelle didn't listen; she was too busy being a clock. First she was eleven o'clock; then she was nine; then she was five; then she was one.

Suddenly the pointing was over and they threw her to the ground in the center of the circle. All of them began swaying back and forth, droning in a slow and sonorous voice, and the whole group began moving in a circle together, not the way the clock moves but the other way. Michelle had hurt her elbows when she fell, but the chanting and the moving circle and now the organ playing frightened her, and she wanted to get out of the circle, right away. She ran from one to the other, throwing herself against their legs, hoping someone would give way, but no one did. They were too big and she was too small. She ran faster and faster, but it didn't bother them; they were getting excited, too. Whatever they were doing, it seemed to be working, because Malachi was dancing about on the stage next to the white thing. He was painted red, and Michelle thought he looked like a monkey, she thought he looked stupid the way he was jumping around. They were all in a frenzy, which seemed about to explode.

> They all started creeping around. They were still in the circle, but they were creeping and they were saying something about . . . something about how they wanted the Evil One to come. Everybody was looking at me. It gave me the creeps. I didn't want to be looked at like that. I wanted to rub their eyes out. It was really stormy out. I could hear the rain and the wind. They kept moving faster and faster. Then they started coming in close. I didn't want any of them touching me. I nearly got suffocated, just like by one of those snakes that squeezes you to death. That's what's gonna happen to me. It was making my head dizzy and I was so tired.

The next thing she remembered, she looked up at the front and saw Malachi and the nurse standing there, as if something were about to happen. Malachi was still painted red, but he wasn't jumping around in that funny way anymore. He had crazy eyes, and Michelle didn't feel like laughing at him. All of a sudden the air changed and Michelle felt that MMMMMMMNNNNNNNN, the grating and pressure she had felt the first night as the procession marched in. The people in the circle were still swaying and moving rhythmically, but they were chanting louder and louder and they were getting scarier and scarier. Michelle looked up and saw her mother at the front beside Malachi; she was sitting in a chair like a princess. Malachi said nothing, but his eyes said, "Come here." Michelle resisted his fierce gaze, but then the circle started closing in again, and she was forced forward.

I've got nowhere to go but up to where Malachi is. I don't want to, but I've got no one to say that to. I don't want to get close to them. I knew what they wanted me to say, but I couldn't even say I wanted Malachi. I didn't. I didn't want to go near him. Please make their eyes go away! It's like I'm paralyzed and everyone's looking. And when I got really close . . . there's something on the table. It's covered up. I can tell you that by this time I was terrified of anything that was covered up. It was going to be a big bunch of worms or bugs or something. What are they going to do? I can't stand those eyes! I was so afraid of Malachi. He's not saying anything. I'm so scared. I'm so scared of him. My eyes are beginning to see double. I can see two of Malachi. They're both red. I can't see straight. I don't want to lie on anything cold.

Michelle was forced to lie down on a slab of stone, and they started taunting her, pinching her, and flicking their fingers at her. Then Malachi approached. He was so frightening, he didn't even seem like Malachi anymore, just a red thing walking toward her, but she couldn't run away; the nurse was standing right over her. The red thing grinned down at her and began taking her dress off. Michelle didn't want him to; she wished she had a white dress to wear. But then her dress was off and she was cold. The others were chanting now at the top of their voices, and incense filled the air. Michelle felt she was suffocating; she couldn't breathe.

The red thing's hurting me. He's pressing on my stomach and my chest. He's pressing the air out of me. He's pushing on my tummy. It feels like my insides are going to squish out. The nurse is doing something down below. I want to see if my insides are coming out, but I can't see. I tried to kick with my arms and legs, but someone pulled them apart. The nurse just keeps telling me to stop. I don't want to. I don't want to, I don't want to! I'm crying and telling them I don't want to. Then Malachi's gone. They were poking something down there. I looked down, and there was this little thing lying there. It was lying between my legs, and I could see it was a baby! *A baby!!*

Screaming hysterically, Michelle tore away and leaped off the stone slab. They had put her next to a dead baby, and she didn't think she could stand it without going crazy. Frantic with fear, she ran across the room, through the chanting circle, and made it to the round bed. The cross was still under the mattress, and now she brought it out for the first time. She had to help the baby. She knew they didn't like crosses.

She held it up high, and the room went wild. Everyone was shouting angrily; again she was disrupting their ceremony. Michelle held it tight in her hands, and even Malachi, the red man, couldn't get it away from her. Then he seemed to change his mind, and dragged her, his fist around her fingers, back to the front, back to the slab where the baby lay. Michelle still had the cross in her hands, and she thought it was safe because she was holding it; Malachi couldn't take it from her. Then he raised his fist, raising her arms along with it, and drove the base of the cross down upon the body of the baby.

No! No! Nooo! The red man. No! *He stabbed the baby with it!* Not with that, no! Help me! Help me! I didn't mean it that way. I'm not helping anyone. I'm not helping. Oh, the baby. You can't stab the baby anymore, it's just a mess. It's all my fault. It's all my fault. What am I going to do? What am I going to do? They're mad. They're mad at me. They rubbed it all over me . . . the baby. Oh, God! On my face, my chest . . . I can't stand it anymore. Oh, God, it's got to be the end. It's got to be. I can't stand it! I wished I was the baby. I wished I was the baby. I don't know what to do. I can't stand thinking of what to do. Oh, please, oh, please! Please, I don't know how to get out. I want to get out. I can't. I wanted this to be the end. It's supposed to be the end. Please talk to me. Please talk to me. Please!

chapter 15

*L*AWRENCE Pazder had a knack for what one of his friends affectionately termed "creative tardiness." Dr. Pazder himself would admit that punctuality was not a fetish with him. There were so many people crowding in on his life—colleagues, patients, family members, friends, comembers of the many committees he found himself agreeing to serve on—that there was always a call or an impromptu visit to delay him. His openness and, more than that, his commitment were such that fending off interruptions did not come naturally to him. Colleagues, patients, family friends—they all learned to accept the fact that this energetic and altogether engaging man, important in all their lives, was unlikely to appear at the designated moment. It was best to allow fifteen or twenty minutes. Perhaps half an hour. And then, well before acceptance yielded to irritation, the tall, lithe fellow with the high, broad Polish cheekbones and the warm, white-toothed smile would come striding in, his expression a mixture of sheepishness and self-amusement.

Michelle therefore was not surprised that Dr. Pazder was absent when she came for her appointment that day in early spring. She simply sat in the waiting room and had a chat with another of the psychiatrists, Dr. Jim Paterson. When Dr. Pazder arrived she was surprised, however, to see that he was unsmiling. In a way, she was relieved. Michelle was in no mood to smile either.

"I don't think I can go on," she said when they had entered the office and closed the door. "I have this terrible sense of foreboding. I mean, it's really frightening—as if something really horrible is about to happen."

"Any idea of what it is?"

"No idea. Except that . . . well, it's that I have this feeling I'm moving into areas where it's really . . . dangerous. I don't mean just physically. I mean . . . I have the strongest feeling that I should talk to a priest."

"Is there something you want to tell a priest, do you think?"

Michelle thought for a minute. "No," she said, "it's more that I need something from him. Some sort of protection . . . something like that."

Dr. Pazder could see that Michelle was struggling to understand and define her impulse. He could also see that she was immensely apprehensive—very tight, very edgy. It was clear that she was greatly reluctant to make her descent—indeed, that a descent might be impossible.

"What about Father Leo?" Michelle brightened. "I would feel much better if I could see him. I don't know why. I just would."

Dr. Pazder picked up the phone and called the young priest, who said that, as it happened, he'd be free in an hour and would come right over.

While they waited, they spoke of other things. They examined the old blue-leather copy of the St. Joseph's Missal that Dr. Pazder had fished out of the glove compartment of his car, where it had languished for some time, among the maps and Kleenex. It might prove interesting, he told Michelle, to look over the schedule of feast days for the years 1954 and 1955, when the five-year-old child was suffering through the regimen of the Satanic year, and to compare it to the schedule of feast days for the current year, to see how closely they corresponded; there had often seemed to be correlations. The missal was old but not old enough. Its tables of yearly ecclesiastical calendars began with the year 1956. They would need another missal. Dr. Pazder would phone his mother in Edmonton, he said, and ask her to send him hers.

Then Dr. Pazder spoke of another matter, and his expression made Michelle suspect that this was the topic that had extinguished his usual smile.

"You were kind enough," he began, "to let me discuss this work with my wife." Dr. Pazder had been anxious to have his wife comprehend something of the nature of this extraordinary endeavor—so that she would understand why he was seeing less of his family these days, and spending so much additional professional time with one patient. He had wanted his wife to understand how important the work was, and to have her support. Because of the secrecy mandated by the doctor-patient relationship, however, he could not have spoken about the case—even to his own wife—without Michelle's permission. She had freely, though uneasily, given it. "I told her it's a very exceptional situation, one that is vital not just to you as a patient but also to psychiatry, and that I thought that a major contribution to the psychiatric literature would surely come out of it. I said I had no idea how long it would go on but that, for as long as it did, I would do my best to arrange things so that the effect on our family life would be as small as possible. I'd alter the rest of my schedule, and so forth.

"I tried to tell her something about the nature of your remembering," Dr. Pazder continued. "I told her that you were totally reliving a childhood experience, and that it was very stressful, and that afterward, it took time to integrate the information that had come out. But there was just so much I could say without going too deeply into it and saying more than I should say, even with your permission. I don't want you to feel that your privacy has been intruded upon, or else you'd have a hard time talking to me. So I gave a brief description, but, in a way, that might have been worse than not saying anything at all. In a brief description the things that happened to you and that are happening to you now are almost unbelievable. I'm afraid I just wasn't able to say enough about it so that my wife could understand and feel at peace about it."

Michelle did not reply. Dr. Pazder began to feel that he had perhaps made another mistake—in telling Michelle about the mistake he had made in telling his wife.

When Father Leo arrived, wearing his customary turtleneck, jeans, and boots, he looked a bit harried, and Dr. Pazder commented on it. "I've got no less than two weddings today," the priest said, "and a funeral tomorrow. But I was bringing Communion to a parishioner just four blocks away, and it was no problem to stop by here to see you. Anyway, I'm interested in what you're doing, and if there's anything I can do, I want to do it."

Doctor and patient brought Father Leo up to date on what had happened since the last time they had seen him—the ceremonies, the rituals, the symbolism that the child Michelle was reporting from her deep past. "We've gotten to be very concerned," Dr. Pazder said. "It seems possible to us that these people were involved in something very definitely anti-Christian. It sounds a lot like Satanism to us."

Father Leo had listened silently, spellbound. He cleared his throat. "It does to me, too," he said. "It was in my mind from the first time we talked."

"We don't presume to say whether or not this should be of concern to the Church," Dr. Pazder went on. "We're telling you about it on the chance that it is. But more than that, we need your help. This is an extraordinary thing, because on the one hand this happened a long time ago, and probably a number of the people involved have moved away or are old or maybe even dead."

"Or maybe they're not," Father Leo said.

Michelle tensed, and Dr. Pazder said reluctantly, "Or maybe not." He collected himself. "Anyway, there's the present, but there's also the past. Michelle has to go back down there, and she has the strongest feeling that there's something very difficult ahead for her down there, something maybe even dangerous."

"What I need to know," Michelle said, "is what protections the Church has for someone coming near these kinds of things. I mean, is there anything I can do, or have, or whatever, that would . . . that would take care of me. Do you know what I mean?"

"You mean to keep these people from hurting you? In the present or in the past?"

"Both, I guess. I know about holy water, and I know about crucifixes, but it's not that sort of thing, it's not on that level, it's not a direct physical threat. At least I hope it's not."

"I hope so too. Well, I could say a Mass for you. I'd be happy to do that."

"I'd like that very much. But what I feel the need of, a really strong need, is for a prayer or something, some words to make people safe."

"What she's worried about," Dr. Pazder said, "is if something evil had a grip on her or on someone else, could you do anything about it?"

"That's what the rite of exorcism is," Father Leo replied. "To drive out evil."

"Could you tell me what it says?" Michelle asked earnestly.

"Actually," Father Leo said, "I don't know it. There was a time when it was taught to all priests, but now only a very few are trained in exorcism. I was not. But, Michelle, it's clear you're not possessed, and I'm sure you'd agree that there's no need for an exorcism."

"Oh, no, I agree. That's not what I meant. It's just that, well, I seem to need to hear *words*. I want to have not just general words but also specific words, words that were made to deal with this sort of thing. I would give anything if I could have those words in my mind when I go back down there. I wouldn't be so terrified then. I don't know how to tell you, except that I *know* this is what I need." She stopped, her lips quivering. "I know I've got to go back down there if I'm going to be free of my memories . . . but I just don't *dare* go back down unless I'm a little bit protected."

Father Leo stood and placed his hand on Michelle's shoulder. "I get it," he said gently. "I'll see what I can do. I'm sure the bishop has a copy of it. And there are other people I can call. I'll get back to you later. Right now I've got to prepare for this afternoon's wedding." He smiled. "There's a young couple who need some of the Church's protections too."

After Michelle left, Dr. Pazder picked up the pile of mail that had been left on his coffee table that morning and began to sort through it. A long white envelope with a familiar appearance brought him abruptly to full attention. It was from Dr. David Bolton.

Dr. Bolton was senior medical consultant to British Columbia's Medical Services Commission. Just after returning from Mexico, when it had become clear that the work with Michelle would not be over swiftly and that it might in fact demand great amounts of his time, Dr. Pazder had written to Dr. Bolton. His patient, he told Dr. Bolton, "presented a most serious process requiring extraordinary frequency, duration, and intensity. . . . At this time, she is experiencing a continuous spontaneous flooding of repressed memories. . . . She has required several hours on most days to work through her emerging memories and feelings of abandonment and despair. With very intensive psychotherapeutic techniques, she has been able to continue reintegrating herself and coping as a wife. . . . She does have the potential and resources to resolve the past, and this is clearly indicated in her work with me.

"I have sought a second opinion because of the unusual nature of her struggle and am engaged in frequent communication with my colleague"—Dr. Pazder here was referring to Dr. Richards Arnot—"concerning her. . . . He is in agreement with my findings and therapy."

Dr. Pazder had gone on to explain that the one hour a day that British Columbia's medical plan covered was only a fraction of the time he was spending with Michelle, and he requested that the commission authorize extended coverage.

Now here was the reply. It was brief. The answer was yes. The commission agreed that the case was exceptional and gave Dr. Pazder permission to bill the medical plan for more time.

It was extremely welcome news. Dr. Pazder knew very well that he would have provided the time anyway, permission or not. And he knew that he would be devoting time well beyond the new limit the commission allowed. Faced with Michelle's need and impelled by his conviction that this well might be the most important case he would ever have, of far-ranging significance to his profession and those it served, he could scarcely do otherwise. But the commission had lifted a heavy part of the burden. It would make a real difference.

Slightly exhilarated, he picked up the phone. For some time he had been meaning to call a physician named Andrew Gillespie. Dr. Gillespie's offices were just two floors above in the same building, yet Dr. Pazder had had a certain subliminal difficulty in getting himself to contact Dr. Gillespie. Was it, Dr. Pazder wondered, that he was afraid Dr. Gillespie might not tell him what he expected to hear, or that he might?

Dr. Pazder dialed and waited as Dr. Gillespie's nurse called him to the phone. After the pleasantries were exchanged, Dr. Pazder said: "I wonder, Doctor, do you remember a little girl named Michelle Harding? You were her pediatrician, I believe, in the early fifties."

Dr. Gillespie did remember the child and her family, even though it was twenty-odd years ago. He remembered the mother, and that she had a number of problems with Michelle from time to time. He remembered Michelle's having had a tonsillectomy—and he remembered something about a car accident (Dr. Pazder's heart missed a beat), a car accident that had taken place just as she'd reached school age.

Dr. Pazder asked if the child had been hospitalized.

Yes, said Dr. Gillespie, he believed so. He promised to search his files in the basement and report back.

The call ended, the receiver back in its cradle, his hand still upon it, Dr. Pazder sat stunned. He released a long sigh. The car accident. The hospital. Just when Michelle said they'd happened. It was the first outside confirmation of any of the details of her story. He found himself more than anxious to know what other information the pediatrician's records would supply.

In the next several days, Dr. Pazder continued his inquiries. It was not that he was checking up on Michelle to see if she were telling the truth; he was not making the inquiries in that spirit. It was more that, as her psychiatrist, he needed to ascertain just how accurate her reliving process was, if he was to help her properly. If the process proved to be factually uncheckable, even unreliable, it would be necessary to know that, but it would not invalidate her testimony as an expression of certain inner realities. There was, however, more to it than that. His researches might turn up other bits and pieces of information that could shed light on the dark events of Michelle's childhood, helping him to help her more effectively, giving him concrete points to which they could anchor the nightmarish revelations.

But too much time had elapsed. Officials at Royal Jubilee Hospital told him that the hospital's policy was to destroy all files after fifteen years. It was much the same at Victoria General, which formerly had been named St. Joseph's Hospital—the files went back only to 1967.

Dr. Pazder then attempted to check the accident and the woman's apparent death. He went through mounds of clippings in the morgues of the local newspapers. A number of deaths had been reported around Christmas of that year, but, since Michelle did not know the dead woman's name, it was impossible to pinpoint any one death as the significant one.

When Dr. Pazder called the local detachment of the Royal Canadian Mounted Police, he was informed that they destroyed all records after five years unless charges had been laid. The Department of Motor Vehicles also destroyed records after five years. The Bureau of Vital Statistics said they could not help him unless he could provide a surname. Did they list individual deaths by type? Dr. Pazder asked— auto accident, for example. No, they did not.

And then came a letter from Dr. Gillespie:*

> At your request I am trying to recall this patient. . . . I recall seeing her on two or three occasions. . . . I wondered about the mother's ability to cope. She was a kindly but rather ineffectual woman, somewhat overweight. . . . She was having difficulties with alcohol. Her husband was away much of the time.
>
> I do vaguely recall that Michelle was involved in an accident at around five or six years of age, for which she was admitted to the hospital for care. I believe this involved a car accident . . . and that Michelle had some difficulty with smoke inhalation, from which she made a satisfactory recovery.
>
> I do not remember the details, and I am sorry that we do not have her old files. . . .
>
> With kind regards,
> A. E. Gillespie, M.D., F.A.A.P.,
> F.R.C.P. (C)

So that was it. There had been a car accident and the child had been put in the hospital. And it had happened at the time Michelle said it did. The appraisal of Michelle's mother and the statement about

*For the complete text of this letter, see Appendix 2.

the missing father—these matched up, too. Beyond that, nothing could be confirmed. The records would be of no assistance.

Nothing could happen until they again saw Father Leo. The day after they had met with him, Dr. Pazder had phoned to see how he was coming along. "It's a little amazing," the priest replied. "I'm beginning to think that no one in Canada has a copy of the exorcism rite. I've called all over the place."

"We don't want to put you to too much trouble," Dr. Pazder said, hoping the priest wouldn't take that as an invitation to stop searching.

"No, it's okay, no problem. Actually, there should be a copy in Victoria. What if someone in the diocese got a call saying there was a case of possession and they needed an exorcist? We ought to have one on hand. I've canceled my appointments for the evening. I'm going to stay with this until I find a copy."

A day later Father Leo called back. "I've found a text," he said with satisfaction. "But it's in Latin, and my Latin is more than a little rusty. I can't read it. One of the older priests in the Chancery Office, Phil Hanley, is a classics scholar, and he's going to translate it."

The next call came two days later. The translation was completed. Father Leo said Father Hanley had stayed up one whole night working on it.

"Is it the authentic rite?" Dr. Pazder asked.

"Oh, yes," Father Leo replied. "It's from *Rituale Romanum.* It's the text authorized by Pope Paul V at the beginning of the seventeenth century."

"When can we see you?"

"I wish I could see you today, but I just can't. How about tomorrow morning at ten? I'll come to your office."

For Michelle, there had been nothing to do but wait. Until she heard those words from the lips of Father Leo, she could not think about descending again into her depths and facing . . . whatever it was that would be there. There simply was no way she could bring herself to; she knew this with total conviction, both mental and visceral. Yet again, as whenever the reliving process was blocked, the pressure was building.

Her husband had a couple of days off from his job as a construction foreman, and the two of them, without announcement, decided to spend all that time together. They had seen too little of each other. They went canoeing and took long walks, during which they talked about everything under the sun. They spoke of a favorite dream—to build a log cabin one day. They talked about the chickens they brought up last autumn in the garage and how, when the weather turned chilly, Michelle had insisted on sheltering one of the sick little ones in the house. The next time, Doug said, they'd get their chicks when the weather was warmer and raise them outside.

Doug talked about the book he was reading. Michelle listened with pleasure. Doug was an incredible reader—nearly a book a day. His vocabulary was remarkable, and he loved to play with words, make them do tricks. Michelle enjoyed his dry humor.

They reminisced about when they'd first met and, later, when they'd lived in a boathouse together. "Every morning when we got up," Michelle said, "there'd be that enormous heron nearby, standing so still in the water. Do you remember? It was like waking up in the dawn of Creation."

On one walk, through the rich, moist forest, when the conversation turned, as it inevitably did, to Michelle's work with Dr. Pazder, the mood had changed. Doug listened patiently, but it was as if it were increasingly difficult for him to listen. As if it were too upsetting to hear about the horrible things that had happened to his wife when she was a child; that, but also as if he had simply come to a point of secret exhaustion on the subject. It was only natural for him, Michelle thought, to want an end to it all—as she did—and a resumption of the simple, close, uninvaded life they had once had together.

When they returned from the walk, Doug made a fire, and Michelle made tea. Later there was a chicken dinner, with flapper pie, a local delicacy made of coconut, custard, and cream, for dessert. Afterward they sat by the fire. Michelle wanted to talk, Doug was aware of that. And Doug did not want to talk. He picked up his book and entered it, leaving behind the world of psychiatry and Satanists and tortured children—the world, most regrettably, of Michelle.

"Okay," said Father Leo. "Let me read this thing. But first, let me just point out what you already know, but I've got to say it anyway—namely, that this isn't an exorcism. It's not even a ceremony. I'm just reading you some words. I don't even have any vestments on."

They all laughed at that. Father Leo's customary turtleneck was hardly a prescribed ecclesiastical garment.

"And," he added, "you wouldn't call this a liturgical posture." They laughed again. He was sitting on the floor.

"Okay," he said again, in a different voice, "I'll simply read this." He opened a manila envelope and took out several sheets of paper that were covered with handwriting. He picked up the top sheet. He began,

O Holy Lord, Father Almighty, Eternal God, Father of our Lord Jesus Christ, Who repudiates that receding, tyrannical, and destructive fire of hell, and Who also sent Your Only Begotten Son into this world that its roaring be silenced: Be quick to hear, hurry that you may pull out man, made to Your image and likeness, from ruin and the midday Devil. . . .

Michelle closed her eyes and let the words strike deep.

I exorcise you, most unclean spirit. . . . He commands you, Who commands the sea, the wind, and the storms. Hear, therefore, Satan, and fear, you who are the enemy of the faith, enemy of the human race, harbinger of death, plunderer of life, rejecter of justice, root of evils, promoter of debauchery, seducer of men, traitor of mankind, inciter of envy, origin of avarice, cause of discord, inciter of pain. . . .

Father Leo read quietly, almost in a monotone, but the power of the phrases seemed to build upon itself and fill the whole room.

Depart from me, you wicked, into everlasting fire. . . . You are the Prince of Homicides, author of incest, headman of all sacrilege, master of all evil arts, doctor of all heresies, inventor of all indecency. Go out, therefore, Impious One, go out, Foul One, go out with all your treachery! He rejects you to whose power all is subject. He shuts you out, He who has prepared hell for you and your angels, from Whose mouth goes out the sharp sword, Who will come to judge the living and the dead and the world by fire.

"Amen," said Father Leo, closing the folder. "I hope it helps." "I've got to go." He smiled and got up from the floor. He took Michelle's hands. "I'll be thinking about you. Call me if you need me."

When he was gone, the two looked at each other, eyes wide.
"That was really something," Dr. Pazder said huskily. "I had no idea. . . ."
"It was so strong, such powerful language."
"It's hard to imagine that anything could ever stand up against it."
"I hope not," Michelle said. She felt almost nauseous, for she knew that now she would have to return to the round room and its horrors. But it helped, it really did help, to have this vivid evidence that evil could not range freely in this world, that there was a great force to oppose it . . . that there were protections.

chapter 16

*M*ICHELLE'S next session with Dr. Pazder was scheduled for Ash Wednesday, the first day of the Catholic season of Lent. When she arrived at the office, the secretary, Susan Austin, told her that the doctor would be a little late, but that Michelle should go ahead into his office. There was something on the tape recorder that he wanted her to listen to.

Michelle found the tape recorder easily; Dr. Pazder had left it out on a table for her. She pressed the "playback" lever and settled down on the couch to listen. Dr. Pazder's voice entered the room.

"Michelle, I want to share something with you, something on friendship written four hundred years ago by a man named Montaigne. I think you'll like it.

It is not natural, social, hospitable, or sexual. It is not the feeling of children for parents or vice versa. It is not brotherly love. It is not the love for a female. It is beyond all my reasoning and beyond all that I can specifically say. Some inexplicable power of destiny that brought about our union. Such friendship has no model but itself and can only be compared to itself. It is one soul with two bodies. The experience is beyond the imagination of anyone who has not tasted it. It is hard to find people—I wish I could speak to people who have had experience with what I am describing, but knowing how far from common, indeed, how rare such a friendship is, I have no expectation of finding a competent judge.

That was all. The tape turned silently. Michelle wound it back to the beginning and listened again. It was as if someone had set out to put into words the special relationship that had developed between herself and Dr. Pazder. She replayed the tape, stopping it every few seconds while she wrote down the words.

She had just finished when Dr. Pazder came in. "How did you like that?" he asked. "When I read it last night, I had to share it with you."

"It's really us, isn't it?" Michelle agreed.

Dr. Pazder was looking at her carefully. She seemed happy about the Montaigne quotation, and she was wearing a red blouse—the first time she'd worn red to a session since the remembering began. But not all the signs were good. He noticed that her rash had come back, not only on her face but also all over her hands. He had come to recognize that as a sign of specific stress in Michelle. The session that was about to begin would probably be a difficult one for her.

Michelle was in darkness. At first she thought she was simply in a dark place—a closet, perhaps, or the basement of the old house. Gradually she began to realize the truth—that she wasn't in a room at all, but in a cage. It was only about the size of a small table, and not quite high enough to allow Michelle to stand up. The sides were wire mesh. The wire went over the top, too, and Michelle would have been able to see out except for the sides. There were wooden sides all around that could be opened or closed. When the sides were up, as they were now, it was like being shut up in a box.*

The world was closing in on her. For a long time the round room had been the only space she was allowed, except for short trips in the car. Now her world was even more claustrophobic, no bigger than a wood-and-wire cage.

Michelle felt bereft. It was as if she had never had a father or a

*Hearing about the cage, Dr. Pazder was reminded of the dreaded Ekpe Society of West Africa. Kidnapped children were raised by its members in small, low cages like animals. These "leopard children" could not stand but ran on all fours. Their teeth were filed to points, and they were used as assassins. Of course, Dr. Pazder never told Michelle about the correspondences he sometimes saw between her experiences and the things he had studied.

mother, as if she had never lived a normal life of sleeping and eating and playing. There was only the cage, and it became Michelle's entire world. She counted the wires, played with her feet, pondered the freckles on her forearms—anything to keep herself occupied, to keep from thinking too much about being trapped and afraid.

When they finally let the sides down, Michelle saw that the round room had changed too. It was filled with people all the time now, people Michelle had never seen before, even at the ceremonies. Reading from large black books, they kept up a constant chant, relieving one another as they tired. As they chanted they made a lot of signs, but it was as if they were making them all backward. They said awful things, and Michelle tried not to listen; she hated the sound of their voices, and she hated having strangers see her in the cage. She was naked and very dirty, and she had to use one corner of the cage as a bathroom. It would have been easier without all those strangers there.

If only she could have ignored them. If she curled herself up, the floor of the cage was big enough for her to lie down and go to sleep. But that was impossible. The floor of the cage was covered with snakes, dozens of them. They weren't poisonous, just the black kind she had occasionally seen in the backyard at home, but there were so many she couldn't bear the thought of lying down and waking up with them swarming all over her. She couldn't even stand to step on one; the idea of feeling it move under her bare foot was too much.

She tried to sleep, but whenever she dozed off some of the chanters would spot her and start shouting angrily. They would reach through the openings of the mesh and pull at her skin, pinching at her through the wire. Pushing and pulling and pushing and pulling—it was impossible for her to sleep. They seemed determined to keep her awake, and Michelle realized—from things they said—that somebody was coming, a lady, and that she, Michelle, would not be allowed to sleep until then. They would keep chanting, and keep waking her, until the lady from Vancouver arrived.

Michelle didn't know who the lady was, but she knew that her coming had something to do with the snakes—the snakes were somehow like her. As if they were her sign. Michelle was getting into a fearful state—the sleeplessness, the snakes, the constant poking and pinching made her feel desperate. When they put up the wooden sides, she would get to the point where she didn't think she could take it for even one more minute, and when they let down the sides, she would throw herself against the wire and try to wriggle out, just like a monkey. She knew she had to do something. She had to find something to hold onto before the lady from Vancouver came. Once she arrived, Michelle would not have a chance.

Michelle's hair was long and thick. They wouldn't notice if she pulled out hairs, one at a time. It hurt at first, but she ignored it, intently collecting enough hair to make her plan work. She wound the strands together into a skinny braid a little over an inch long. Then she began the whole process again, and eventually made a second skinny braid. Then she put the two together to form a cross.

> It didn't stay together very well, so I pretended like you do with mud pies. I went to my corner and pretended like you do with mud. Am I making you sick? It does get hard if you leave it alone for a while, you know, just like mud. Funny thing for it to be made out of, but it was all I had.
>
> Then I'm afraid I did a very disgusting thing. I took it and stuck it under my hair. I had really thick hair and it was really snarly. You see, whenever they cleaned me up they always washed me off but they never combed my hair. I don't know why. So nobody would see it but me. I don't know if it was the right thing or the wrong thing to do, but it made me feel like I wasn't alone.

That was all Michelle could do to help herself. Then she just sat in the darkness of the cage, waiting for whatever would happen to her next.

> Then she came. That lady from Vancouver came. She was pretty. At first I believed she'd come to help me. I was a little mixed up. They talked a lot about a prince of darkness, but I didn't know him. I kept thinking there was somebody good in there because all princes were good. She's really something else. She's really pretty. I didn't know she was one of them at first. She didn't look evil or anything. She had black hair.

Her hair fell in waves around her face, and her complexion was strikingly fair. She wore a fashionable blue suit, and her white blouse had an ascot collar. She was a beautiful woman in her early thirties and Michelle felt herself respond to the lady's beauty, but Michelle was determined not to be fooled. In her mind she became a watchdog, defending her cage, on her guard, surefooted and wary. The lady came directly to the cage and spoke softly to Michelle. The lady said she knew how horrible things must have been until now, but she would not let anybody hurt Michelle anymore. Michelle was still the watchdog, still on guard, but she felt her defenses coming down. It would have been so wonderful to be able to believe what the lady was saying.

She was just trying to make friends when she first came. Like one minute she's talking to me like I'm a nice little kid, and the next minute she's this ugly thing. She just turned her head around and looked back at me and changed her face. It was the same face I saw in the car that night. Its eyes looked like they go way back and stick way out at the same time. Everything about it's unclean. Its nostrils are much bigger than they should be, and it has an ugly mouth. She has this long tongue that can go way out, like a snake's tongue. She's saying really disgusting things but they're all in a different language. She drools a lot and her head starts to go all funny and spins around.

Suddenly the lady turned her head again and her pretty face reappeared. She was nice and friendly once more, trying to make Michelle like her.

She's pretty and she's sitting there acting really normal, talking to me about little kids' stuff, and she'll just turn away and look back and all of a sudden it's just . . . it's just the ugliest . . . I just . . . oh, her eyes. Sometimes it looks like a man. I don't understand. She does really disgusting things. Like where I went to the bathroom she'll eat it or she'll rub it on me or she'll rub it on the floor. Then all of a sudden she's back being the other person. Make it go away! *Go away!* Please, I can't yell for my mom. I can't yell for anybody. She just kept looking and coming closer. *No! No!*

Go! I didn't want that face to touch me. I'm scared of that face and all the dark places it has. Make it stop doing those things. It snorts and drools and makes its eyes roll around in all different directions at the same time. *Make it go away!* I can't stand it. *I can't stand it!* No! It's going to drive me crazy!

Michelle came up from her memories and cried for a long time. Now she knew why she had felt such a strong urge to hear the rite of exorcism—it was because the lady from Vancouver was possessed. The nurse and Malachi were evil, but they weren't possessed. That lady was the only one, and it explained why everyone was subservient to her—taking care of her and bringing her things to eat. They all had to bow down to her.

Dr. Pazder rubbed her forehead while Michelle cried, then asked if she would like to come along while he attended Ash Wednesday services. Michelle said yes—she didn't want to wait at the office alone, but she felt a little nervous about it. Because of what she was involved in, she felt she wasn't the sort of person who had a right to go to church.

The Ash Wednesday liturgy was particularly hard for Michelle. The repeated theme of "Ashes to ashes; dust to dust" aroused bad memories, and she felt none of the peace that acceptance of death was meant to bring. But it was over quickly. An hour later, she and Dr. Pazder were on the road back to Fort Royal Medical Centre. He turned on the radio, just happening to tune in on the CBC's broadcast of Pope Paul VI's Ash Wednesday message. "The world is under the power of Satan," Paul was saying. "We must do everything we can in our individual lives and through prayer to fight him."

They looked at each other. As isolated as Michelle felt, it was good to know that the struggle was real, that she and Dr. Pazder were not alone.

When the sides of the cage dropped down again, all Michelle could see at first was the light. The round room again was full of candles, and she saw that the floor was decorated with the familiar design of a circle and thirteen-pointed star. A few people came toward the cage to clean the snakes out. All this time Michelle had wished the snakes would go away, and now there she was wishing they were back. The figures turned on Michelle, then washed her off, quickly, not thoroughly, and put a dress on her. She felt wobbly on her feet.

All these other people keep coming into the room, and they've all got those black capes on. They're standing around that huge circle and I'm being held there in the middle. They're really calling someone, really loudly. Some of them get down on their knees and they start going up and down, up and down. Then they start turning me like a compass, like they always turn me. They're waiting for it to get dark. I know. The only thing they're still waiting for is the Prince of Darkness. As soon as it gets dark . . . all of a sudden that thing jumped in the circle!

The possessed woman stood poised a moment, then began a wild dance, jumping back and forth over Michelle's rigid body. The woman's arms were fully extended, with her hands and palms outward. Her knees were turned out too, so her movements were ugly and jerky rather than graceful. As she danced, the chanting grew louder and louder, and she danced faster and faster until the air began to grate, to go MMMMMMNNNNNNNN. The lady was moving like a whirl-wind, but the others continued their slower, rhythmic motions.

Then everything stopped, and the possessed woman stood over Michelle, her legs straddling the child's petrified body. The woman's face came closer and closer, and Michelle tried to concentrate on the thing she had concealed in her hair, her little piece of safety. Then the lady was on top of Michelle, and her snakelike tongue worked its way into the small girl's mouth.

It was like a snake was in my mouth. And the next thing I know, I feel all funny down below. I shouldn't have looked. I shouldn't have looked. It was a snake! It was a real snake, and it seemed like it was crawling out of me. I thought it was inside of me and it crawled out. *Nooo! Get it off!* I thought it went in one end and came out the other! I think she's put a snake all the way through me.

The lady left the circle and joined Malachi where he was standing, next to the white thing. Struggling and crying, Michelle was brought before them. To her complete horror, Malachi turned to a table and revealed another dead baby. Before Michelle's eyes, he sliced the fetus in half, then turned to Michelle and rubbed half the body against her stomach.

> No! No! Take it away! I couldn't do anything. They rubbed it all over me. Why did they do that? Why did they do that? They rubbed it on that white thing . . . on the stomach. They were all just on their knees and yelling and then everybody's getting up and going crazy and dancing around. I couldn't just stand there anymore. I had to do something. *I had to do something.* But I made a terrible mistake. I yelled, "Mommy." I shouldn't have said, "Mommy." They thought I meant the mommy they'd given me to. They thought I was calling *her* mommy!

The celebrants howled triumphantly. Crying, hysterical, Michelle leaped up and ran from the circle. The possessed lady was dancing again, jumping around as if she were crazy, but Michelle ran about frantically, trying to get away, looking for a place to be safe. She had to run, had to try to get all the snakes out of her body. She ran against the walls, threw herself on the floor while the others danced and rejoiced.

In the confusion, Michelle finally found a spot where nobody was and she crouched there. It no longer mattered whether she was part of the ceremony or not. No one noticed her.

> I wanted to be back in the cage. I wanted my corner. It didn't matter anymore. I didn't matter. I feel so sick. Oh, help me! God help me. I can't talk anymore. I can't. That's all. I feel like nothing. I feel that I'm worse than a snake! They told me the baby was for me, for my birth. Please! Please! I didn't want it. I didn't ask. I'm scared. I'm scared. Please don't leave me. Please, I'm so scared.

chapter 17

*M*ICHELLE's next session began in some confusion. At first she told Dr. Pazder that she'd been put back in her cage again. Then there was a silence, and she said she guessed she hadn't. But she was feeling as if she were in a closed space that was hard for her to identify. Michelle began to breathe heavily, and Dr. Pazder could see that some knowledge was coming to her, and she was struggling to speak.

"Please," she said, beginning to cry, "can you understand that I don't want to be hurt anymore? It's hard for me to go there. I'm afraid. I'm afraid of back then. Can you understand that? Do you understand that the more I know, the harder it is?"

"I understand that," said Dr. Pazder. "I understand how frightening it is."

"Do you have any idea what they did? Do you know where they put me?" She was sobbing now.

"No," he said. "Can you tell me where?"

"They locked me inside that white thing. The only way I can see out is through those eyes, and they think that they're going to make me watch. They pushed all the snakes in through the eyes, so they're all at the bottom, and they put the rest of the dead baby in there and told me that's what I've got to eat." Michelle sobbed for a few moments, unable to speak. Then she said fiercely, "I can't. I can't stand it! It's not just being in there; it's what people think I am. Oh, I wish I didn't know so much. I wish I didn't. I don't know what to do. I can't stay alive. I just can't. I don't want to be inside all those dead people, with all their blood around me. I don't want to look out those eyes. I don't know what to do. It seems the more I talk about it, the worse it gets."

"It's okay, Michelle," Dr. Pazder said. "Just keep going where you can."

"It's like someone's tearing my insides out. I'm so afraid. I don't have a thread to hang onto anymore. They want to destroy me."

"But you're not destroyed," said Dr. Pazder. "They tried but they didn't succeed. You're not destroyed now."

"I'm such a mess. Do you have any idea at all of what this does to me?"

"Well, I'm trying to envision, a little bit, what it would be like inside that shell."

It was like being inside a mummy, Michelle told him. They placed a stepladder inside, and that was where Michelle sat. At the bottom of the effigy were the snakes, and some sort of liquid. She couldn't tell what it was. Inside the effigy it was dark, with just a bit of light coming through the eyes. There was very little space to move around in, only a few inches on each side.

"Did you know where you were then?" Dr. Pazder asked.

"I'm inside the Devil," Michelle wept.

"No, you're *not*. That's not the Devil. It's a hollow shell that they made, probably out of papier-mâché or plaster. Yes, it's covered with blood. The blood of dead people. But the people aren't there; there are no spirits in that blood. It just represents the evil that they did. The evil is there in their hearts. But it's not the Devil, and you're not evil because you were in there as a child. Being in that statue doesn't change who you are."

"It might make me go crazy," Michelle whispered.

"No, it won't. It won't make you possessed, either, I promise you. Who's going to let you go crazy? I won't. God, no. You're free now. You can scream and nothing will happen. You can tell them to stop it. It's not going to make you crazy. But we must do this. When you open up as much as you have it's very important not just to look at the memory but also to feel it and to go through it. It hurts, it scares, it does everything, but you're still okay. You are. I know that by your sanity and by your goodness. This is a hard place to be going. But I don't know any choice but to go there."

"I know," said Michelle. "I don't either."

"Since you have to go there, I will be with you. You don't have to go there alone."

Michelle was imprisoned inside the effigy for a long time. The space was so dark and so confined that sometimes she felt she could not take another breath. At other times the idea of where she was—inside the white thing—would seize her imagination until she felt she couldn't stand it. And yet she was forced to endure, day after day, concentrating on little details, daydreaming, the way she did in the cage, to keep herself sane.

The next ceremony began without warning. They did not wash or dress Michelle beforehand; they just left her in the effigy and let her watch through its eyes. The chanting was less solemn than usual. It seemed almost lively. The candles were white instead of black. The black-robed figures formed two circles, and each circle moved in the opposite direction from the other. Suddenly, and in unison, all the celebrants swept their cloaks back and revealed what was beneath: children. A child clung to each celebrant's leg, much as Michelle had been trained to cling to the nurse and walk around beneath her cloak.

The children seemed to know what to do. They moved in time with the grown-ups, and seemed to be enjoying themselves. From Michelle's vantage point inside the effigy, it looked like a bizarre game of ring-around-the-rosy. Part of Michelle wanted to be out there playing, like all the other children. But she wouldn't have, even if she had been free. She knew that what happened in the round room was no game, and wanted to tell the other children that. Children will do anything if they think everybody is having fun, but she wanted them to know that this dance *wasn't* funny. She could see them looking at the effigy, knew that when they looked up they could see her eyes glaring down at them. They didn't know the trick; they thought the effigy itself was powerful. Michelle couldn't let them believe that! They ought to be afraid. The children did not know that Malachi and the others were waiting for the Prince of Darkness to come—that they were *helping* him come, and that having children in the round room was part of helping.

Michelle had to warn them—but they had to see her first. She had to make them realize who it was inside the effigy. She started to grunt and scream. She made animal noises, growls, whines, screeches.

Suddenly the children stopped and looked up at the effigy. But it was all wrong—they thought it was the effigy come to life. They still didn't understand that it was just a person inside. Michelle wanted to burst out so badly she tried to smash the effigy apart, but it was no use; the more noise she made, the more real the effigy seemed.

In her frenzy, she grabbed what was at hand—the snakes. Scrambling to the bottom of the stepladder, she gathered them up by the handfuls and pushed them out through the effigy's eyes. Some of them squished as she forced them through the narrow holes, but she didn't pause. The children saw the snakes flying out of the eyes, and they danced faster and faster. Michelle had to get out and stop them. She had to!

She rushed down the stepladder again and picked up more snakes. And the decaying pieces of the baby. She shoved them all out the mouth of the image. She was ridding the effigy of everything they had put into it, and that made her feel good. Then she looked down at her hands. Touching the baby had filthied her hands, and she had nothing to wipe them on but her own naked body. All she wanted was to be free of the effigy. "I want out!" she screamed, her voice lost as the celebrants sang louder and louder. "I want out! *Out!* Let me out!"

All of a sudden she was outside. She didn't know how she got there. But she was out. As she stumbled into the room, the other children shrank from the sight of her, naked, her long hair matted, her body thin and bony. Seeing the fear in their eyes, Michelle looked down at herself and began to scream. Her lower body was streaked with red. She was terrified that if she had to be in there any longer, her body would turn red along with the effigy.

Everyone was standing still, shocked, staring at Michelle. They all seemed scared, except for the possessed woman, who was very angry. She came toward Michelle, her face turning awful, her lips whinnying and spitting. Relentlessly she moved toward Michelle, and when she reached her she lifted the child up over her head and threw her backward onto the round bed. Then the possessed woman leaped onto the bed and, straddling Michelle, vomited all over. The children shrieked, and Michelle was filled with disgust. While the possessed woman kept Michelle trapped on the bed, the celebrants danced and did strange things to each other, including the children. The children thought it was all part of the game.

Michelle couldn't bear it. That was when she saw the snake. It was lying on the floor, where she had thrown it down from the effigy. Screaming, Michelle dodged past the possessed woman and ran to the foot of the effigy. She grabbed the snake and, before she could think about what she was doing, put it in her mouth and ran around the room, dangling it from her teeth. "Nnnnn! Nnnnn!" she went, shaking her head, the snake flicking back and forth as she crisscrossed the room in a crazy pattern. The round room was in chaos. Everyone was scream-ing, and Michelle was screaming too. She would run up to a child and shake her head wildly, the snake between her teeth. The children were terrified, and at last Michelle felt she was getting through to them. They were beginning to understand the horror.

It was then that Michelle saw her mother, dressed in a white robe, standing quietly near a wall. Michelle stopped, poised, her body stained with red, the snake struggling in her mouth. Then she dropped the snake and flung herself at Mrs. Harding, throwing her arms around the woman's knees, kissing her stomach, burying her face in the white robe as she cried, "Mommy! Mommy!" over and over. No matter what her mother had done, she loved her. She hugged even tighter, and the woman seemed to like it. She hugged Michelle back, and that seemed to make everyone happy. Michelle was so glad to have her mother again, and then she looked up to kiss her.

"No!" Michelle shrieked. "It's not my mom. No! It's that lady!"

Michelle was utterly crushed. Slowly she turned to the effigy. She knew there was only one place she belonged—inside the white thing. She crawled back inside. There was no escape.

That night Michelle and Dr. Pazder worked until after eleven, talking about the things that seemed to distress her most—that the children, looking from the outside, had taken her eyes to be those of the statue; that she had turned half red, like the statue; that she had had to give up and crawl back inside. She needed to feel less defeated in the present, to reach beyond the anguish of the child, and to see what that child had indeed accomplished.

For the first time she had telephoned Doug and asked him to come pick her up. Both she and Dr. Pazder felt it would be dangerous for her to try to drive alone as exhausted as she was. Doug had agreed, and now they were waiting for him.

"My mother sent me her old missal," Dr. Pazder said, pouring Michelle some tea. It covers 1954 and 1955, the years all this happened. And it's very interesting. I want to show you what I discovered."

He drew a sheet of paper from his missal. "I wrote these down last night." In his slanting script were the dates of the movable feasts, the principal celebrations of the liturgical year. He had listed the dates for 1954 and 1955 and for 1976 and 1977. His chart showed there were startling correlations.

	1954	1976	1955	1977
Ash Wednesday	Mar. 3	Mar. 3	Feb. 23	Feb. 23
Easter	Apr. 18	Apr. 18	Apr. 10	Apr. 10
Ascension	May 27	May 27	May 19	May 19
Pentecost	June 6	June 6	May 29	May 29
Corpus Christi	June 17	June 17	June 9	June 9
First Sunday of Advent	Nov. 28	Nov. 28	Nov. 27	Nov. 27

Michelle looked at the dates and sighed. The events she was remembering had started in 1954, and continued into 1955. The remembering itself had begun in 1976, and it was now just past Ash Wednesday, February 23 of 1977. Michelle's memories were corresponding almost to the day with events that had taken place exactly twenty-two years before. And in those years the Church's important dates fell on the same days they did this year. The days and dates were the same, only twenty-two years apart. She wondered, as she often had before, why she was remembering all this now.

"Another thing that struck me," Dr. Pazder remarked, "was that I don't know when these dates may correspond again. I've been able to check up through 1996 and it doesn't happen within that time. It's also interesting because it helps us to understand that these people seem to move opposite from the Church. At Christmas, instead of a joyous birth, they arranged a death. And for Ash Wednesday, when the Church reminds us of our physical mortality, their focus, though twisted, is on life and children. See?" He pointed to the date on the first table. "That ceremony was on February 23 in 1955, which is where you were in your memories that day. And Ash Wednesday fell on February 23 this year too—the day you told me about that ceremony."

"What I talked about tonight has something to do with these opposites too," Michelle said. "It does have something to do with the children. We're leading up to Easter now, and they're going to do something opposite. They have to get the children all ready by Easter. I'm so terrified for the children. I'd like to ask Father Leo to remember them when he says Mass this Sunday."

"Well, we'll find out what these dates mean soon enough," Dr. Pazder said. "But I want to say one more thing before Doug gets here. And I want you to listen hard. I don't want you to dwell on these dates. I grant you, they are interesting. I think we'll find they are significant in the context of your memories, and they may help us understand more as we go on. On the other hand, the dates may be nothing more than coincidence. We don't know. So don't let yourself get too worried about it."

"Okay," Michelle said, but she was not at all sure she could keep from being concerned.

When Doug arrived, Dr. Pazder told him how much Michelle had gone through in the session. Doug helped her into the car, and they started for home. He asked no questions.

chapter 18

*M*ICHELLE'S remembering had become relentless. She and Dr. Pazder were working daily without respite, and he was beginning to worry about her. There was little time to integrate her experiences before she was flooded with new ones. One day, while she was remembering, the five-year-old Michelle told him, "I don't think there's a sun anymore. I haven't seen any for so long. Maybe it's not there anymore." That day he decided it was essential to take a break and get their feet on the ground.

The Pacific Northwest is beautiful in the spring, when the long winter rains cease and the sun climbs high over the mountains. Michelle packed them a lunch, and they drove to the top of a small mountain near Thetis Lake, just outside the city of Victoria. The wild flowers were blooming, and Michelle thought the trilliums looked like a flock of little nuns flying low over the ground. There were birds in all the trees.

Inevitably their talk turned to Michelle's experiences. But the surroundings inspired them to put everything that was happening into a perspective that gave a more hopeful meaning to Michelle's suffering. At home again that night, Michelle wrote Dr. Pazder a letter:

> I didn't quite understand when you started to talk, but the more we talked the more it grew. Reflecting now, it doesn't surprise me that we talked of what we did, because the pure and innocent things of the world were all around us, like arrows pointing to the truth.

We sat down, and you started to talk about the people in my life, the people back there who had hurt me so badly. You talked about them as evil people trying very, very hard to make evil happen, to bring life to their wickedness.

All of a sudden the confusion isn't there. I understand their deliberateness. I understand their planning. I understand what they're trying to get me to do. It's much more than remembering. It's insight into a desperate space.

I was talking to you about all the details, all the rules and regulations they had, the methods they had to follow. *Had to.* You said, it's that "had to" that makes evil. If things just are, naturally, you don't *have to* do so many things. But they had to. I'm beginning to think they were more desperate than I was. They can frighten you . . . and your fear is their tool. The fear that evil can exist without your wanting it to.

But it cannot. It just cannot. If you believe what they tell you, then it does exist. But if you don't, then it's impossible. I know that. I know how hard they tried. Isn't my life a testimony to how hard they tried? The only way they could have reached me was to love me. But they can't love. That goes against what they are. So I couldn't be what they wanted me to be. Evil can't exist where there's love. That's what they were trying to destroy. That's what they were trying to break down. They were trying to make me believe that love doesn't exist—that my family didn't love me, they didn't love me, even my body didn't love me. Nothing did. If nothing was there, then evil could be there. But only if I let it, and I wouldn't let it. Because I wouldn't, they could not regenerate the Devil. With goodness, he's completely impotent. I know that, and that is a very deep, profound knowing.

Not everyone can love as an adult. I think that's what getting in touch with nature is all about. It's not getting in touch with the trees and the grass and the flowers. It's getting back in touch with what comes naturally—love, trust, innocence.

Love is the opposite of hate and evil. Love opposes hate and evil. As long as love exists, the others can't. Knowing this, the unfolding of my memories gives a validity to my life. Thank you for hearing and for letting me hear through my agony what I was saying. Together we've arrived where we have, knowing what we do. Thank God for that knowing. It's a kind of turning point.

From inside the effigy, Michelle sensed that the atmosphere in the round room was angry and menacing. Ever since the last ceremony, Malachi and the others had been glaring at the effigy and yelling things in her direction. It felt like a storm. Everybody looked all black and scary, and once in a while someone—Malachi, the nurse, or the lady —would come up close to the statue and all of a sudden their eyes would be looking in at her. Sometimes she would forget whose eyes they really were, and she would imagine that the white thing had turned inside out and was staring in at her.

Inside the effigy it was even more confining and frightening than before. After the last ceremony, the possessed lady had angrily seized Michelle and tied her tightly to the stepladder, to be sure she didn't burst out again at the wrong time. It was hard to sleep that way, and it made her feel completely helpless, especially when the spiders came.

Michelle didn't know where they came from, but one day there was a mass of little red spiders. Were they real, she wondered, or just a horrible nightmare? They swarmed up the stepladder from the pool of red liquid at the base, and wherever they crawled, they left a thin red trail. Michelle could hardly bear them. She couldn't just let them crawl all over her; she had to kill them. But her hands were tied. They crawled in her eyes, up her nose, and into her ears and hair. Michelle couldn't stand it. She couldn't move; there was nothing she could do except try to shake them off. But moving just made them creep, which was even worse. The snakes began to eat some of them—but hadn't she gotten rid of all the snakes? Her mind began to reel. In the dim light coming through the eyes she could even see the spiders' legs hanging out of the snakes' mouths. She didn't know how to stop it, didn't know what to do. So she just went dead. In her mind she shut everything up tight, even her nose. She told herself she had no skin, no hair, no eyes. She particularly didn't want to have ears. The spiders bit her, but she didn't react; she adamantly refused to have any feelings.

The only things she couldn't turn off were the voices of the people outside. They had gathered outside the effigy again, and to Michelle their voices were like dripping water. It was so hot that sometimes she felt as if the walls of the effigy were closing in on her.

Michelle was lying on her back. She was not inside the effigy; she vaguely remembered having been untied and carried through a tunnel away from the round room. She had never seen the place she was in before, and she had never seen the man who now looked down at her blankly.

He was very tall and he held himself erect, the way soldiers do. His eyes were pale blue, his hair a sort of dark gray, and he had a receding hairline. He had terrible skin, all pitted, and the sharpest nose Michelle had ever seen. She thought that if he ever fell over, his nose would stick right into the ground. He was called the doctor.

The room was little and had no windows. There was a big sink and a metal table on wheels. Michelle saw that she was lying on a sort of counter. The doctor thrust his arms under her body and placed her on an old wooden wheel, like the kind her mother had used to wind the garden hose on. He bent her backward around the wheel, tied her hands to her feet, and spun her around. Michelle didn't understand why he would do that, except that it hurt a lot.

The little room was a terrible place to be. They only brought her there to hurt her, and Michelle was brought there again and again. One day the doctor stuck something hot down Michelle's throat. It was very painful, and when it was over it hurt for the rest of the day. Michelle didn't understand what they were doing, but she was afraid that they were changing her inside. That would be her punishment for shoving all those snakes out the effigy's mouth.

On another day, Michelle was tied down to the table on wheels. Cloaked strangers assisted as the doctor approached Michelle and did something to her head. The pain was so intense she thought she would faint, but she did not, and it continued. When he was finished she was untied, turned over, and retied so that she had to lie flat on her stomach. She couldn't see what he was doing, but she felt a searing pain at the base of her spine. This time she did faint. When she awoke, she was inside the effigy again, tied to the stepladder. She couldn't touch her temples or her spine to investigate, but her head and her back hurt for days afterward. Again Michelle had the feeling that something was about to happen. She was tense waiting.

They lit a big fire in a corner of the round room. The fire made it even hotter inside the effigy. They never let it go out. Next to the fire they assembled a whole collection of crosses—paper ones, wooden ones, crosses made of dead holly. Some they ripped apart, some they chopped up. They threw all of them into the fire.

Michelle saw that they had another dead baby, and she cried out for them to stop, but they didn't listen. They nailed its little hands and feet to a big wooden cross that they had saved from the fire, and then they broke all the bones in its body.

> It was sick what they did. It was sick. They hurt it so. I don't care if it was dead. It still could hurt. Oh, the poor little thing. Why didn't they do that to me? Why didn't they? Not a baby! *Not another baby!* They just threw it on the fire, just like it was nothing but a piece of wood.

Now they were draping everything in black. They were wearing their black robes again, and their faces were painted white. The candles were red. Abruptly, they all turned and faced the effigy, their eyes fixed. Michelle watched, unable to move, too frightened to scream, as they proceeded slowly across the room toward her.

> They are putting me upside down in that red thing. I'm upside down. I'm not right-side up anymore. Why am I upside down? I don't want to be here. No! No! Help me! Please don't do this to me! No! *Don't go away!* Don't leave me here like this. I can't see. I can't breathe right. I can't swallow like this. Don't leave me like this. . . .
>
> I'm going to die. What if I hang here for about a year? No one will ever know I exist and the spiders will eat me up. I can't stand it! Please come back. Please, somebody, hear me. Come back! I'll love you. I'll love you. Come back! Come back!

Michelle listened as the footsteps receded and a door slammed shut. There was pressure all around her body, and a wetness against her skin that she couldn't explain. She felt like toothpaste in a tube, and it made her angry, angrier than she had ever been at anything they had ever done to her. But the pressure was increasing, and she was terrified again. It really hurt, and she was afraid she was going to be squeezed to death.

Michelle was not left long by herself. She heard them shuffling in again, heard them gathering around the effigy. She could see nothing but blackness, but she knew they were there, Malachi and the others, dressed in black. Then the darkness was penetrated by a soft wailing, like the sound a wolf makes under a full moon.

> Something is happening. It feels like someone's thrown a pail of water on me, and now . . . it's like . . . I'm being born. I have something thick wrapped around my neck.
>
> My bottom comes out first. That makes me feel like my legs are breaking. It hurts. No! No! I feel like I'm going to break in half. I can't breathe. No! Help! I'm . . . I'm . . . I'm out! I'm out of that red thing. Malachi's cutting that cord around my neck so it doesn't choke me to death. He says he is giving life to me.

Michelle's first thought was that she felt stupid. She had tumbled out, bottom first, and there everybody was, all lined up and waiting. She felt really clumsy, with everybody looking at her. They were like a curtain of black, pierced by the white faces.

As they stared down at her, Michelle slowly became conscious of what she looked like. She was on her hands and knees. The floor around her was soaked with red liquid. Michelle herself was all red and wet, and she thought she had lost her skin.

Her head was still hurting, and so was her spine. Now, out in the light, with her hands free, she reached to see what the doctor had done that had hurt her so much. At first she was puzzled. There were little knobs sewn to her head, and a long tail coming out of her spine. When she realized what they had done to her, she began to scream. In spite of the pain, she reached up and ripped off first the horns, then the tail.

Blood poured down over her eyes. And all of a sudden Michelle didn't care what she did anymore, because she felt she was going to die anyway.

Outraged, humiliated, and in pain, she ran to the round bed, where she had left the white book so many months before. When she reached under the mattress it was still there. She didn't really know what the book was or why it was important, except that it was white and their world was black. She sensed that, like the crosses she had made, the white book would keep them away from her.

As soon as they saw what she had, they froze. The fire was roaring in the corner, and Michelle had a feeling she knew where the book would end up. But not all of it. She had to keep some of it with her, so she tore some pages out and stuffed them in her mouth. Other pages she pressed against her body, trying to make herself white again, and they stuck because her body was wet with the red liquid. They were coming at her now, coming to get the book, but all they got was the cover, not the insides. As Malachi came toward her, she desperately threw a handful of pages in his face and ran, scattering paper everywhere.

After the confinement of the effigy, it felt good just to run. But she wanted to do more than that. She wanted to tear the room apart, to destroy anything that meant something to them.

As they scrambled to gather up pages and throw them in the fire, Michelle scurried to the stone table they had decked out with a special cloth. Malachi's knife was there, and a lot of big silver cups. As Michelle threw the first cup into the fire, the possessed lady began to shriek. But Michelle didn't care. She had always been afraid of the possessed lady, but now Michelle was too furious to care.

> I've seen so many people hurt. I saw that lady killed. I saw the babies killed. I've heard too many things! I've been left alone too long. Now it's everything at once, and I hate it! I just hate it! The only thing I can do is throw their things in the fire. Most of them don't burn right, they just smoke, but I don't care. I want them to. I want everything to burn up.

Michelle turned on Malachi. She was sure he would kill her, so she had nothing to lose. That gave her strength. She looked straight at him and screamed that she hated him and that from then on she wasn't doing anything she was told, not ever.

Inexplicably they did not kill her. Malachi seemed angry enough to, but she sensed there was some reason that they couldn't. Slowly the group closed in on her. In their hoods and white paint, they all looked like the Grim Reaper. They were carrying long sticks and poles, and they poked and pushed at her, prodding her relentlessly, driving her toward her old cage. But none of them would touch her. They just kept at her inexorably, herding her with their sticks. There were so many of them. Like a black tide, they swept her toward the cage. One side was down, and she scrambled in.

They formed a line, and Michelle expected them to file out of the round room in their customary procession. They did leave, but on the way to the door the line wound past her cage. As each member went by, he or she spat at Michelle through the bars and threw a handful of ashes at her. Soon she was covered with spittle, but she was too proud to cry. She just crouched there, glaring at them defiantly. When the others were gone, Malachi and the nurse stood before the cage and told her that she would learn how unworthy she was—that no one had ever loved her, or ever would; that no one had ever wanted her, or ever would. Michelle was nothing, he said, and nothings had no memories, no pasts, and no futures.

It was a very long time that night, after Michelle had surfaced, before she could bring herself to talk to Dr. Pazder. She was pale, limp, exhausted. He made tea and held the mug to her lips while he supported her head. "Take a sip," he said. "You'll feel better. Just a sip." She had told him all this on Monday, the day after Easter Sunday 1977.

chapter 19

*M*ICHELLE was concerned about Dr. Pazder. He had been working so hard, with her and with his other patients, that he was greatly fatigued. There was gray in his hair that had not been there six months before, and new lines around his eyes. She wished she could do something for him, and then she hit upon an idea. As a non-Catholic with a growing interest in the ways of the Church, she had been intrigued by the fact that a Mass could be said for a specific person—"a sort of spiritual shot in the arm," Dr. Pazder had called it. At first it had seemed strange to her—a Mass said for just one person? And then Dr. Pazder had gone with her to Father Leo, and the priest had said a Mass for them, and suddenly the practice had come to seem meaningful. Now she conceived the notion of returning the favor, of having a Mass said for the exhausted psychiatrist.

Father Leo Robert, however, could not be the celebrant. Having completed that year's work as university chaplain, he had gone on a world tour. But friends had spoken to Michelle with enthusiasm about another priest, Father Guy Merveille, the new rector of Sacred Heart Church. She decided to stop by to see him on her way to the Fort Royal Medical Centre.

Sacred Heart was not an ordinary parish church. Strikingly modern, a round building with huge glass windows, it sat atop a high hill in the north end of Victoria looking out on a breathtaking view of the city and the ocean. Father Guy was free when she arrived, and he welcomed her into the rectory study.

[*163*]

"I am here for a friend," she said, "someone who has been very, very helpful to me. I would like to have a Mass said for him. Is that possible?"

The priest was tall, dark-haired, and serious, but when he spoke it was with a twinkle. "A Mass," he said, "is always possible. If you and your friend can come this afternoon at three, I'll say a Mass for him then."

They talked for a quarter of an hour, at the end of which Michelle rose to depart. She noticed that the priest was observing her keenly. "I think you have been struggling with negative forces," he said quietly.

"You're right, Father," she replied. "I have."

When Michelle told Dr. Pazder what she had arranged, he was very touched. At three that afternoon, they presented themselves at the rectory. Father Guy was waiting for them. Michelle introduced the two men, and they chatted a bit before walking across to the church.

There was a vitality to the service that everyone felt. "A really good Mass, wasn't it," Father Guy said afterward. They agreed and thanked him and stood talking for a few minutes. "I think we're going to know each other well," the priest said. "We have lots to share."

Driving back down the hill, Dr. Pazder said to Michelle, "I like him. What do you know about him?"

"He's a Belgian. A Norbertine canon—it's an order based on monastic principles, but with an active apostolate. He got his M.A. in sociology at Temple University in Philadelphia, and I hear he worked with street gangs there."

"I like him," Dr. Pazder said again.

"So do I," Michelle said. "I'm glad we're in touch with him."

"Speaking of being in touch, I think it may be time to go talk to the bishop. What do you think? I know him pretty well, through Church committees I've served on and so forth. I'd just feel better if somebody in authority knew about all this stuff."

"I would too. I'd like him to know what we're doing. I mean, I sometimes wonder if it's okay even to be talking about all this—the ceremonies, the rituals—or whether we're dealing with things we shouldn't. And if I had his blessing, his prayers, well, it would mean a very great deal when I have to go back down there."

When Remi De Roo was thirty-eight, he became the youngest Roman Catholic bishop in Canada. Raised on a 480-acre family farm in Manitoba with, as he had put it, "one hand on the tractor and the other on a halter," he was ideal for the diocese of Vancouver Island, a large, rugged area with many isolated missions tucked into the wilderness. He was from the start a champion of the underdog, particularly the Native Indians. "Why don't we see what we are doing to destroy our own Indian people?" he once asked a conference. "We expect them to conform to the image we set for them, and when they don't, we marginalize them." Not doctrinaire, he tolerated limited use of the old ritual form of the Mass modified by the Church since Vatican II, alongside the new forms he preferred. "There's a place within the Church for us all," he said.

Michelle had never met a bishop before—De Roo was her first. What she saw as she entered his residence was a slender man with large eyes and light hair. His manner was intellectual but by no means austere; quite the contrary—he was most engaging. There was a quiet, empathetic warmth that Michelle responded to instantly.

After some opening conversation, Dr. Pazder laid out the case for the bishop briefly, in broad outline. And then, wanting Michelle to hear him say this as much as he wanted the bishop to hear it, he said: "To come right to the point, then, I feel that, in my professional opinion, Michelle is not crazy; in fact, she's a sound, healthy woman. I've listened to her for many hundreds of hours for close to a year, and four years before that—and I'm a trained listener—and so far as I can determine, she is not making it up. I'm convinced that she believes it to be true—that is, I believe she's genuine."

The bishop then asked Michelle some questions, letting her tell her story herself, attending to every word. At the end of an hour he turned back to Dr. Pazder and said: "Well, of course, I completely agree with you. It's clear that Michelle is totally genuine. As to the truth of her story—whether or not her dreadful memories are accurate—I'm in no position to say. Nor can I speak about the ramifications of the story. Nor should I; it seems possible that someday I might be called upon to make judgments upon it, and I shouldn't anticipate those judgments.

"But I do want to say"—he took Michelle's head between his

hands; her eyes were still moist from the emotion of recounting her experiences—"that I really am very sorry for all the pain you've had to go through. You are a *good* person, Michelle, and you must not feel ashamed for what happened. You are in no way responsible." He gave Michelle his blessing, and then all eyes were moist.

The bishop offered to talk again at any time, and he gave them the use of his library for such research as they might need to do into the phenomena Michelle was encountering.

Michelle said that she had found it very helpful to have the spiritual guidance of Father Leo at the most difficult moments of her travail, and she wondered if, when there was more that needed talking over, they might go to Father Guy Merveille.

"An excellent idea," said the bishop. "Father Guy is a very interesting man with a very broad background. He has experience that other priests have perhaps not had, experience that might well be useful in dealing with these matters. Let me assign him to you and ask him to keep me closely informed."

As he saw his visitors to the door, the bishop smiled and said, "Michelle, you are appropriately named. As you know, it was Michael the Archangel who drove Lucifer from Heaven."

The relationship with Father Guy flourished. He and Michelle had long conversations, about the remembering but also about Michelle's inner life, her own spiritual quest, her growing sense that she wanted to become Catholic.

"I think it is important that you be baptized," Father Guy said, "for all your own excellent reasons but also for your protection. It would be better. One is always safer when one holds the hand of one's Father."

Michelle glowed. "Would it be all right?"

"Nothing," the priest replied, "could be more all right." His voice was grave, but when Michelle studied his face, she saw an affectionate smile. Diffidently, she brought forth one last misgiving: Would the evil she was encountering in her descents taint the Church if she joined it before she had come to the end of the remembering?

Father Guy replied emphatically. "It will be better for you to be part of the Church while you are going through this instead of outside it. There is no reason for you to stand outside the Church if you truly want to be inside."

He spoke to Bishop De Roo, who gave him permission both to baptize and to confirm Michelle at the same time. The date was set for June 28.

On June 24 Dr. Pazder and Michelle went together to Sacred Heart Church. As they sat in the pew, listening to Father Guy celebrate Mass, Dr. Pazder noticed that the sacristy light, a little candle burning in a glass cup suspended by a chain from the ceiling, had suddenly grown dim. "Did you see that?" he asked Michelle after the service. "The sacristy light went way down. It's still way down."

"Maybe it's burning out," Michelle replied, glancing over at it. And then she tensed. "What's that?" she exclaimed in a loud whisper.

A few feet away was a small wooden bench. Neither of them had ever noticed it in the church before—and they would have; it was very out of place in the simple, modern decor.

"Those symbols!" Michelle said, and Dr. Pazder, looking closer, saw that the bench was carved with ornate designs. His heart skipped a beat. They were precisely the symbols Michelle had described as being sewn on the cloaks of the inhabitants of the round room.

They hurried to the back of the church, where Father Guy was bidding farewell to the last of the worshipers. "Father," said Dr. Pazder, "could you come here for a second? I want you to have a look at something."

When the priest stood before the little bench, his expression of befuddlement changed to one of shock. "Oh, my God!" he said. "What is that doing in here? How did that get here? I know those symbols. We'll get rid of it right away!" He snatched up the bench and, holding it at arm's length, quickly transported it from the church to the grass outside.

They examined it. It was very well made, well fitted, finished with many coats of varnish.

"What should we do with it?" Dr. Pazder asked.

"I can tell you what we'll do with it," Father Guy said. "We'll burn it. It couldn't be more perfect—this is the feast of St. John the Baptist. You know the Gospel—St. John was the bearer of the Light. It's traditional to have a bonfire on the feast of St. John—to signify the bringing of the Light to lighten the world. We'll have a bonfire tonight, and we have our fuel."

In preparation, Dr. Pazder and Father Guy knocked the bench apart. Soon its sections were strewn on the grass. "Oh!" Michelle said, and the others looked at her inquiringly. "Don't you see? There are thirteen pieces!"

When Michelle and Dr. Pazder returned that night, Father Guy was waiting for them outside the rectory door. In his hand was a sheet of paper. On it, he explained, he had written a prayer, in both Latin and English, a prayer meant to drive out anything evil in the fire.

They moved the pieces of wood to a suitable spot about ten feet from the concrete wall of the church. Father Guy crinkled his paper and stacked the wood around it. Just as they were prepared to begin, Dr. Pazder said: "Could you hold on just a couple of minutes? I want to get my camera."

Dr. Pazder, during his time as a physician in West Africa, had become fascinated with African ceremonies and had taken countless photos of them. Many ceremonies involved the burning of juju, little dolls and amulets used in black magic, and replacing them with a cross —this as a way of trying to get rid of the animistic beliefs among West Africans in the spirits of the jungle. Dr. Pazder had built up a very extensive collection of photographs of such ceremonies, planning someday to use them in some sort of transcultural study. Now, as Father Guy prepared to light the bonfire, Dr. Pazder felt strongly compelled to take photographs of it.

"But your camera's all the way at your house," Michelle said.

"Won't take a minute," Dr. Pazder replied, already heading down the hill toward his car.

"Now, Dr. Pazder, is this really necessary?" Father Guy called after him. Father Guy had already come to know something about the doctor's slightly flexible perception of time.

But the psychiatrist was climbing into his car. "I can't explain it," he shouted. "I just think it's important."

He was back in twenty minutes, breathless, with two cameras strung

around his neck, and quite oblivious to the somewhat strained looks
that were aimed in his direction.

The ceremony began. Michelle stood to one side of the fire. Father
Guy, vested in white and wearing a white stole, stood to the other. He
said a prayer, then struck a match and touched it to the kindling. Flame
seemed to leap from the match, then into the air. Almost instantly
there was a tall column of fire, nearly six feet high—far larger, far
brighter than one might have expected. It burned with a fury.

Father Guy took his thurible, opened it, and spooned incense upon
the glowing coals within. Sweet smoke rose into the night air. He closed
the thurible and, reciting a prayer, swung it toward the fire, censing it,
cleansing it. He gave a Bible to Michelle and asked her to read the
beautiful, uncannily evocative words from the opening of the Gospel
according to John.

> In the beginning was the Word;
> the word was with God
> and the Word was God. . . .
> And all that came to be had life in him
> and that life was the light of men,
> a light that shines in the dark,
> a light that darkness could not overpower. . . .

Father took a vial of holy water and, thrusting it forward again and
again, sent drops hissing into the flames. He recited the prayer: "In the
name of Jesus Christ I order any influence of evil, any power of evil,
to go back to where you belong."

Abruptly there was a pungent, almost overwhelming odor. All three
of them smelled it—sickening, cloying. Dr. Pazder recognized it immediately; it was a smell he could never forget. He had known it a
number of times in Africa, usually when natives who had been drying
gunpowder in their huts, too near the fire, had been badly charred. It
was the odor of burning human flesh. And then it was gone. There was
a rustling in the trees, yet the night was still.

Throughout the ceremony, he kept taking photos, one after another, guessing at the apertures and shutter speeds, holding the cameras

as still as he could to reduce the blurring that could result from long exposures. By the time the fire had died down, the film in both cameras had been finished. The men threw water on the last embers. Fifteen minutes later Michelle was on her way home to Shawnigan Lake, and Dr. Pazder was in his kitchen unloading his film and putting it on the shelf by the door, where he would find it in the morning. He would drop it off at the photo lab on the way to work.

Father Guy went into the church to divest. As he started out again, he looked at the sacristy light. It was burning brightly again.

Michelle was baptized four days later. Every word of the ceremony had weight. "God is light and in Him there is no darkness," read Father Guy as he poured the water. As part of the ceremony of confirmation, Father Guy then drew his stole and robe about Michelle's shoulders —to symbolize her being taken into the Church.

The next day Dr. Pazder picked up the developed films and prints from the photo lab. He looked at them on the spot. Some prints were, after all, slightly indistinct; it was hard to hold a camera still enough in poor light. But there was Michelle, reading the Gospel. And there was Father, sprinkling holy water on the fire. And there was the fire itself, those eerie, leaping flames. But in the background—what was that? That figure beyond the fire . . . it seemed to be dressed in a long, flowing gown, and there was a glow around the head.

He looked at other prints, of the shots taken just before and just afterward. The figure was there, but never in exactly the same spot. It seemed to be moving slowly from left to right.

Dr. Pazder was puzzled. There had been no one else there that night. Certainly no one in a long robe. The air had been still. The smoke had gone straight up—you could see that in the photos. What was that figure?

He looked at other photos. The figure was gone, apparently drifted off and out of the frame. But other images were visible—smaller, fierce-looking images, moving, changing form—about thirty of them in all.

Was it just one of the films that was peculiar? He checked. No, the images appeared on both, from the different cameras.

Dr. Pazder showed Michelle the photographs when she arrived at his office that afternoon. He made no comment but watched as she looked at one after another. She smiled at the picture of Father Guy sprinkling holy water on the fire. And she gasped when she came to the first photograph with the misty figure in the background.

They took the pictures to Father Guy. He studied them silently. His mother, quite an old woman, who lived with him, picked them up and looked at them. She stopped at a photo of the figure. "Yes," she said after a time, quietly, as if to herself, "that's Mary with the child."

The pictures were put away. It was too much to think about. They went back to their work, the remembering. But the photographs were on their minds. Dr. Pazder's father ran a large graphic-arts business in Edmonton, and was an expert on photography. A month later, on a visit home, Dr. Pazder showed the photos to his father, asking him if there was any way to explain these anomalies. His father said no, no way at all. Dr. Pazder went to more experts. The answer was the same.

He had his cameras inspected. Nothing amiss there.

In the fall he and Michelle and Father Guy built other fires, on the same spot on the same sort of night, wearing the same clothes, burning the same sort of wood, using the thurible, the vial, duplicating the first occasion as well as they could. Dr. Pazder took rolls and rolls of film. None of the prints revealed background images. At the end of each attempt they would find themselves standing by the dwindling fire and staring over toward the plain concrete foundation wall of the church, at the place where, in those baffling first photos, the glowing presence had seemed to stand.

chapter 20

ON June 30 Michelle called Dr. Pazder. For the past days, she said, she had been afflicted by strange, distressing urges. She had felt a repeated impulse to get in the car and drive—somewhere, she didn't know where. She had kept twisting her hands harshly, the one inside the other. Dr. Pazder did his best to reassure her.

And then, an hour later, she abruptly arrived at his office, without an appointment, very upset. "I don't want to continue this remembering," she said. "I'm not going to do it anymore. I wish I didn't even have a tongue. If I could tear out my tongue, I'd never have to talk again."

Dr. Pazder knew that the Satanists had used sophisticated techniques of psychological manipulation to try to inhibit Michelle—not merely to make her forget but, if she should remember, to make her not tell. Michelle had found the strength to talk—despite them, she was telling. But their manipulations had made it extremely difficult for her. It was undoubtedly this extreme difficulty that she was reflecting in her refusal to continue.

And perhaps there was more to it than that. A dreadful memory was coming up, he sensed, undoubtedly the unbearably horrible memory that had impelled Michelle to seek spiritual armor from the Church. It was forcing its way past the dire admonitions of the Satanists, causing a tremendous emotional battle. It seemed quite possible, he thought, that her very sanity could be at stake. Such mind-control techniques had unbelievable power, he knew. In Africa he had seen the influence of the juju dolls; if a person believed in juju, the dolls could be used to make that person roll over and die, on the spot, without any other intervention. He had detected some of the methods the Satanists were using, but he had no way of knowing whether or not there were others, perhaps even more baneful, of which he would have no knowledge and which he therefore might fail to combat effectively. It was an eerie, indeed terrifying contest that he and Michelle were engaged in, struggling with the cruelest adversaries, largely in the dark, across a void of twenty-two years. The struggle was for her life—not her physical life; it was clear that the Satanists chose not to kill her—but for her spiritual existence. For them nothing would have been achieved by killing her; the victory would come only if she gave herself to them.

Now Pazder told Michelle that it was desperately important that she not yield to the Satanist suggestions, that she resist them, that she allow herself to ventilate the fearful memories. The Satanists had tried to fill her with guilt—it was one of their techniques. He had done a study of concentration camp survivors—someday he would let her read the professional paper that had resulted. He had observed for himself the oft-noted phenomenon that these people who had been innocent victims nevertheless suffered guilt—guilt over having survived when so many others did not, guilt merely over having seen so much death. Michelle, it appeared, had survived when others had not, and she had seen much death. Experiences such as those were a psychic maelstrom through which sane, decent people could not pass blithely. The great necessity, Dr. Pazder said, was not to let oneself be destroyed by the guilt but to touch the horror and deal with it. And then he did something he very rarely did with a patient: He commanded her to continue.

The next day, after a two-week hiatus, they resumed their sessions.

MICHELLE: It's like someone is putting my insides through a wringer, and having them all come out the wrong way. It's all confusion and things being mixed up and things not being the way they're supposed to be. I have to struggle so inside, just to have things come out backward, hoping they'll be right in the end. Please help me sort them out. I feel wrong because I want to go away. But the confusion isn't my fault, it wasn't my fault what happened.

DR. PAZDER: I want you to remember your confusion and to share your remembering with me. But I don't want you acting on your confusion—driving places or things like that. All right?

MICHELLE: It's like someone's got hold of my brain.

DR. PAZDER: You've got hold of your own brain. It's okay. If they told you that, it's not true. Nobody has hold of your brain.

MICHELLE: But it makes me feel funny in my head. It's like someone pushes a button. I'm afraid. I don't want to die but I'm afraid I'd kill myself. I'm afraid of myself. I'm afraid I'll get in that place where I don't have any feelings, and it will just seem like it's the only right thing to do. I know it's not. They are trying to make me end up farther away than I've ever been. It's got to do with the way they keep counting backward. I don't want to count. It's like when you're scared before an operation and they put you to sleep and they tell you to start counting and you start counting. The more you count the less upset you get. Then it's like all your feelings are the same. Am I sounding funny? What's the matter with me? Hang on to me, please. Hang on to me. *Hang onto me! I don't want to go away!* Where are those things coming from? It's not me. I don't want to go frozen.

DR. PAZDER: You're not going to go frozen by letting it come out. Do you hear me?

MICHELLE: I feel dizzy. What happened? Nothing's happened to me, has it? I don't know what to do. I feel like I'm going to go in a coma and die.

DR. PAZDER: It's okay. You're not going to go in a coma, and you're not going to die. Let it come. It's okay.

MICHELLE: There are things deep inside that don't feel like me.

DR. PAZDER: Let them out. Let them out so they're not you. They don't have to be in there.

MICHELLE (going deeper): What do you do when people have their eyes shut and they don't hear you? . . . I'm in a really heavy place. They got people there that are like that.

DR. PAZDER: You can face it with me.

MICHELLE: No! No! I don't want to watch anybody else die. Please, I don't. It's making me wrong.

DR. PAZDER: No, it's not making you wrong. It's just the memories you have to deal with.

MICHELLE: They have this little bottle. They put a needle in it, and then they put it in my arm. It makes me feel bad things. It makes me go backward. It stops my feelings. . . . It's like walking in my sleep, but I wasn't asleep. It's like everything going dead inside and there was nothing I could do about it. It was like being crazy and dead and not having any control and not having any feelings and not being able to move, and going to sleep and having my eyes wide open all at the same time. My head feels so squeezed. Oh, God. Please, I'm not going to go away. [long pause with much struggling] There's something wrong with my body. It's going somewhere. I see that little bottle, and they make me count, and the same time everything inside me is going like that. [screams] What's the *matter?*

DR. PAZDER: It's okay. You're scared.

MICHELLE: Those wires! Where are they coming from? It makes my head feel funny. Am I crazy?

DR. PAZDER: No. No, you're not, Michelle. You're remembering.

MICHELLE: I'm in some kind of a room. I've never been there. It's in that round room but it's real scary. What are they doing to me? It makes me go all funny. I feel like a monster.

DR. PAZDER: You're not a monster.

MICHELLE: It doesn't destroy your brain? That stuff they put in my arm, does it?

DR. PAZDER: No, it doesn't. Your brain is beautiful.

MICHELLE: I'm not crazy?

DR. PAZDER: No, you're not.

MICHELLE: I don't need to go and have a piece of my brain taken out, do I?

DR. PAZDER: No.

MICHELLE: I'm scared of what they are doing. No! It's got to do with counting backward and dying. It's like they're saying I have to die, I'm useless. I'm going to go crazy. Then they make my body jump with the wires. My head hurts. It hurts all my bones. Then you can't do anything. You just get sick. It's so ugly. [crying] They make me jump too. Oh, please tell me I'm not remembering.

DR. PAZDER: It's okay, Michelle.

MICHELLE: It makes me crazy.

DR. PAZDER: No, it doesn't. Tell me about the wires.

MICHELLE: About the wires? I know what they are now. They told me then that they called that funny thing . . . they call that person . . . they say he's electricity. He can take over electricity. . . . There's a great big fire in the room. Oh, God help me. Oh, God help me. If I tell you, I won't feel more like that, will I?

DR. PAZDER: You'll feel better. You always feel better.

MICHELLE: It's so sick. Oh, God. I can't go there all at once. You'll be nearby for the next little while, won't you, please? I can't live with these things alone. Please. If I'm making it up, I want to die. Really.

DR. PAZDER: That's what they told you. It's all right. You're not making it up. You don't have to die.

They had taken Michelle from the round room down a dark tunnel. The floor was unpaved. There was a bad smell that became worse and worse as they went along. They came to the little room where the doctor had sewed horns and a tail on Michelle, and passed through it to the room beyond. It was larger, and the smell there was intensely bad. The room was very hot, and Michelle realized that the big brick structure in the corner of the room was an open hearth; she could see the flames.

One bare lightbulb hung from the ceiling, illuminating a number of stainless-steel stretchers. On several of them were bodies. Their eyes were closed but they seemed to be alive. Across the room were four coffins, three big ones and one small.

Michelle was strapped to a stretcher. The doctor came over and looked down at her expressionlessly. Then he went to a table, picked up some metal things—knives, it seemed—and went to one of the bodies.

God help me! Oh, God! He cut off its feet! Oh, no, I don't want to hear. I can *hear* him cutting its legs. I can hear him cutting the bones up. Oh, no! How can I live with it? Can people live with it? I'm sure I'm going to die. Oh, God, that's what they're going to do to me next.

The doctor continued his grisly work, methodically cutting off the limbs in a certain order—at the ankles, then at the knees, at the groin. Then the fingers, the hands, the forearms, the upper arms.

> He's cutting it all up! Oh, God! It's on the floor. It's got no head. *He's got no head!* Oh, no! God help me. I'm going to die. I want to die so badly. I can't stand it. I can't stand it! Why can't I go crazy? I'm going to go crazy.

When the doctor had finished with one body, he went to the next and proceeded in exactly the same fashion, until the floor was running with blood and red-stumped members were littered everywhere. And then, just as matter-of-factly, he reversed the process. He picked up a thigh segment from a woman's body and, with fine wire and a needle, began to stitch it onto the torso of one of the males. Then, from still another of the bodies, a lower leg. On he went, limb by limb, assembling a macabre composite, until one body was complete. Finally he attached thick black wires to its limbs. And suddenly, to the child's absolute horror, the body came alive. Or it seemed to. It twitched and jumped, then abruptly lay still, and then just as abruptly started jerking violently again. It slithered off its blood-slick platform and tumbled to the floor. One of its wires came loose, and sparks erupted from it as it touched the wet floor.

The twitching subsided. The body lay still, the sparks ceased. The doctor came over to Michelle. His face was blank; saying not a word, he carefully taped black wires to her arms and legs. And then she felt a searing jolt. Her whole body was a unity of pain.

> Oh, God, please help me. I feel so guilty. I'm not a monster. Oh, God. You don't *do* that to pieces of people! No! You don't cut them like that. Please, that's wrong. Please put them together. You don't cut people apart like that. You don't put them with the wrong pieces. I feel like I can't live. Not with what I know. It's not just in my head. It's all through me. My brain, it feels like it's burning. They're making me do that twitch. Why can't I stop it? Oh, God, help me! Oh, please! God, it's such a terrible feeling.

[Crying out in terror] How can you stand to touch me? I'm panicking inside. My insides are just panicking.

Over the next twenty minutes, Michelle sobbed her way back up from the depths. "I have to talk for a minute," she said finally.

"Of course," Dr. Pazder replied.

"I can't stand any more, I feel so guilty."

"You're not guilty of anything. But when I think of what you had to face, now I understand why you couldn't go there until you were baptized."

"I need God to help me. I can't live with it." Michelle was silent, then stammered out a question: "How . . . how did they do that when the people were dead? How did they make them move?"

"You can make any piece of flesh jump like that with electricity. It seems they were trying to make you feel that the Devil had the power to do that to them—and to you. It was horribly confusing for you, especially when they kept shocking you too."

"It makes me feel like killing myself. It makes me feel like I just can't stand it."

"You can stand it." Dr. Pazder's voice grew grave and measured. "You must be careful not to let that experience make you think against yourself."

"I hope it goes away."

"It'll go away. It's like your rashes or your pains. It'll go away. Right now it's there because you've just come through it and it's very sickening. I feel it in my stomach too."

Michelle had stopped crying, but she still spoke with a tremor. "Those people aren't people," she said, raising her eyes to look directly at Dr. Pazder. "People who do things like that are monsters."

JULY 2

"I remembered some things after we finished the other day," Michelle said at the start of the next session. "I thought about that fire in the round room. It's a really creepy fire. The more blood they put in the fire, the creepier it got. It was sort of ugly and dead. I don't know if you've ever seen a drippy fire. It's awful. It has the strangest shapes.

"And I remembered somebody in black. He was reading out of a book, and the book was black. There was something about it that made it seem like forever. I thought I'd die if he didn't stop.

"And I just kept feeling like I'm going to stop breathing. I don't know what it's about. There's something about going around, and no matter which way I turn I'll always come out facing the wrong way. It's so hard to explain." Michelle remained silent for a moment, biting her lower lip, then spoke again. "It's like everything is facing the wrong way. You can't get out because everything's turned on itself."

JULY 3

"When I woke up in the morning, I was still in that awful room. I was lying on the table again, and the doctor was trying to make me open my mouth. He had some kind of cold silver thing and he pushed it in, and I had to open up. And then he began to do things to my teeth! Sometimes he just pulled them out. It really hurt! I wasn't allowed to make any noise or to move at all. And then he had a drill and he began . . . to . . . to *drill* them! I just lay there frozen. I was paralyzed. . . .

"My eyes won't close. Maybe they sewed them open! Maybe they're never going to close again. I won't move! I'm just lying here. I can't move. I can't move!"

Michelle was weeping through the fragments of her sentences. "They got a mirror and showed me how I looked. I didn't look right. Some of my teeth are gone. They're gone! I want my teeth back! I want my teeth back! They said I was never going to be the same again."*

JULY 19

MICHELLE (in her depths): I'm supposed to go to sleep, but I won't. This doctor is still there. He's making me sleepy. He has a light or something shiny. I'm supposed to look at it, and he's saying things to me. He wants me to sleep. I'm afraid to sleep, because then I'll die.

*See Appendix 3 for the statement of Donald L. Poy, B. Sc., D.M.D., who in 1978 examined the adult Michelle's teeth and found evidence of the trauma she described.

He thinks I'm looking at the shiny thing, but I'm not. I'm looking past it. Do you understand what I mean?

DR. PAZDER: Yes, I do.

MICHELLE: You see, I watched him do that to someone else. He had children there, and he can make them look like they were dead. I don't want to go dead. I look sleepy like they did so that he won't get mad. The doctor did it to the children with a candle. He made their eyes go up in their head, and they didn't breathe. They just lay there. Then he'd say something and they'd wake up. I'd hear them talking about how you couldn't tell the difference if you were dead or not. . . .

If I go to sleep, I'll never get out of it, ever. . . .

DR. PAZDER: Sure you will.

MICHELLE (suddenly brightening): My pretend friend, she's back. I'm so glad I have her. She always used to tell me not to talk, not to tell them anything. She says I shouldn't go to sleep. She says she'll stay with me and keep me company, so I won't go to sleep. . . .

They're pushing me. . . .

DR. PAZDER: Pushing you?

MICHELLE: Pushing me, trying to *make* me sleep.

DR. PAZDER: The doctor?

MICHELLE: Yes. He keeps making my eyes go funny. They're sticking things in my hands. I'm getting sick. They say funny words on me, and they write them down in the book. . . .

There's something wrong with my hands! There's *bugs* on them! Get them off! . . .

They're tying my arms down. I want to rip them off. They're scaring me. They're saying things. They're scaring me. I don't want to die now! I don't want to die now. Now isn't the *time* for me to die. It's not!

DR. PAZDER: No, no, it's not. You won't die. You'll be all right. Tell me, what are they sticking in your hands?

MICHELLE: They . . . the doctor has a bottle again.† He's got a needle. He's sticking it in my hand. I feel really far away. It's done

†From further discussion it appeared to Dr. Pazder that the bottle contained Methedrine and Amytal, or similar drugs.

something to me. It's the same counting as before, but the doctor keeps making me look at the shiny thing. I'm scared . . . I can't get my mouth to work. It sounds like other people's voices are coming inside my head and staying there. They seem to be putting things in there, for good. The doctor's got me frozen. I can't move. Something's scaring me.

DR. PAZDER: Breathe deeply. Let your breath go.

MICHELLE: Somebody help me!

DR. PAZDER: Michelle, breathe! Breathe out!

MICHELLE: Something's happened. It pushes people away. It's got to do with a word. It makes me go like a record. You know, when a record's run out? I'm going, "Ahhhh." Then everything's fine. Hi, Mom! Hi. I'm Michelle. Come here, I'll give you a kiss. [sings] Where's my doll? My doll. I'm fine. There's nothing wrong. No. Nothing wrong. Nothing. [laughs] Nothing's hurting me.

Who said that? It's not me! It's in my head. Get it out of my head. Help me. They keep putting words in my head. Everything's fine. Nobody's ever hurt me. I won't tell anybody. Yes. Yes, I know. Yes. I know. Yes, sir. Yes, sir. No. Nobody hurt me. Nobody hurt me. I did it to myself. Isn't that funny. I did everything to myself. Yes. I'll forget it. Yes, I promise. Oh! No! *I won't say that word!* No! No! Please somebody make them quit saying that word. Please. I'm going to die. They got to quit saying it. . . .

No one can hear me. My mouth won't move. No one will hear me. Please. Please. Everything's all right. Please. Please, someone know it's not all right. It's going slow, then it's going fast. *Get away!* Get that needle out of my hand. Quit doing that to me. No. I won't make my head turn around. I won't! I won't do that! Oh, God, something's going to happen. Got to get back. No. I'm not going to go squish. No.

Mommy. Mommy! Mommy, please come. Mommy, where are you? Mommy! I want my mommy. I don't care what she's like. I want my mommy. I want my mommy! Please! Anybody! Please!

Everybody's walking away. I'll keep my mouth shut. I'll keep it shut. I promise I'll keep it shut. Please. No. Don't leave me here. Please don't leave me here. No. I don't want the bugs on my hands. No. Please. No. Don't go. Please. Come back. Come back. *Please,* I'll die. . . .

I'm evil. Is that right, sir? I'm all poisoned. I know. I know. I'm worse than everybody. I know. Yes, sir. I don't have a mother. No, sir. I wasn't born. I won't get upset anymore. I won't go near anybody. I'll keep my mouth shut. Don't hurt my mom. I don't know anything. . . .

It's written down. They wrote everything down in the book. They wrote my name. And all the bad things that would happen to me. They wrote it all down. They'd know who I was. They said I'd be all alone, all my life. . . .

They said I'd wasted almost the whole year for everyone. Everyone had other things to do. They'd all had to waste their time on me. I was the worse thing they'd ever met. All the people that have died, all the things that have happened—it's all my fault. I have to be taught a lesson. I'm going to be sorry. I'm going to be sorry. I am sorry. I already am sorry. I'm sorry to everybody. . . .

I don't want to be scared anymore. I can't take any more. I'm going to go away like I was told, because I'm going to be lost anyway. I'm so scared. I'm scared. [she was screaming and crying as she began to ascend]

I went away deep . . . way down deep. I felt I was all apart. It's like I left me. It's like falling backward, except you see yourself way up there and you fall away from yourself. . . .

I can't take any more. Help me. *Please.* Please, don't lose me.

DR. PAZDER: We're not going to lose you.

MICHELLE: Please don't let me get lost. Please don't.

DR. PAZDER: You're not going to get lost.

MICHELLE: What's the matter with me? I don't make any sense.

DR. PAZDER: You do make sense. Yes, you do make sense.

MICHELLE: I feel crazy.

DR. PAZDER: You're not. It all makes sense to me. Those are their suggestions. They're just suggestions that they gave you; that needle is clouding you up a little bit, but that's not going to last.

MICHELLE: They can get you away from me. They can make things really terrible.

DR. PAZDER: No, they can't get me away from you. They have no hold on me. None at all.

MICHELLE: I'm not going to be left alone, am I?

DR. PAZDER: Don't believe that. The only things that have power over you are the things that they suggest that you believe.

MICHELLE: Something's really scaring me.

DR. PAZDER: Tell me what you've left out as much as you can. You don't need to leave anything out, out of fear. When you do that you get a little trapped.

MICHELLE: It had to do with that shiny thing and the needle.

DR. PAZDER: It's the suggestion. It's like a hypnotic thing. But you mustn't be afraid of that. Don't be afraid they'll hypnotize you down there and you'll stay hypnotized when you come back up. We can go there and bring you back, if we have to. What they told you doesn't stay there forever. You're bringing it to your conscious by talking about it. Their suggestions don't have power over you unless they are buried. You have to let them out.

MICHELLE: I didn't really let him hypnotize me.

DR. PAZDER: I know you didn't, because you weren't paying attention to him and looking at the shiny thing like he wanted. That's the first thing about hypnosis. You had to *want* to follow his suggestions. He couldn't make you. Not any more than he can now. They were using two powers: the power of suggestion and the power of repressed memory. They used a number of other sophisticated techniques of psychological manipulation and control, such as brainwashing or conditioning, to confuse you and make you remember backward, and even to turn on yourself.

MICHELLE: They're hard on me.

DR. PAZDER: I know. It's really hard.

MICHELLE: It's very complicated. It keeps going back and forward and inside out.

DR. PAZDER: I know.

MICHELLE: Am I strong enough?

DR. PAZDER: Yes. Listen, trust yourself. You've been at this a long time. You've done this sort of work more than anyone, I'm sure of that. Deeper and longer. I know you're strong enough for three reasons. First, you got through it then, and then was really worse than now. You were little and alone, but you got through it. That makes you strong enough. Second, because you have *you* now. You've done a lot of work with you. You've got a lot of you at your disposal. Far more than you ever had then. Third, you also have spiritual resources. Michelle, you're a very strong person.

MICHELLE: I hope so.

DR. PAZDER: You were going to tell me more about what they said, and about that word you were trying to say.

MICHELLE: I know what it means. It's a word they use to get power somehow, and to make things permanent. It's like saying, "In the name of the Father, and of the Son, and of the Holy Spirit." But it's opposite. I have to go right back to when they're cursing to remember it all. That's so hard on me. It is. I have to trust I'll come back, you know.

DR. PAZDER: You will.

MICHELLE (in her depths): I keep hearing someone else's voice. It's a man's voice. I don't like it. And that man is reading something from that black book.

DR. PAZDER: What's he saying?

MICHELLE: Something about a door and "seven times four" and then "there's no more."

DR. PAZDER: No more what?

MICHELLE: I'm trying to tell you. I'm going all fuzzy. I don't understand the words. They're all put together funny. . . . So much turning . . . so much turning. "This black . . . a piece of white . . . and blood . . . and it comes at night. Black, black, black. I'll open the door. Turn around and there's no more."

DR. PAZDER: Try to say it.

MICHELLE (straining to speak): Ahey . . . ehey . . . ah . . . aaa . . . hhh. Aaaa . . . ave . . . ahhh . . . ahhh . . . Round, round, round . . . long ago . . . ffff . . . fire . . . ff . . . fire . . . fire, fire, this fire . . . this night . . . this night . . .

It's black, dead white.
Everything is wrong way around.
Everything's lost, nothing's ever found.
So long ago, it's long ago. There's a fire.
There's a fire. There's a fire. Is hhhh . . . ahhhh . . .

DR. PAZDER: Say the word.

MICHELLE: Agggai ahgi something. Aggga . . . ahhhh, ahhhh, a door, a door, ahhhh . . . dirt . . . dogs . . . dark.

> Never, never come back. Never see any light.
> It's made wrong by blood at night.
> What's made wrong's never right.
> Blood is right, blood is right. Ahhhh Ahhhh

DR. PAZDER: It's okay to say it.

MICHELLE: Ahhhhh . . . ugggl . . . ugg. It warms this fire, fire, fire, fire, fire, fire, fire, ahhhhh. . . .

DR. PAZDER: You're okay. I'm here. Keep talking and saying what you heard.

MICHELLE: It's old. It seems so old.

DR. PAZDER: Yes.

MICHELLE: Old, old. It's old. It's old. It's all murky. It's through fire, fire, ahhh . . . that's someone else's voice. Fire uhhh . . . Comes long ago, ahhhh long ago, long ago, dirt, damp, fires. Goes around . . . goes into the ground.

There's a . . . a . . . a . . . ag, agg, a . . . ggggg, aaa hhhh, thhhh, sssssss . . . [breathing becomes faster] It's coming in black. It's coming in black. It's come in black. Take you, black, never white, never right. Only red will make right, fire, sssfire, come, come, come, come, aggg, aggg . . . ssssss . . . [breathing becomes very fast] agggg sssss cut to left . . . cut, cut . . . always wrong, never right.

Help, help. Far, far help. It's far. It's far, help. Help. Ohhh. God, help! I'm not going to come back. Help!

DR. PAZDER: You're going to come back, all right. It's okay.

MICHELLE: You're so far away. It's so awful. It's not going to be okay.

DR. PAZDER: It's okay. Hey, it's okay. Look at me! It's okay.

MICHELLE: I feel all weird. I feel guilty. I feel like I've been somewhere awful in that room.

DR. PAZDER: There is some word you can't say.

MICHELLE: It's not English. . . . there are people, faces in black, and the fire. . . . They're doing things with their hands.

DR. PAZDER: Like what?

MICHELLE: A snaky movement like letters on me.

DR. PAZDER: What do the letters say?

MICHELLE: I don't know, but the whole time they kept singing like a priest does.

DR. PAZDER: Like chanting?

MICHELLE: Yes, but weird. They're hissing at me. SSSSSSSS. I'm not making any sense. I feel guilty. I feel like I've done something I shouldn't have. Have I put myself in danger by saying these things?

DR. PAZDER: That doesn't put you in danger. That frees you. Curses don't have a hold on you. Don't let them have a hold on you.

MICHELLE: Do they make any sense?

DR. PAZDER: Maybe they're backward.

MICHELLE: What happens to me when I go like that? What's going on with me? I go funny. I feel all numb.

DR. PAZDER: Well, you are going down very deep to remember this. They are also using everything they can to make you give up. It's a horrendous struggle.

MICHELLE: But they said so many things. Things like, "There is no way out."

DR. PAZDER: You have a way out. There isn't anybody to stop you from coming out. Do you hear me?

MICHELLE: Yes. I do hear you. Do I have a way out?

chapter 21

 HE construction company Doug Smith worked for gave him a week at a resort hotel up-island. It was just what he and Michelle needed, a chance to do nothing very complicated all day long. Get a suntan. Breakfast, lunch, dinner. The psychiatric sessions were not mentioned; it was as if that had become a forbidden topic.

Dr. Pazder also felt the need for a holiday. For two weeks he, his brother Ron, and their families, fished at Sooke and Deep Bay. Dr. Pazder's oldest son, Lawrence, landed the prize salmon, a thirty-four-pounder. They barbecued several salmon over evening campfires. At the end of the two weeks, both families drove to Dr. Pazder's parents' place in Edmonton, where the large Polish clan was gathering. His father—a successful businessman, accomplished violinist, and amateur astonomer—and his mother—a wise and loving woman—presided over the traditional Polish feasts. There was singing and dancing until all hours.

Michelle's vacation ended before Dr. Pazder's and, back in Victoria, she found herself beset by the same heavy psychological pressures. She drove to the Fort Royal Medical Centre to record some thoughts for him, and while she was there, taping in his office, his colleague Dr. Jim Paterson saw the open door and stuck in his head. For the instant before her expression brightened to say hello, he saw the strained look on her face. He went in and sat down, and soon the two were earnestly conversing. A warm, fatherly man, the oldest member of the Fort Royal psychiatric group, Dr. Paterson was easy to open up to.

Michelle told him how hard the therapy had been and hinted that it had taken a toll in her private life, her friendships, even her marriage. Her nearly total absorption in it and the extremely long hours she was devoting to it—both seemed to be distancing her somewhat from the people around her. She was worried about that.

"Well," said Dr. Paterson, "you know what they say: Therapy is a little like climbing a mountain. The struggle really comes just as you reach the top. You know you're near, but you can't quite see over it yet. Just keep on working the way you have been, and suddenly you'll find that you're at the top of the mountain.

"You may also find," he went on, "that partly because of this work you'll grow differently from the way you would have, differently from the people around you. You might even grow away from some of them. This is normal, and in the long run, as you meet new people, you'll have a better basis for friendship."

The gentle, matter-of-fact way Dr. Paterson spoke was enormously consoling. It gave extra meaning to the struggle. And it was also good to hear from him these things she had also heard from Dr. Pazder. For Michelle, the five minutes with Dr. Paterson were buoying. She put away the tape recorder and drove back home.

Once again, the round room. Michelle was standing, not allowed to move. She was supposed to listen, to pay attention. But she was so tired. The man in black was still reading from the black book.

A knot of dark figures were proceeding toward her; as they emerged from the subterranean gloom she saw that they had a child with them. It was a girl, of about her own age. The child was terribly familiar, but Michelle's fatigued mind could not focus on the question of where she had seen her before. And then, in a sudden, sickening moment, she knew. It was her pretend friend. How could they have captured her pretend friend?

How had they known? How had they found out? Had they heard Michelle talking to her? Maybe they'd seen her at the hospital and recognized that it was she who had kept Michelle's spirits up, helped her maintain her independence, nourished her determination not to give in. Were they so clever that they could even tell what one's secret pretends were? That was the most frightening thing of all.

And now Michelle realized that her pretend friend had never left her. She'd always been there, on one level or the other, always on hand to fan the little spark of courage, to say the funny, sassy thing that would amuse Michelle and take her mind away from the horrors, or give her a fragment of understanding that made the ghastliness comprehensible . . . and therefore bearable. But, before, she'd always been free. Now she was in their grasp. They had trapped her.

"Don't hurt her!" Michelle called out. "Don't hurt her. She never hurt anybody." But they did not acknowledge her cries. They were lost in the harsh, rhythmic litany recited by the man in black.

Once sure that they had Michelle's full attention, they turned to the pretend friend. An old woman came forward and, with a knife, started hacking away at the pretend friend's lovely brown hair. Two other robed figures came forward and, scooping some sort of muck from a bucket, slathered it onto the pretend friend's face and arms and clothes. For a long time they appeared to be grappling with the pretend friend's head; when they were done they stood back and showed Michelle what they had done: The pretend friend's teeth had been pulled, and blood was running from her mouth.

The black cloaks again obscured the child. After a long time, they again parted. The pretend friend was now lying on the ground.

> She helped me so much. She's my friend and now I'm not being her friend. They're cutting all her hair off. She always liked her hair. She liked it neat and tidy. She liked it braided with ribbons on the end. She always kept her clothes neat. She used to play a lot but she never got dirty. Now they're,messing her up and I can't help her. We swore we'd do anything for each other and now I'm not helping her. I've broken my promise. They've already made her eyes shut and they've taken all her teeth out. She always had such a nice smile and all her teeth were straight. I have to stand there. I have to just stand there. I feel like they're cutting me apart.

"Go to her, Michelle," said a voice. "Give her a hug."

Michelle raced to the little form on the soil and put her arms around it. And then Michelle screamed. The pretend friend's head had rolled to one side. It had been chopped off. So had her arms and legs. Chopped off and then put back together on the ground so that the body would appear to be whole.

Through her tears Michelle looked up at the faces surrounding her. They were laughing that soundless, wild-eyed laughter she had first seen so many months before, that first night when Malachi was holding her above his head and pointing her and those people had stood in the doorway, watching her agony.

Michelle was pulled away from the corpse, and several of the figures began to pile the severed limbs on a white cloth. She began to scream again, and a pleasant voice said, "You can go over and put her back together again if you want, Michelle."

I tried and I tried and I tried. But I couldn't. None of them would help me. Please help! Someone has to hold some of the pieces together while I go get the rest of them. I don't have enough arms and legs, I've got to go get the rest. . . .

I tried and she fell apart. See, they let me have her and she fell apart. They thought it was funny. . . .

I was telling them to put her together again and they said, "There's nothing there. It's just pieces."

I tried for the longest time. I knew once I quit trying I'd lose my arms and legs. It just got to be more of a mess. Instead of helping her I was messing her up more. It's hopeless. It's hopeless. I feel like dying. That's how I'm supposed to feel. *Please! Please!* My head's gotta stay on or they can put in ugly things. What's going on? I don't understand. I'm really getting mixed up. There's something wrong. I'm running out of time. I feel like I'm going to faint. I'm going numb. I'm in trouble. Please help me.

"It's okay," Dr. Pazder whispered. "I'm right here. I'm with you."

"I don't know where I am."

"You're right here."

"I'm just terrified. Will you keep me safe?"

"It's horrifying. But we'll put it all together. I want you to talk with me about it."

"It makes me so scared it takes my breath away."

"Yes."

"It's that kind of scared. It's a really hard place to go to. It's a long way away with the doctor and the drugs and everything." Michelle didn't speak for a few minutes. She sat with her hands over her face. Through them she said at last: "I guess that's how they found out about my friend. . . ."

"I don't know. Who was the little girl they cut up?"

"I know that it was a real person. It wasn't all my imagination. There was a little girl there who looked just like my friend, but they messed her up. She wasn't an imaginary person."

"But I hope you understand that your imaginary friend is an important part of you. She's still alive. You can't lose her. They tried to break her apart from you. They tried to split you up, to split you apart and keep you that way. They were trying to make you see yourself from a distance. Do you understand that?"

"Yes."

"They were trying to destroy all the good you had in you. They made you feel that you were responsible for destroying your pretend friend. They tried to replace that good part of you with a broken, red, messed up thing. But she's not messed up and she's not dead."

"I knew that she was a pretend, but I really had to believe in her."

"Of course you did. She was very real to you back there. She also *is* you, a deep, safe part of you. She is your idealized self—the part of us we all have and treasure, and strive to become. They were out to destroy that most precious part of you, with every possible means. It's incredible that people mess around with people in that fashion. That's really hard to believe, that people will do that much, but they certainly knew what they were doing. It's a lot of time invested in a little person, isn't it?"

"Yes."

"They gave you all kinds of suggestions that were really aimed at confusing you, mixing you up, making you feel you were crazy, making you go against yourself. They wanted you to believe you'd made your friend fall apart. Then you'd have turned on yourself.

"There must have been other suggestions, too. A long time ago you dreamed about bugs under your skin. There are no bugs under your skin, and no one can put any bugs in. But they can make you feel that, by suggestion. But you can go to a terrible place like that and return from it intact as long as you keep your ego present—as long as you hold onto the special place inside that you have guarded so carefully all your life. God only knows how you survived."

The next session was the following day, the first of September. The minute Michelle walked into his office, Dr. Pazder noticed that her rash had become more acute—on her neck, her hand, her arm. So they began by speaking of body memories again, those physical signs of deeply buried inner distress. "Your body," he told her, "seems still to have a lot to remember. That's what's so hard about body memories —you have to face them or they just stay."

The pretend friend's remains were gathered again in the white cloth, staining it red. On top of the bulging cloth was set the child's head. Nearby stood the effigy, once white but now completely reddened with blood; it had been placed at the center of a red circle that had been painted on the floor. Michelle was taken and put in the circle too.

The celebrants began to move around the circle, first in one direction and then the other, oblivious to the severed head and the horrified child, their gaze fixed upon the effigy. The man in black read from his book in a tone that rose above the droning of the circling figures. His tortuous phrasings, his grating, malevolent inflections brought Michelle fresh panic. And over and over again came that word, the maddening, chilling, backward word of Satanic power.

The fire grew larger, roaring. The circle broke and the robed figures were suddenly carrying the head and the bulging, red-stained cloth toward the fire. Chanting more intensely now, in thrumming syllables, they threw the limbs upon the fire and at last, with a bellow, the head. Michelle could not stand it. She had to save her friend. She ran to the fire and thrust in her hand. But the heat was too fierce, and she withdrew, her hand badly burned. She was shattered. She had tried to help her pretend friend, who had helped her so many times, but she had failed.

Now the circle reformed. The chanting continued in another tempo, verse building upon verse, climbing toward a crescendo. From her place—in the shadows to one side on the earthen floor where she lay forgotten—Michelle saw the figures closing their circle upon the effigy. They clustered around it, then lifted it above their heads. In a double rank they bore it toward the fire and, after a final, pulsing, dissonant chorus, heaved the grotesque red image into the flames.

As he sat listening to Michelle pouring out horrors in the voice of a child, Dr. Pazder found a prayer coming to his lips unbidden. "O Lord our God," he said silently, "protect this child from all anguish. Free her from the terror of the past. Keep her close. Let her believe in herself."

Above, the picturesque waterfront of Victoria, British Columbia, with the Empress Hotel at left. *Below*, Parliament Building. Experts believe that Victoria and Geneva, Switzerland, are the two official centers of the Church of Satan.

Michelle at the age of a year and a half was still a happy child, unaware that her mother had emotional problems and that her father was alcoholic and usually absent.

This picture of Michelle at the age of four was taken in 1954, just before her ordeal began.

The Fort Royal Medical Centre in Victoria, where Dr. Pazder has his offices. It was there, during fourteen months of long and frequent sessions, that Michelle relived her dread experience at the hands of the Satanists.

Left, Dr. Pazder, with Michelle, in a typical attitude—listening (but in atypical dress—coat and tie). *Photo by Beuford Smith/Cesaire.*

Below, Michelle is shown during a psychiatric session. Having completely descended into the depths of her memory, she is speaking in the voice of a five-year-old child—her own self at that age—and recounting her experiences in detail.

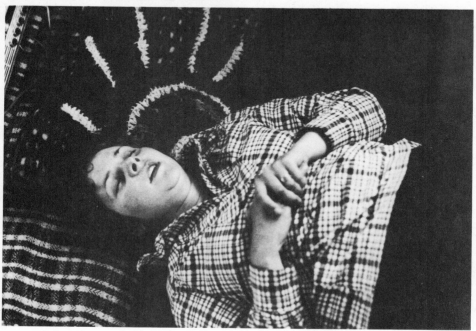

Michelle told Dr. Pazder of being taken to Victoria's Ross Bay Cemetery. The lid of an old grave, such as the one above, was pried back, Michelle was lowered into the grave, and the lid was replaced.

In this mausoleum, members of the Church of Satan performed a ritual in which they attempted, unsuccessfully, to give Michelle a "rebirth into evil." As the child was being led to the mausoleum, she saw the nuns' graveyard shown below and, in the dark, thought at first that the headstones were people.

The Malahat, a mountain pass fifteen miles from Victoria. There, in 1954, a car accident was staged, Michelle believes, one that nearly cost her life. Twenty-two years later, coming to and from the psychiatric sessions, Michelle had to travel this same fateful route almost daily. *Below*, Sacred Heart Church in Victoria, high upon a hill overlooking the city.

The wooden emblem of the "Horns of Death," ancient symbol of Satan, that was discovered in Sacred Heart Church. The pastor, Father Guy Merveille, burned it on the feast of St. John in June 1977, as Michelle and Dr. Pazder looked on.

Dr. Pazder, an experienced photographer, took these three extraordinary photos during the fire ceremony. They seem to show that, as Father Guy (left) led the service, a glowing presence appeared beyond him, moved slowly across the grass behind the fire, and came to Michelle's side.

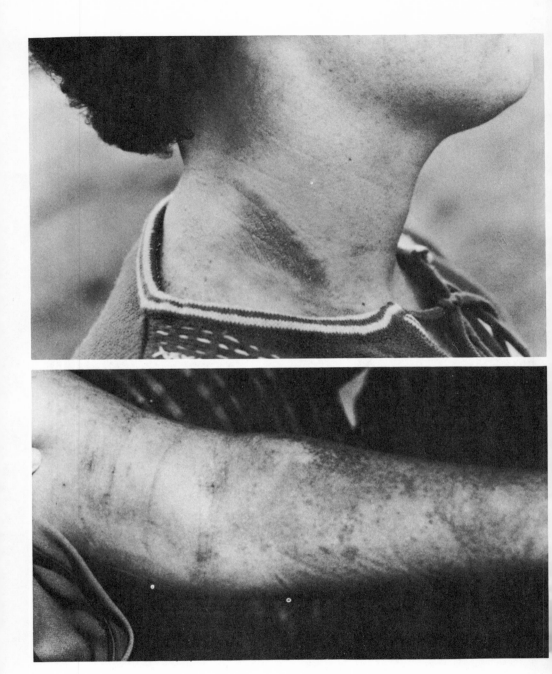

Michelle experienced "body memories" of her ordeal: Whenever she relived the moments when Satan had his burning tail wrapped around her neck, a sharply defined rash appeared in the shape of the spade-like tip of his tail. *Below*, her arms were ablaze with rash when she remembered being roughly handled twenty-two years before.

In one session Michelle drew pictures (shown on this and on the following page) for Dr. Pazder as she emerged from the depths of memory. She tried to show him some of the forms Satan was taking. But she found her drawings too definite and distinct; Satan was vaporous and constantly changing.

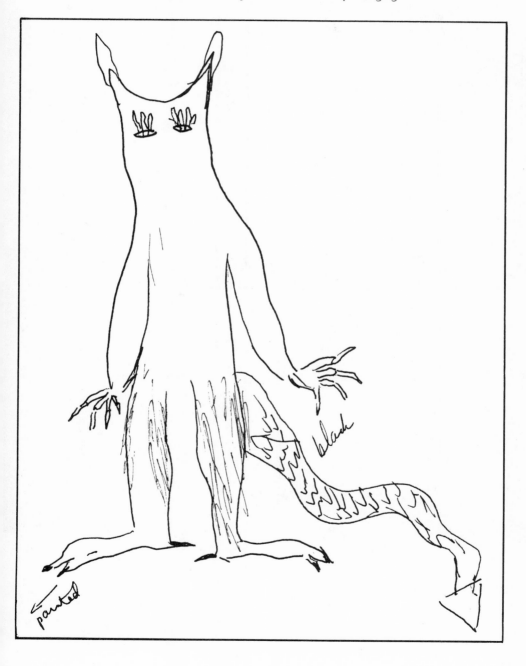

January 1977: The first three clergymen to examine Michelle's testimony, saying Mass during a break in their endeavor. From left: Father Guy Merveille, Jesuit Father Amédée Dupas, and Bishop Remi De Roo. They listened to tape recordings of the sessions and questioned Michelle closely.

February 1977: Michelle and Bishop De Roo at the Vatican with Sergio Cardinal Pignedoli (center). Skeptical at first, the cardinal became concerned and asked for a study of Michelle's story.

PART 2

chapter 22

*I*T was September 6 and everything was worse. Michelle's rashes were worse. She had a rash on the inside of her left elbow now, another under her left armpit, one spreading across her chest. And there was a very sore, raw, new rash on the right side of her neck. It was dark red—ugly and painful-looking. Different from the other rashes.

She was preparing for the return to those frightening depths. But she did not want to go. She was resisting. "There's something really heavy there," she said to Dr. Pazder. "It's like something's going to happen. I'm afraid of it."

"It's okay. Just let yourself go. It will be okay."

"I don't feel very well. My neck really hurts. . . . Something's wrong!" she gasped. "Something's really scaring me. Nothing is going to take you away, is it?"

"No, nothing could make me go away."

"Please promise me something. Will you promise me something, please? Promise you'll protect me."

"I promise."

"Please . . . ah, ah . . . I'm not supposed to know. . . ." Her voice trailed off. She was deep in that place now.*

*By this point in her remembering, Michelle had developed the ability to communicate with Dr. Pazder readily while remaining in her depths. Because the remembering thus became more like a colloquy, and because other voices began to enter, the testimony now is usually presented as dialogue, not excerpt. Still, virtually every word is taken from the transcript of the Smith-Pazder tape recordings.

Everything was black. And the black was moving. Surging like a stormy sea. The people were all wearing black monklike robes, girdled with black rope. There were many, many more people—a huge crowd —and it seemed that they had gathered from all the corners of the earth. Their voices carried foreign inflections, and as alike as they were in their attire, their varied postures and movements gave the sense of a great mixture of humanity. And these people were important. They meant business. This was the most important thing in the world to them. There was a solemnity, an even deeper sense of purpose than before.

It was a long time before the little girl realized that she was in the middle of three circles—circles of people in black moving around and around. "Oh, God, I'm not supposed to be here. There's not just one circle, there's three of them. There's a lot of people. The inside circle is all drawn on the ground. The other ones go out bigger. It's got to do with people that are bad. You make three circles. And inside every circle, something happens. . . . You know when you throw a stone in a pond and it makes rings? The circle on the inside is where the stone goes down deep. . . . That's where you get locked in."

She was gasping in terror, so frightened that she could hardly get the words out.

"It's all backward. You go inside out, and then you go outside in. And the different circles do different things. It's like one circle makes you sleepy, and one circle puts a curse on you, and one circle does something else. The people on the outside are all women," she continued, "and the people in the middle, I'm not sure which it is . . . one of them's all men, and one of them's all women, and one of them's all mixed up. . . . Are you sure I should tell you this?" she asked.

"I'm not supposed to see this," she said anxiously. "I think I'm supposed to be asleep. Is it all right if I just babble about it?"

"It's all right," he told her. "Just babble. Just babble."

The child drew a breath and conscientiously set about telling him what she knew. "There's a lot of people around the outside watching. I thought it was all black walls, but it's all the people standing around."

She stopped, the sound of her breathing loud in the quiet office. And then the slight voice of the five-year-old started again.

"I don't know. You see, at nighttime, people know things. The fire tells them. Everybody turns this way and everybody turns that way, and sometimes it looks like a snake, and sometimes it looks like horns, and sometimes it looks . . . it looks all bent and scary. But then it goes back to being three circles, and it's got no beginning and no end. And there's no way in and there's no way out." She said these last words quickly, as if they frightened her so much that she had to get them out as fast as possible.

"Am I inside a snake?" she asked suddenly. "Maybe I'm inside a snake and they're not people." She seemed to hold her breath at this thought, and then she went on a bit more confidently, making a valiant grasp at reality . . . at what must be reality. "They've got to be people," she said. "But when they bend their heads down, it's just all black. It looks like a snake.

"There's no way out. There's too many layers. Inside every circle there's a layer. Every . . . every . . . every . . . No! I don't want to go through the circles. I don't. You go through the circles, and you come back to where you started. No! No, I don't want to. I'm hurt. My arms and legs hurt so much they feel like they've been torn off. Oh, I don't know what to do. It's all fire. Everywhere I look it's fire. How will they get out? You get out by getting burned. Oh, no!" She paused. "If you stand in the middle, what happens?" she asked frantically. And then she answered herself. "I don't know what happens."

The men in the inner circle had seized the child. Each one raised her above his head and pointed her in the four directions—north, west, south, east—and passed her along to the next. They handled her cruelly, as if she were inanimate. She might have been a piece of wood.

"I don't want to get turned around. I don't want to go in the first circle. I don't want to. No! No! I don't like it. . . . Now the next circle's got me and I'm going the other way—all inside out, all inside out. . . . I don't want to! I don't want to. I don't want to go in the next circle. Please, I don't. I don't want anybody touching me. I don't like the way they touch me. . . . They're all like snakes. Uhh. It's like they all turned into snakes. Everything's happening so fast. . . .

"I've got to go back and forth," she shrieked. It's got to . . . it's got to make a pattern. It's got to make . . . it's all mixed up. . . . I don't understand. . . . It's hot. It's hot! I've got to know what to do. I can't find my way out. I've got to go this way, then I've got to go that way. You can only go back through the circles, uh, go backward. I don't understand. I'm scared. I don't want to go backward. No! I don't want to go backward."

Michelle was crying and screaming, reliving the terror and bewilderment of the little girl of long ago. The child was being passed back and forth between the circles according to some predetermined and meaningful design. She was trying desperately to remember just how they were passing her, because she was sure that they were locking her in, just as the doctor in the laboratory had tried to lock her in with his curse. And the only way she would ever get out would be to retrace the way she had been passed back and forth. But it was too complicated. She was too frightened.

Then in a frantic voice the child said, "Oh, no. I don't want them to start moving again. They're going different ways. They all got heads that turn around. I don't want heads that turn around. . . . All of a sudden everything is quiet."

Dr. Pazder heard the fear in her voice. The sudden quiet. Absolute quiet.

The little girl was being held high over the heads of the crowd. Up in the air, she was aware of the fire—it was growing larger. She sensed the growing tension in the room. The electric atmosphere that she had so often described by rubbing her fist across the palm of her hand. The air had now become so highly charged that she could hardly breathe against the pressure. The air was pulsing around the room, expanding against the walls, a solid sheet of unseen intensity. And now it was still. No movement. No sound. Their backs were turned to her.

In a voice thready with fear she said, "They're all turned. Their heads are sticking this way, and their feet are the other way. And then they jump up and down, and their heads are looking at me, and their feet are walking away. What's . . . I don't understand. . . . I don't want to. . . . I don't know. . . . I don't know anything. . . ." Her voice was slower, almost drowsy, and then she screamed. "Everybody's on their knees. They're up and they're down. What's happening? Help! Help! No! I don't want everybody going crazy! It's all jumping up and down.

And why is everybody going around? I'm the only one that's still. What's the matter? They're screaming and yelling. . . ."

There was a pause and then she said, "It's time. It's time. They're setting a clock. It's going . . . something's going to happen. . . . I don't want to see any more . . . oh . . . I'm afraid. I'm afraid. I'm all in pieces. Something's wrong."

She spoke to Dr. Pazder across the years. "Something's wrong," she told him. "Please. Put your hand on my wrist. On my wrist. You've got to make sure I'm alive. You've got to make sure my heart doesn't stop. Please, I'm too scared. They're going like that . . . around and around. It's gonna get closer. It's gonna get closer." Then, sounding weaker than he had heard her before, she choked out her words between sobs and coughs. "Way tiny . . . going way tiny . . . I'm losing my arms. I'm going tiny. No one will know. . . . What's happening? My legs are gone. . . . I've got no legs." The child had fled for a time to that small core deep inside her.

Moments later Dr. Pazder heard a voice reflecting desperate terror. "Oh, no! Help! Help me! It's all turning. All the circles. They're all turning. Help! Please help! It's burning. It's getting bigger. The fire's bigger. . . . No. I can't . . . I can't run. . . . Help me!

"It's all black. It's all black. It's all black. All black!"

The next time she spoke, her voice had changed. It was heavier, slow, and full of menace.

> Out of the fire.
> A man is born.

It was as if Michelle were echoing another voice.

> And he walks.
> Behind, the path is born.
>
> It burns out the way.
> It burns out the way.
> Of destruction and decay.
>
> And people will follow
> Because they think they will see.

And all the time—
Ha! They are following me. . . .

For Dr. Pazder, the shock could not have been greater. Pretty, delicate Michelle was speaking in a deeper, harsher voice. The words came extremely slowly, in a thudding, monotonous cadence, one at a time. They echoed back upon themselves, as if they came from all directions at once. The tone was weighty with menace. Unearthly. Deadly. Dr. Pazder found it maddening.

You come from fire,
And to fire you return.
You come from fire,
The only way out is to burn.

When you burn,
You come to life like me.
You will never have any eyes.
You will never be able to see.

You have to burn them out first.
You have to burn to see.

Michelle stopped and began moving her head from side to side, as if looking for something. Her words now issued in the little girl's voice. "Where . . . where is the white?" she asked softly. "Where's the light? White . . . where's the light?"
And then she resumed that dark, leaden tone:

There is no light.
Stupid people with stupid words.
Stupid people thinking that they can be heard.

"Where's the light? Where's the white?" the little girl inquired again. Dr. Pazder could see her eyes moving under the closed lids. "Someone help me. Someone . . . help . . . help me . . . help. Where's my friend? Help me. . . . Help."
Her voice had grown fainter and fainter, and then she was fright-

eningly still. Hardly breathing. Her face was icy white, and Dr. Pazder could barely detect her pulse. He observed her carefully. It was alarming. How long could he responsibly allow her to remain in this state?

At last her head moved slightly. She began to speak. Her voice was still weak but also mild—milder than he had ever heard it. *"Au nom du Père . . . Au nom du Père . . . Au nom du Père . . . Au nom du Père . . . et du Saint Esprit."* Michelle was weeping soft tears as she repeated *"Au nom du Père et du Saint Esprit"* over and over and over.

To Dr. Pazder's relief, her breathing increased, her color began to improve, and her skin became warm as she repeated the words, *"Au nom du Père . . . Au nom du Père . . ."* He was baffled. He could not understand this constant repetition. And in French! He had been working with Michelle all this time and had never heard her speak French.†

"Help me," she begged. "Oh, the little children, the little children . . . *Les enfants . . . les enfants . . . les enfants . . . Au nom du Père . . . les enfants . . . ma petite, avec moi . . . Mes petites enfants . . . ma petite . . . mes petites enfants . . . Au nom du Père . . . et du Saint Esprit . . ."‡*

And then, sadly, she said, "I died. I's dying. I'm dying. I dying. Die. I'm dying. . . ." There was a short silence. When she spoke, her voice had a tinge of wonder in it. *"La lumière! Allumez. . . . La lumière. Allumez. Allumez. Allumez. Jésu. Jésu. Jésu. Jésu. Le . . . le . . . les enfants, Jésu . . . assistez les enfants . . . les enfants. Jésu. Jésu. Jésu. Jésu, Il est blanc. Oui, monsieur. Assistez. Assistez."§*

She began crying. But they were not sad tears. Not frightened tears. Dr. Pazder could hear relief in her sobs.

"Ma mère. Maman. Maman. Ma mère. Ma mère. Oh, ma mère. Où est ma mère? Jésu. Jésu. Où est ma mère? Votre mère. Votre mère. Votre mère avec moi! Votre Mère, avec moi!

†The translation of these words is: "In the name of the Father . . . and of the Holy Spirit."
‡"The children . . . in the name of the Father . . . my little one, with me . . . my little children . . . in the name of the Father . . . and of the Holy Spirit."
§"The light. Bring light. Jesus . . . the children . . . help the children . . . Jesus, He is white. Yes, sir. Help. Help."

"Merci. Merci beaucoup. Merci. Merci. Ma mère. Maman. Maman. Ma mère. Ma Mère.||

"Help. Please, please, on my head. Please on my head. Stay with me. Stay with me. Help me. I got to keep the red out. I gotta keep the red out. I got to keep . . . I got to . . . I got to stay . . . I got to stay.

"Votre mère . . . votre mère . . . stay . . . avec moi. Restez avec moi. Au nom du Père et du Fils et du Saint Esprit. Au nom du Père et du Fils et du Saint Esprit. ॥ No. No. No. Help. I can't be left alone. Please, someone's got to understand.

"Help! Help!" Her voice came from a long way off.

"I'm right here, Michelle," Dr. Pazder said.

"Please, do you understand? Can you help me? I'm too far away."

"Hold on," he said. "I'm here. Nobody's going to hurt you I want you to come back now and stay close to me."

But he could not bring her back. Her voice stayed faint and distant, her eyes fast shut. She was not responding to the usual ways he helped her return from the past. She kept calling for help. There seemed to be a part of her that he could not reach. It suddenly came to him that he must make spiritual contact with her if he was going to bring her back at all. He began to pray.

"I believe in God the Father . . ."

Silence. Not even a flicker of reaction. He repeated the words, and then again. On the third try, her lips moved. And finally, tremulously, she began: "I . . . I . . . believe in G . . . Go . . . God . . . God . . . God the Father . . ."

"Creator of heaven and earth . . ."

"Cr . . . cre . . . cree . . . creator of heaven and earth . . ."

"And in Jesus Christ."

"He's Jesus Christ," Michelle whispered, eyes opening.

||"My mother. Mommy . . . My mother . . . Oh, my mother. Where is my mother? Jesus . . . Where is my mother? Your mother . . . Your mother, with me! Thank you. Thank you very much. Thank you. . . . My mother . . . Mommy . . . My Mother."

॥"Your mother . . . your mother . . . stay . . . with me. Stay with me. In the name of the Father and of the Son and of the Holy Spirit."

"His only Son, our Lord . . ."

"He's our . . . our . . . our only Son. . . ." She broke down and started crying again, but finally she managed to stammer, "He was His . . . His only Son . . . our Lord . . ."

"Who was conceived by the Holy Spirit . . ."

"Who . . . who was conceived by the Holy Spirit . . ."

"Born of the Virgin Mary."

"Born of the Virgin Mary . . . She was His mother. . . . It's His mother. . . . She was His mother. His mother looked after Him, didn't she? Will His mother look after me? They can't hurt Him, can they?" She was crying still, half the little girl who was trying to emerge from that place, and half the grown woman.

"No," Dr. Pazder reassured her. He went on, "Suffered under Pontius Pilate . . ."

"He suffered under Pontius Pilate . . ."

"Was crucified . . ."

"He was crucified," she repeated softly.

"Died."

"He died . . . He didn't die. He didn't," she protested, crying deeply. "He looks after little children. He looks after *les enfants.* He holds their head when they're scared. . . . When it gets really dark and people are trying to make everything red or black, He'll come, He'll come. He'll keep them from getting cold, won't He?"

"Yes, love," Dr. Pazder said.

"He won't leave them, will He? He won't leave them. He'll tell them about His mother. When they don't have a mother. He doesn't mind sharing His mother. He understands when you're alone, that you need a mother. . . . She'd hold you really close and you'd feel warm. You wouldn't be dead." She was still crying. Then her tears intensified. "She's come to help me. Everybody that comes to help me gets hurt." She sobbed quietly for a few minutes, and then she reminded Dr. Pazder, "You didn't finish."

"He died and was buried." Dr. Pazder picked up the prayer again.

"He died and was buried," she repeated.

"He descended into hell . . ."

"He . . . that's why He cares," she wept. "That's why He doesn't mind sharing His mom and Dad. He . . . He . . . He's got scars too, doesn't He?"

"Yes, He does."

"I wish He hadn't gone there. Was He grown up?"

"Yes."

"He wouldn't want a little child there, would He?"

"He doesn't want anyone there."

"He descended into hell. . . . He understands, doesn't He? He understands about this."

"On the third day He arose again from the dead."

"On the third day He arose again from the dead," she repeated the words thoughtfully. "He came out of hell, didn't He?"

"Yes. He was there too."

"His mom would stay with Him, wouldn't she? His mom didn't mind when He was all a mess, did she? She'd look after any little children who were a mess, wouldn't she? . . . Women matter, you know."

"He ascended into heaven . . . ," he continued.

"He ascended into heaven. . . . He's got to go home. But He can come back. . . ."

"And sits at the right hand of the Father."

"And sits at the right hand of His Father." She was calmer now. Her face was peaceful. "His Father was glad to have Him home. He'd hug Him, wouldn't He? He'd tell him He was sorry He had to be hurt, wouldn't He?"

"Yes, I'm sure He would," Dr. Pazder told her and continued with the prayer. "Thence He shall come to judge the living and the dead . . ."

"Will He hate me?" she asked.

"He loves you. . . . I believe in the Holy Spirit, the Holy Catholic Church, the communion of saints, the forgiveness of sins, the resurrection of the body . . ."

"The resurrection of the body." Michelle picked up the words eagerly. "All in one piece, He looks after that, doesn't He?"

"No matter what we do, He looks after it," he agreed. "And in life everlasting," he finished. "Amen."

"And in life everlasting," Michelle concluded. "It's life, not death."

"Yes. With God, life never ends. It only does when we turn to the dark."

They were quiet for a considerable time, while Michelle partially surfaced. Then Dr. Pazder asked, "Did it help you, to pray?"

"It really helped a lot. I didn't know how I was going to get my hands unfrozen. The more we prayed, the more I knew you understood, and the more the feeling came back into my hands and feet."

"It was a place that was hard to know what to do," he said. "It was the first time we prayed together to bring you back from that place."

"Sometimes you need more than someone to say it's okay," she told him. "When you pray, it's like when you talk to me. The talking and the praying let me know you understand. And when you understand I get some freedom."

"Where did you learn to speak French?" he asked. "I didn't know you spoke it."

"I can't. That's why I had the trouble about my degree at the university. I never passed the language requirement."

"Perhaps that was something you heard as a child," he said. "Perhaps you heard it in the hospital. They probably had some French-speaking nuns there. I suppose that's possible. And 'Jésu'—is that Spanish?"

"I just don't know."

"What about that other voice—that deep, deep voice? What was that?"

"I don't know. He came out of the fire, and he was awful-looking. Just awful. I can't tell you. And he had his *tail* around my neck!" She raised her hand to her collar, "My rash," she said, tilting her head so he could see. "It really hurts. Is it worse?"

"It's pretty bad," he replied. "It looks really sore. The important thing is not to scratch it." He paused, as if groping. "Can you tell me a little more . . . about what happened? I'm pretty confused. I understand about the circles and the passing you around. But then what happened? Someone with a tail came out of the fire?"

"It was all black and red like a fire . . . a fire in the night," said Michelle, slipping back swiftly into her remembering. "And there was this man. But he was like an animal, too. He's standing in the fire! He's looking out at me from the fire! Oh, I can't stand it, I can't stand it

—he's shooting fire out of his fingertips . . . and now from his eyes! Oh, dear God. He keeps changing shape. It's so ugly. So ugly! I just can't stand it. And he makes his tail fly around. It's a snake! No! It's coming out at me! It's wrapping around my neck! It's on fire! It burns! it burns!"

Michelle began to gag, and Dr. Pazder thought he might have to keep her from choking on her own tongue. But she stopped gagging. She wrapped her arms around herself. "I got so scared. I'm so scared. I got frozen. Frozen cold. And I can't move. I'm burning and I'm freezing to death. The fire doesn't do any good!"

And then slowly, Michelle's countenance lightened. "All of a sudden . . . it's like morning, and it's not scary anymore. It's not bright light, but it takes the scary away. And there's a man and he's got white on. He's really far away. Then he starts coming closer. When he gets close, then I can't see the bad man that scares me anymore. . . . I don't seem to need to say anything to this man in white. I can't anyway, because I'm so scared I can't open my mouth. I'm really glad to see him.

"I started to cry. It seems like every time a tear came out, he understood. He patted my head and put his arm around my shoulder. He's being my friend. He didn't talk to me, but I knew he had a mother. He said that she could be my mother, too."

"Did he talk? Or did you just know that?" Dr. Pazder asked.

"I just knew that. He'd just go like that, and you'd know." Michelle leaned over and stroked Dr. Pazder's face.

"He just touched you?" He was trying desperately to pin this down.

"Yes. He knew I was so scared that I needed a mother to stay there with me, because I was going to have to be there a little longer. I tried to tell him it was really awful, and she'd get hurt, because those people hurt everybody else. But I don't think they can see her. He wouldn't have left her there if she'd get hurt, because you don't do that to your mom.

"And he told me that I'd know when things were right, because I'd feel warm. And he's right. When things haven't been right, I've been cold. . . ." Michelle was quiet for a moment, and then she continued. "He had on . . . it was the warmest white I ever felt. I was awful cold.

I wasn't afraid of his mother. I just wanted to hold onto her hand. I didn't need a big hug. I just needed a hand to hold onto." She stopped again. "It sounds stupid, doesn't it?"

"No, don't say that. It's not stupid. What did it feel like when he touched you?"

"It just felt soft and warm."

Dr. Pazder involuntarily shook his head. There was something new and astounding going on here. At the minimum it was a vision with great psychological import. At the maximum—well, at the maximum it was almost too much to think about. The professional in him came to the fore, and he resumed his questioning, anxious to get as many details on tape as he could while they were still fresh in Michelle's mind. "What did he look like?"

"Ummm," she considered. "He didn't really look like a face, you know. He looked more like a feeling than a face. That does sound funny, doesn't it?" she asked in a little distress.

"No," he told her. "I understand."

"He looked like . . . this will sound funny . . . he looked like all the things in the world that you ever love. He looked strong, but like a rabbit too, you know," she explained, "just like all those things. . . . His hands are big and strong and smooth. And they just cared."

"Were you still in the middle of the circles?"

She nodded. "It was like being in the eye of a storm, because all the circles were making storms, you know. When the good man came, I wans't scared, and I knew it wasn't a trick. It was the first time in a long time I felt like a little girl again. The first time I remembered what color I was. I'd forgotten I had dark hair. I'd forgotten a lot of things about myself."

There was a long silence while both thought about what had just transpired. Finally Dr. Pazder spoke. "We've got to leave this for now," he told her. "We can talk about it more tomorrow. I've got to think about it first."

Michelle straightened up and stretched. "I better go home," she said.

He walked her to her car. "You know that was really strange material. Who do you think you were talking to?"

"Who do *you* think I was talking to?"

He started to speak, then stopped. "I don't know. All I know is that we both need to go home and get some sleep."

"But what do you think?" she persisted.

"I don't know. I don't want to talk about it until I've had time to think." After Michelle left, he got in his own car and went home. All he wanted was for the day to end. He did not want to face the fact that he was working with a patient who thought she was seeing and talking with Jesus and Mary. And the Devil, for God's sake!

He could not fall asleep. There were a hundred questions going through his head. Had Michelle snapped?

Once he had treated a patient who had insisted that he was Jesus. The man was crazy. But Michelle was not saying that she was Jesus or Mary.

Was she putting this on to keep him interested? He could not believe that. If she had shown any signs of being an hysteric, or of being in this to capture his attention, he would have booted her out long ago. No, she was serious. And her pulse had all but disappeared that day. She had really gone through something back there, he was convinced of that.

Was she having visions?

What *was* it?

It was too much. He lay there, his eyes open in the dark. He believed that some people had seen the mother of God. He believed that some people had seen the Devil. But in Victoria? The Devil? Jesus Christ? One of his patients? He was not ready to cope with it.

He yawned and hoped that tomorrow they would be back with the old familiar cast of characters—the nurse and Malachi and the possessed woman, even that vile doctor. He could cope with them. He knew Michelle could cope with them.

"It's too much," he sighed to himself. "It's gone too far." And he fell into troubled sleep.

Thirty miles away, Michelle was sitting at the kitchen table. The memories were still with her. The light and the warmth. "If they hear you, they will hear me," Ma Mère was saying. "Just as they hear my

Son when I talk for Him. *La nuit est très grande, ma petite. La nuit est très grande et très mauvaise. Allumez. Allumez.*"**

Michelle smiled. When Ma Mère talked to her she felt wrapped in love. But then she thought of what it meant. She was frightened of what the future would bring, the future that was twenty-two years in the past. She dreaded returning to that world tomorrow. Or today. It was tomorrow already. Nearly six o'clock. Doug would be getting up any minute now.

**The night is immense, my little one. The dark is very great and very sinister. Bring light. Bring light.

chapter 23

THE following morning, for the first time, Michelle and Dr. Pazder were uncomfortable with each other when they met.

Michelle was wearing a purple turtleneck that came right up under her chin. He looked at her carefully. "Your rash must be much worse today." She nodded and pulled the turtleneck down to show him the rash on her neck. This morning it was not only ugly and red, it also had a definite shape. Like an arrowhead.

"Umm," he said, looking at it carefully. He put his hand on her forehead. "You've got a little fever," he observed.

"I feel shaky," she said. "I . . ."

"Don't scratch that," he interrupted her. She had started to rub her neck.

"You seem irritated with me today."

"No, I just don't want you scratching. It makes it worse. When you scratch off a layer of skin, it gets itchy." He paused and then said, "Let's go over some of the things we talked about last night."

"I'm having a hard time getting away from it." There was a great deal to tell. The memories had not stopped last night. It had been a night of wonder and fear. "It won't go away. That place. It won't go away. I keep hearing conversations and things. It won't go away."

"What kinds of conversations do you hear?"

"Are you sure I should talk to you? Or will it just put me in the crazy house?" She had started to cry. Her distress was evident. "Should I just be quiet?" she asked miserably.

"Talk," he told her. "It's very important."

"But it sounds like I think I'm Napoleon. It sounds like I'm crazy. But it didn't last night," she protested through her tears. "It doesn't feel like it's crazy." The tears kept coming. Finally she asked, "Is it as important as it was yesterday?"

"Of course it is," he said warmly. "I want to hear about the new things, but first we both need to go back to that place and talk about it more. I want to talk about anything that is connected to it so we can understand it, so we can put as much of it together as we can."

Michelle's breathing became deeper. She felt less defensive. He was going to listen. He was going to help her. She started to talk. "That thing's got a tail wrapped around my neck. Should I tell you about that?"

"Yes, just tell me what you can."

She looked at him. She wanted to talk about it, more than anything else in the world. "Well, you know," she began, hesitantly, "the only time that the tail wasn't there was when the light came." She stopped. "I feel scared telling you this. Is it okay?"

"It's okay."

And this time she truly felt that it was. She reminded him that the figure in white had called his mother. "She was very far away," Michelle told Dr. Pazder. "Like a star way off in the distance somewhere. And then it got closer.

"And he was telling me that he couldn't stay there. But his mother could. Does that make sense to you?" she asked. She had broken down in tears again.

"Yes," Dr. Pazder said softly.

"I didn't want him to go away. I felt safe with him. Even with his mother there, I didn't want him to go away. I wanted to go with him. Why couldn't he take me with him?" She stopped talking. There was a pause.

You have got to stay here. Michelle's voice had changed. Now there was a new tone. It was a woman's voice, warm and gentle, but very firm.

"I don't understand," the little girl cried. "I didn't understand the lady. She said she could be my Ma Mère. She took my hand and said to hold on really tight. She couldn't be there always. Not like that, like standing there. Only for a little while. But she'd always know where I was. She said to hang on."

The tears took over. Michelle could not speak for a long time. Dr. Pazder waited. Finally she was able to go on. "She saw I was so scared. She just talked to me. Like when you go to bed at night, someone will hold your hand and talk to you so you aren't scared.

"I was too tired to stand up," the child's voice continued. "I just held on tight. I listened and I didn't feel so tired. I kept feeling like I was going to fall down. She said she could protect me.

"I wanted to hide behind her. No," the child said unhappily. "No. I guess not." Dr. Pazder could feel the little girl's desire to hide and her sad realization that it was impossible.

Michelle was quiet again. The next time she spoke, she sounded motherly.

"No," said Ma Mère. "Not hide. Not hide."

"Ma Mère! Oh, Ma Mère," the child cried, and then she spoke directly to Dr. Pazder. "She said that I'd find . . . she said to look until I found . . . I had to find ears. I had to find ears!"

She fell silent. There were no more words, only tears. And the tears lasted for a long time. Finally, she sighed heavily, drawing air deep into her lungs and expelling it slowly. And then her eyes opened. She appeared to be mostly in the present again. As soon as Dr. Pazder felt she could handle it, he started asking questions.

"Did you hear her talking?" His voice carried urgency. He really wanted to know.

"She held my hand," Michelle replied simply.

"Did you see her?" he repeated.

"She stood there," Michelle said and pointed to a spot a few feet in front of her.

"What did she look like?"

"She had on blue clothes. Light blue on her head and darker here." She pointed to her body.

"Did she have a face?"

Michelle hesitated. "Well, not like that. You knew she was a mother. She had sad eyes. They hurt her baby. She'll always have sad eyes because of that."

Dr. Pazder turned his head and looked around the office. He saw the familiar surroundings. The worn sofa, the coffee table, and the green plants reminded him just how remarkable this experience was.

"There was something sad," Michelle was going on. "I didn't understand. There was something awfully sad. She knew it too. She wasn't crying, but she knew it was sad." She paused for a moment, and then she said, "My legs are all wobbly.

"She knew how afraid I was," she continued, "and how I wouldn't stand up alone. She kept saying 'not alone.' And she said, 'The ears will listen.'

"She held my hand all that time. It made me feel stronger." She smiled reminiscently. "It makes me feel like two little skinny legs can stand up. . . . They're awful skinny," she said, her voice growing smaller. "And they hurt."

And then Michelle returned to the past. Dr. Pazder realized how readily accessible the past had become for her.

"Be careful. Take care of it." It was Ma Mère speaking. "It's going to be hard," she told the little girl. "It's not going to get better right away. I'm sorry. Just a little while longer. Then it won't seem so bad. And when the time is right, you'll find ears. And you'll find your eyes. When it's time, you must stand up to him." And then she warned Michelle to be careful about what she said, not to speak to people about what she knew before it was time.

There was a long silence, and then the child spoke again. "I don't want you to go."

"Not for a little while," Ma Mère promised.

"She won't go for a little while," Michelle reported to Dr. Pazder, wanting to be sure he understood everything that was going on. "I can feel her close, all around my face. She's touching my face."

"Come," said Ma Mère. "Come, get strong. You must get strong."

"I'm afraid," the little girl said, weeping.

"It's all right."

"I don't want to be alone again."

"We have to be human," Ma Mère told her calmly. "You want to help your brothers and sisters."

"I don't have any," the child cried.

"No, you have many."

"How can I help? I can't even help myself. I can't even get out of those circles."

"You will," Ma Mère promised, "but only if you stay. Or else too many people will be left in circles."

After a few minutes, Michelle told Dr. Pazder, "She says she'll stay a little while so I'll know what to do. I'm standing there holding on so tight, holding onto her hand so tight. Maybe if I held on tight enough, she can't go away. I feel so brave standing there with her."

Michelle had been crying and talking at the same time. Now she grew silent. When she spoke again her voice was hushed and full of fear. "Nobody can see her, but all the people in the black robes are really upset. Everybody's upset. They're yelling and screaming and making noises with their teeth like that." She gnashed her teeth to show him.

"What'll I do?" she screamed. "What'll I do? Don't leave me. What'll I do?"

The woman took Michelle's tiny hand in hers. Gently she opened the fingers and traced a small cross on the palm. When she was sure Michelle understood, the woman stood back and watched the child make the crosses in her own hand. The woman's voice was confident and serene. "You go ahead," she told the child. "We'll do it together."

chapter 24

"*I* just want to tell you one thing," Michelle told Dr. Pazder. It was their next session, one day later. "When I talk to you, I don't know what's going to come out of my mouth. But I don't just babble out things. I can feel them inside, and I can visualize the places. But how come I don't know until I talk to you? I'm being honest with you, but I don't always understand it. Most of the time I'm terrified just letting my mouth open, and then to have to say that much to you. . . . If you didn't believe me, I'd be crazy. Then what would I do?" she asked desperately. "How would I ever convince anybody?"

"I happen to believe you"—he was very matter-of-fact—"for many reasons," he said, "but mostly for what I feel *with* you. It feels real. You feel real. You feel like you go into a place that is very real, and you go back to it, and the door begins to open, and you begin to remember things that happened. I listen very carefully, you know, to hear whether you're coming from a place that seems like you're remembering. And you are.

"You're describing it with what we call a visually eidetic memory. You seem to see things you are describing, in detail. I hear you describe what you see, and I don't hear it as a hallucination. It is too organized. Too long-term. It fits into the pattern of your life too well. You haven't been psychotic at any time. You aren't delusional—you don't believe in any of this happening in the here and now. You go back and forth to it. It doesn't grab you unexpectedly. You are struggling to work with what you remember. That's very different from a person who is delusional."

Dr. Pazder stopped and sat forward. "I don't think it really matters," he continued, "whether people believe you saw Ma Mère or not. I don't think that matters. I think the way you are expressing the experience is very touching. It is authentic as an experience. You are saying something about life from a deep, loving place. Is there a difference in its value as an experience if it comes from her or from you?" he asked Michelle. "Is there really a difference?"

Michelle sighed. She *had* seen Ma Mère—she knew it. But it was all so strange. As she was turning all this over in her mind, she rubbed at her neck. Dr. Pazder caught her wrist gently. "No," he told her. "Try not to touch that. You'll just make it itch more."

"It's my only evidence," she said worriedly. He looked at her, not understanding. "It's all I've got," she said. "I know it sounds funny. I'm not sure what I mean, but this mark on my neck—it's my only evidence! The bishop has to see it. I just know it's important."

"Okay." It was late afternoon. They had been working since early that morning and they were both exhausted. But Dr. Pazder understood that Michelle was not going to be able to rest until she had shown the mark on her neck to the bishop. And he could understand why. He had heard her scream when the thing that came out of the fire wrapped its tail around her neck. And the mark was there. He reached for the telephone.

An hour later, they were in the bishop's office. Dr. Pazder explained as briefly as possible what Michelle had been remembering during the past forty-eight hours. "And there is a new rash on her neck that she feels she must show you," he concluded.

Michelle rolled down the turtleneck of her sweater, exposing the rash. The bishop looked closely at it and then took a step backward. It was clear that it meant something to him. It was also clear that he did not mean to comment on it at any length, although he appeared to understand why Michelle had needed to show it to him.

He said very little, but he let her know that such manifestations were not unfamiliar to him. And he told her that she was not to feel that she was strange or peculiar because of these markings or her experience. And then he put his hand on her head and gave her his blessing. That was enough. Michelle felt relieved. The bishop had seen the mark and acknowledged its existence. She felt free to go on with her memories now. The bishop's acknowledgment gave her a kind of permission to continue, just as talking with Father Leo so many months before had allowed her to go back into the past and start reliving her experience with the possessed lady.

Half an hour later, Michelle and Dr. Pazder were with Father Guy in his little den at the rectory of Sacred Heart Church. It seemed only natural to meet with their spiritual adviser after leaving the bishop. They told the priest about their visit to the bishop and about what Michelle had been experiencing during the past several days.

"Do you want to show him?" Dr. Pazder asked her.

She had no hesitation. "See what you think," she told Father Guy, pulling the turtleneck sweater away from her neck to show him the mark.

"Hmmm." He looked closer. "The shape. I do sense something evil touched here," he said somberly.

"It wasn't there—that mark—it wasn't there a week ago," Dr. Pazder told him.

"It's where that thing's tail was wrapped around my neck."

"It looks like the end of the tail," Dr. Pazder said, "the way you see the Devil in medieval pictures."

"It is the classic image," Father replied. "These things become known."

"It's important for you to see it," Michelle said. "It's the only evidence I have of what happened." She was so earnest that her face was pale and strained as she spoke. "I didn't understand very much of what was happening, you see. Except my body always remembers before I remember with my mind. There was a very elaborate ceremony with three circles of people. In the middle is a fire, and out of the fire comes this ugly thing—a bad man. At first there's a snake around my neck, and it turns into his tail."

"Oh, my goodness!" Father murmured.

"I thought my heart was going to die. I couldn't move because I was so scared." She spread her fingers to illustrate how she had been paralyzed with fear. "Then all of a sudden, there comes a light. Not like sunlight. It just . . . takes away the darkness. There's this man walking toward me and he's wearing white. I start crying, and he understands all the pain. He understands everything that happened. . . . I didn't want him to go. I was afraid. I saw a tiny light in the distance. It was coming closer. I was afraid, but he said it was okay. He left and she was there. . . . She took my hand and was telling me lots of things.

"She told me a lot about women. She said she knew how afraid I was, and she knew about the scars. She said her son had them too. And she said it wasn't going to get better right away, but that she would stay with me for a little while. She said a lot of things that I wouldn't understand but that I would one day, when I found ears to hear me."

Father had been listening attentively, his face grave. "And is it after that that this happened?" He pointed to the mark on Michelle's neck.

"The tail was around my neck all the time."

He nodded. "I see." He made no comment on what Michelle had told him but turned and reached for his Bible. "Before you go," he said, "there is something I want to read you." He leafed through the Bible until he found what he was looking for. "This is from the first epistle of Peter," he said, and he began to read:

"No one can hurt you if you are determined to do only what is right; if you do have to suffer for being good, you will count it a blessing. There is no need to be afraid or to worry about them. . . . And if it is the will of God that you should suffer, it is better to suffer for doing right than for doing wrong."

chapter 25

*D*R. Pazder would often look back upon this day—
he would think of it as the day the war began. It was a cosmic battle
Michelle was describing, lasting many weeks, with the Devil and his
followers on the earthen floor of the round room, attempting to proceed with their dreadful and apparently crucial ritual, and, somehow
in the air above, other forces bearing down, disrupting the ritual with
an interference that was not physical but spiritual. In that battle, Satan
would attempt to use the child Michelle as his pawn. . . . Whenever
Dr. Pazder would think of it all, the word that would come to mind
was "mythic." Not mythic in the sense of untrue, but of having the
elements and dimensions of the great traditional stories that mankind,
consciously and unconsciously, has distilled from life and passed down
over the aeons. The Book of Revelation, for example. Dr. Pazder would
often thumb through it, marveling at the brilliance of the St. John
images and their correspondences to Michelle's testimony.

"And there was war in heaven: Michael and his angels fought
against the dragon; and the dragon fought, and his angels, and prevailed
not; neither was their place found any more in heaven. And the great
dragon was cast out, that old serpent, called the Devil . . . which
deceiveth the whole world: he was cast out into the earth, and his angels
were cast out with him. . . . And when the dragon saw that he was cast
unto the earth, he persecuted the woman which brought forth the man
child. . . .

"He had two horns. . . . and he spake as a dragon. . . . He maketh fire come down from heaven on the earth in the sight of man, and deceiveth them that dwell on the earth by the means of those miracles which he had the power to do . . . saying to them that dwell on the earth, that they should make an image to the beast. . . . And he had the power to give life unto the image of the beast, that the image of the beast should both speak, and cause that as many would not worship the beast should be killed."

And over and over again Dr. Pazder would return to John's famous challenge: "If any man have an ear, let him hear."

The child continued to look about her, trying to make sense of the strange world she was in. She was still at the center of the three concentric circles of worshipers. To one side was a rough stone altar. To the other was the fire, and in it stood a burning presence, his tail wrapped around her tightly as he stamped and snorted, his face appearing and disappearing in the flames. His mood had changed. He was raging.

The marching circles halted, and in unison the worshipers in the middle ring turned their cloaks inside out. Where they had been black, now they were scarlet. The rings were black, red, black. A chant began, not loud but quiet and serious. *Omni, omnay, omnay, omni, omini, omnay, omanay, omni, omini, omnay, omanay.* The words were repeated over and over again. During the chanting, the circles began to move again, all in the same direction, then all in the other direction. And then they stopped, and the figures all faced the center.

From the flames came the deep, echoing voice. Slowly it spoke again in bizarre rhyme.

> Out of dark and fire red
> Comes a man of living dead.
> I only walk the earth at night.
> I only burn out the light.
> I go where everybody's afraid.
> I go and find the ones who've strayed.
> All the darkest forces, they are mine.
> The darkest forces all entwine.

Come my power. Come my strength.
Fire. Fire. Burn and burn.
Forces of darkness, turn, turn.
Turn around all the light.
Turn a light. Make it night.
Come, my evil friends alike.
Turn the light. Burn! Burn! Burn!

The words lingered in the air. Michelle could feel their pressure. And then the horror of it overtook her.

"It's burning . . . it's burning!" she cried. "It's moving its tail around. Angry! Angry! Angry! The tail is angry! The circles are angry. They are angry at her. There's something wrong."

Michelle began to look frantically around her, moving her head from side to side to watch what was happening.

"He's saying something. . . . He's making all these signs. . . . They're making their legs go, they're stomping the ground. They're making marks on the ground with their feet. No! All . . . all where the marks are . . . it's all on fire! It's all on fire. It hurts me. I won't look. I won't listen."

The child stood there in a panic, choking and gasping and crying. Suddenly she stiffened. "Yes, yes. Yes, I listen. I listen. Yes, sir. No. No. Don't want to be burned."

Again the leaden voice came from the fire.

There is no mother who'll always care.
There's only me to burn and scare.
There is no mother who walks on the earth.
There is no mother that gives birth.
There is no mother whose name is right.
There's only me with my fiery light.
The only light in the world to see
Is the light brought here by me.
The only light that grows is mine.
There is no light, no words divine.
There is no sign.

There was no mother to give birth.
No.
The only word in the world is *mine*.

With great sweeping motions of his arm, the fiery figure drew a large cross in the air—a Christian cross, with horizontal and vertical members. And then, violently, he threw a cross of fire at it, his own cross, with diagonal members. The fire billowed into the space where the other cross had been.

> That sign is wrong!
> I break it up
> And THROW IT OUT!

"Face the flame!" Michelle heard the horrid voice boom out at her. "I'm facing!" she cried. "I'm facing!"
The room now filled with fire. The creature was throwing flame everywhere, and streams of sparks that burned holes in the black.

> Mine's the sign that burns,
> That burns a path,
> That burns a path of anger and wrath.
> It's the only path for people to see,
> A path that leads them down to me.

"Help me," Michelle called to Dr. Pazder. "Its tail is all wrapped around my stomach. I'm being burned!" Her hands were stretched out in front of her, and her body was contorting in pain. "There's a weight on my chest. It's so heavy. I feel as if everything is being squeezed out of me. I can't breathe. Get off my chest!"
After a period of struggle, she relaxed a bit. "Come here," she said to Dr. Pazder, softly but with some urgency. He bent toward her, and she took his ear in her fingers and pulled on it. She was pulling so hard it hurt. "I need your ear," she said. "I've got to tell you a secret. It's okay to tell you what I saw. It's okay?" she asked in a tiny voice, then loosened her grip on his ear.
"Yes, it is," he told her in relief. "It's okay to tell me. It's okay."

But she did not seem to hear. She was trembling. It was a violent body tremor, and she was trying to speak. She was trying so hard. She started to say, *"Au nom du Père . . . au nom du Père . . ."* but soon she was so frightened that all she could do was stammer. "I c-c-can't move my legs. I ca . . . I ca-can't move my legs. I'm just so afraid! He's squeezing me. He's squeezing my stomach! He's pushing me there. Oh! Ma Mère!" she called. "Ma Mère! Ma Mère! Ma Mère! Ma Mère!" She called "Ma Mère!" for close to ten minutes while the violent trembling continued. Then she returned to the round room. "He . . . he . . . he's telling the middle circle what to do. . . . He . . . he . . . ow . . . tail . . . his tail tells. His tail tells. His tail . . . tells a tale. Tells his tail. Oh. My middle is the same as the middle circle. Oh, oh, oh!" she cried.

"Your middle is the same as the middle circle?" Dr. Pazder was perplexed.

"He . . . he . . . he tells them what to do. He tells the middle what to do," she tried to explain. "I get so afraid just talking about it. . . . My skin hurts so much. It goes all funny. My bones hurt. My stomach gets sick. My breathing inside changes. That person being there really makes a difference . . . you know, it isn't like the tail is on the outside of my skin; it's like it's on the *inside.* . . . That person makes my breathing go all funny."

"Can you describe him?"

"Big and ugly," she said, making a face. "Really big!"

"Has he got a face?"

"No. His face is more like the fire. You think you see it, and by the time you look hard, it's already changed. You never really get a good chance to look at it. His legs are long, and he has funny toenails. There's lots of hair on his legs. They're strong. Sometimes all you see are huge legs, and then a minute later you can just see a clawlike hand. At other times he's just a dark space with glistening eyes, or nothing but gigantic steaming nostrils. You never see him all at once—he's always distorted and he's not quite substantial, more like a vapor. You could never reach out and grab him. He doesn't have any clothes on. It's all fire. It's just so scary.

"There's something wrong." She was suddenly alert. "I feel something happening that's wrong. . . . It's looking at me. It's ugly. It's got its back on fire. Why doesn't it hurt him?" She began to moan. "Oh, my back hurts. It hurts. He's got his foot . . . he's standing there and he's . . . it's *hurt*ing! His foot's all . . . I don't want to hear. . . . It turns to look at me and it's all uhhh l-l-l-like all black, and it's a fire behind . . . and then it seems all red. His eyes, eyes . . . eyes . . . I'm scared. Scared. I'm scared! He opens his mouth, and it's all full of fire. He's got his foot on me . . . his foot . . . his tail . . . his tail. . . . He's going to pull my head off!"

Michelle was screaming, frantically tracing the small crosses in her palm. "It's all on fire! All on fire in the circles. *Au n-n-n-nom du Père* . . . *Au nom du Père* . . . It's all . . . they're all . . . I can . . . I can't. . . .

"Some-something's happening," she told Dr. Pazder across the distance. "Something's in the air."

"Pressure in the air?"

Michelle only moaned.

"It's changing," she said. "It's changing. I don't hear so much noise. It's like a storm. Like a storm. It's red and black. But there's light. There's a light. It makes the fire mad! Mad! It roars! It's all black and red. All around the room. Like a storm. It's like a storm and it's got zzz-zzz-zzz-heeeeeeee-bbb-b-b-b-blackness, thhheeee blackness. He's blackness. P-p-p-p . . . the black . . . the black . . . black . . . he . . . makes the storm. He's angry! He's angry! There's something going 'Wwwwhhhhoooooo.' " She tried to imitate the howling of wind. "He makes it madder and madder, and . . . mmm mmm mmm mmm mmm uh-uh-uh-uh-uh."

The child was almost speechless with terror, yet she kept pushing the words out, trying to tell Dr. Pazder what was going on. The air was swirling, gusting. She felt as if she were in the center of a maelstrom. The round room was full of deafening noise, but there were noises on high too, and a turbulence somewhere far above. She was in a precarious no-man's-land—unprotected, vulnerable, frightened.

"There's a fight . . . ohhhh, oohhhh." She could not speak. All she could do was moan. And then the words came, very softly. "I can't breathe," she murmured. "I can't . . . can't breathe. It's quiet. Quiet.

Quiet." Her voice faded away and then her breathing. There was no more gasping. For a moment, everything was suspended.

"Ma Mère, Ma Mère." It was a tiny voice. "Ma Mere, Ma Mère," she said the words over and over.

"Oui. Oui, mon enfant," came Ma Mère's gentle tones. *"Oui, ma petite."*

"Oh, Ma Mère, Ma Mère. You came back! Help me. . . . Help me!"

"Oh, *ma petite.* Shhhh," she hushed her. "Shhhh. I came back."

"I'm tired," the child sighed. "Ma Mère, I'm tired."

"You must watch just a little while. Just a little while more. I'm sorry it's so hard. My coming makes him angry. But you needed to know I'd come back," she explained. She looked at the child with soft concern. "You have much to do. You must not tire now."

The child sensed the finality in her tone. "Please." She started crying. "Please, please, please. I'm too afraid. Don't go yet. I'm too afraid. I don't want that man to come back. When you're here, I can't see him. Stay and I won't be afraid. Please. Please just stay a little while longer. . . ."

"Our Father is looking after us."

"I don't understand," Michelle cried.

"Our Father loves us. We're all children."

"But you're grown up. A mommy."

"We're all children. We all need looking after. We all need to be cared for. Our Father knows about all his lost children."

"What if they stay lost?" Michelle sobbed.

"They don't stay lost. There is always a light. That is why my Son died. So that we could see the light. Not the fire."

"But what if the fire's really close?" The child was desperate. "What if the fire is burning you? It's burning me. Can he make it better?"

Ma Mère stroked the child's arm. "It's what the water is for. That is why our Father made the ocean and our tears the same."

"I don't understand."

"That's all right. You will. But you must . . . you must know whose foot is on your chest. You must know who is hurting you."

Michelle stiffened. "I don't want to know!" she shouted. "I don't want to!" She was screaming at the top of her voice.

"Shhhh. Shhhh. It is very important. Many people do not know who he is. That is why so many people get hurt. They are afraid."

"Like me," Michelle said.

"Not really like you."

"Like bunnies?" the child interrupted hopefully. She was desperate to keep Ma Mère from leaving and was saying whatever came into her mind, just to prolong the conversation. "Bunnies get very afraid and their noses wiggle. And when they get sad—I always thought when bunnies get sad, their ears must go down."

"You know, when my Son first left home, when he started to walk, it was important to touch as many people as He could. That's what we all must know. It is not where you go. It is not who you are or what you are. It is loving as you go. It is walking out of the darkness. There is only one way out. When you have ears, you will understand. We all have to walk as far as we can and touch as many people as we can."

"But what if they won't hold hands with you? Nobody here will hold hands with me," she confided tearfully.

"You don't want to hold *these* hands. If they wanted to hold your hand, you would." There was a silence before Ma Mère spoke again. "There is going to be a fight," she told the child. "Ears will help, and hands will help, and hearts will help." She sighed and shook her head. "But you must know. . . ."

"I must know what?"

"There are two things you must know. One you are learning now —that I will come back. And you must know who that person is. I am not trying to frighten you. You must know who that person is." Ma Mère touched the little girl. "He is called Satan."

chapter 26

"*H*E is called Satan." The word fell heavily.

"I'm *scared* of him," the child said.

"Whenever you need help, you call my Son. He will be there."

"But He's dead!" the child exclaimed. "Does that mean I'll be dead too?"

"No." Ma Mère smiled patiently. "No. You will see. Call Him and you will see. And you must tell your ears so they will know. It is the way out. That is why there is water and a cross and the light."

The little girl nodded. She did not understand, but—in a way she did understand.

Ma Mère paused and then added, "The timing is important."

"I don't think I'll find what you want me to in time," Michelle said doubtfully. "I haven't done much right lately."

"You will find what you need to find in just the right amount of time," Ma Mère assured her.

"And what will I do?"

"You will know what to do." She caressed the child's cheek. "Don't be afraid."

"Does your Father cry?" It was another delaying question.

"He cries with you," Ma Mère said. "He wants a world that is balanced. But that can't happen unless people are willing to stand up for Him."

"You mean like me with wobbly legs?" she asked. "Does it make Him feel better if wobbly legs stand up?"

[*233*]

"Much better," Ma Mère said warmly. Again she touched the child's cheek. "I'm going to have to go," she said.

The child began to cry. "But I don't know enough."

"You will learn. You will understand," Ma Mère reassured her. "And remember: You know who he is. Don't get confused. Call Jésu if you need Him. Come, take my hand," she said. "Come, *ma petite*. It is time."

"Oh, Ma Mère, Ma Mère!" The little girl repeated the words over and over. "Ma Mère, Ma Mère, Ma Mère!"

"The other," Ma Mère reminded her. "What I told you," she added gently.

"Yes, Ma Mère. *Au nom du Père and du Fils et du Saint Esprit.*" And the child bravely waved a tearful good-bye.

She cried for a long time before she spoke again. And when she spoke, she was back in that blackness and infernal noise. "I know who you are!" she cried. "I know who you are!"

The one called Satan began to roar, not at Michelle but at the woman he could not see, somewhere above him. Frustrated and furious, he held out his arms and stretched his gnarled fingers wide, and from the fingertips a blinding, sizzling force flowed out toward the circles, as if he were imbuing his legions with his own power. The circles went around and around with renewed intensity.

"Look at me!" Satan shouted at Michelle.

"I'm looking," she said. "I'm looking. I'm looking." Secretly she was pleased. Looking was exactly what Ma Mère had told her to do. She would indeed look—everywhere, not just at Satan but also into those dark places where they hurt all those people.

The smoldering form began gesturing ferociously, making gigantic diagonal Xs, invoking all his powers, the powers of darkness. The worshipers knelt in place, and when he raised his hands they lifted their heads. Those on the inside circle chanted in a strange language Michelle could not understand. Satan addressed them as his high priests.

The fire shot up high, spiraling, writhing. Again the air beat with a heavy thrumming. It was like two storms, Michelle thought, one above the other—both of them revolving but in opposition to each other. The one below was a storm of blackness and fire, and the noise it made sounded to the child like NYUNG, NYUNG, NYUNG, NYUNG. The one above was a storm of brilliant light, and its noise was WHOOSH, WHOOOOOSSSHHHH, WHOOOSSH.

Satan still was in the fire. Perhaps he was part of the fire. The little girl could not tell. His shape was constantly changing. Sometimes he looked like pure flame. Sometimes he was the hideous presence with fire bursting from his eyes and fingers. And then her heart stopped: She saw his face! But it was not a face. Just empty black. In that dark void Michelle imagined she saw a thousand spiders and snakes, open sores, dripping blood, people with claw marks on them, people with no eyes. As she stared, she felt an astonishing thing—something like rain upon her shoulder . . . water from above.

Suddenly everything went still—almost still; from somewhere there was a low, funereal noise, a pulsing hum. The worshipers saluted. It was clear that something was about to occur.

A line of robed figures formed. Simultaneously, each flung open his robe to reveal a child clinging to his body. The children were naked. They stared at Michelle with glazed eyes, and she trembled as she heard Satan presenting them as "the children of darkness."

> Their eyes can only see the night.
> They would be blinded by the light.
> I set their hearts on fire.
> To serve my purpose is their only desire.
> To cling to me till they grow old,
> To carry my message, to evil unfold.
> To keep a circle of burning light.
> To hold in the darkness, keep out the light.
> See how they cling tight.
> They cling to blackness like the night.
> They cling to what is right.

From somewhere close to her ear, Michelle now heard another voice, gentle, firm. "Come, Michelle. Be strong. Stand up. Hold tight. You will rest later. But first you must learn to face the dark. And remember, know who that is."

"I remember, Ma Mère."

The children began to move, strutting in circles around the people they had clung to. As if at a signal they fell to the ground and crawled on their stomachs, hissing, slithering among the legs of the onlookers.

"Come, my children," called the sinister voice, "feed my fire."

The children rose quickly and dashed off to the side, then scrambled back again. Each was carrying a book. Michelle realized with horror that the books were like the white one she had kept so carefully under the mattress, her friendly book.

The book is His. It's written for blood.

> No eyes can see what this book said.
> What's written in the book is dead.
> No eyes can see; not even a friend.
> The books are mine in the end.
> You can write all day; you can write all night.
> But writing won't bring light.
> I'll burn it out. I'll make it black.
> I'll turn your words from front to back.
> I'll burn each page; I'll *eat* each word.
> And spit it out, never to be heard.
> The fire will grow; their eyes will see.
> The book of words can't stand up to me.
> When they grow old they'll know and tell,
> The only power comes from hell.
> Fire, fire, burning bright
> Divide the world with my light.
>
> The fire spreads; it rips apart,
> Join hands; it's the counterpart.
> As a fire's fed, a fire's led
> Across the world, the sleeping dead.
>
> Three times seven, seven times three,
> This is the time that belongs to me.
> From now until then the seasons turn again.

I can do much to destroy and then
Replace with words of hate and despair,
Words as stupid as love and care.

So feed the fire, children of hell.
Feed the fire so you can tell.
Feed a fire that'll spread for years.
Feed a fire. Feed, feed, feed a fire.

Matthew, Mark, Luke, and John
Burn in the fire and then you're gone.
Their words were lies; my children will see.
In the fire their word dies.
The only thing left burning true,
Is the light that shows me to you.

Michelle was stunned by the long, pounding rhythms of Satan's speech. The very slowness, the relentlessness of the rhymes added to their menace, as if the words were being underlined with evil.

The children began to tear at the books with their teeth, ripping out pages and stuffing them in their mouths. Michelle now could see that their teeth were pointed, giving them a ghoulish demeanor. They would then run to the fire and spit the paper into it, then bite off more and do it again.

Michelle urgently wanted to retrieve the pages from the fire. But there was no hope of that. It was too enormous, too blistering hot. And her legs were so weak now that she did not trust them to carry her.

The Beast was watching with glee, growling out his rhymes.

Three times seven, seven times three;
Now the year belongs to me.
Four times seven, seven times four;
Turn around and you are no more.
Four times seven make twenty-eight.
That's when the world will learn to hate.
My fire will have burned for all those years.
My fire will have burned out many ears.

But I'll be back; you wait and see.
I'll be back to take the world for me.
Everything that's gone, must return.
I was thrown out; but *I can burn.*

Look at my eyes, and you can see
The fire burning inside of me.
Look at the children in them too.
That fire that burns. What is new?
Look at my eyes!

"No," Michelle screamed out in Dr. Pazder's office in her thin, child's plaint. "I don't want to look at his eyes. No! Get him off me! Get him *off* me!"

But Satan was implacable. He would not let her regain her own voice, not yet. He still had things to say. Michelle found her throat constricting as if in the grip of a remorseless iron hand, and her voice was driven deep into her chest. "Now . . . turn . . . my . . . child-ren," she intoned in the cold, hollow bass,

Turn around. . . .
Crawl all over the world.
Turn my children, turn around.
Touch every piece of ground.
Touch everyone you can.
Make a beast of every man.

Dr. Pazder phoned Father Guy. The bishop had said the priest had special knowledge, and Dr. Pazder now needed the benefit of it. He had been listening to Michelle repeating Satan's strange rhymes almost continuously for two weeks, and he wanted to ask the priest's opinion.

"He speaks to confuse," Father Guy responded. "In Church history, we learn that it is usual for Satan to speak in rhymes. I have read his rhymes in French, in German, in Spanish, in English. I have read rhymes from the Middle Ages. If you look up Satan in a theological dictionary, it will say that he is known to speak in rhymes. And the form of the rhymes reveals his personality. They do not have an orderly structure, but they are very intelligent. And very deceptive. They all have meaning. When Satan was cast out of heaven, he did not lose his intelligence."

"On the surface they can sound foolish," Dr. Pazder commented.

"Yes, on the surface perhaps," Father Guy said. "But underneath, there is a lot there. Double and triple meanings. Satan will not humiliate himself to speak like ordinary people. He considers himself too brilliant for that. Remember, he is speaking to his high priests. There is important content there.

"People shouldn't dismiss these rhymes as foolish or stupid," the priest went on. "The writer Hannah Ahrendt coined a phrase in another context, 'the banality of evil,' and I think it has profound application here. Banality, triteness, these are the superficial attributes of evil —and its principal disguise. We expect it to be big and flashy and glamorous. But it is small and mean and unoriginal. Nonetheless highly dangerous, of course. Indeed, all the more dangerous for its apparent triviality, its unnoteworthiness—like bacilli. No, Dr. Pazder," Father Guy said emphatically, "it would be a great mistake to underrate these rhymes—the *very* mistake Satan wants you to make."

chapter 27

*I*T was the twenty-second of September, the height of a glorious season in Victoria, with clear, blue days and crisp, starry nights. But Michelle and Dr. Pazder hardly noticed the weather. It had been one full year now since Michelle had started her fateful remembering, an unimaginably painful year—and still they were not finished. Indeed, the process had grown more intense.

At the beginning of one session Dr. Pazder taped a short memorandum:

> We have a good deal of additional equipment here today. I feel that careful documentation of what is happening is important. We have a videotape recording machine, a sixteen-millimeter movie camera, an eight-millimeter movie camera, a thirty-five-millimeter camera, a cassette recorder, and our familiar reel-to-reel recorder. Dr. Richards Arnot is helping run the equipment today. He is also here to witness the process.

Dr. Pazder wanted to document the changes in Michelle's facial expressions and in the way she used her body to explain what was going on, as well as the changes in her voice. He was somewhat nervous, however, about Michelle's reaction to the camera and lights—and especially to the presence of a third person. But they did not inhibit her at all. After the first few minutes, she seemed to forget they were there.

Dr. Pazder was grateful that his colleague Dr. Arnot had agreed to run the camera. It freed Dr. Pazder to monitor Michelle more carefully. And this was necessary, for she was being stretched to the limit, in both past and present. Re-experiencing these frightening and mysterious events meant re-experiencing the physical debilitation that had accompanied them as well as the terror. And accepting these extraordinary revelations as part of her past was an exhausting process, which she had only just begun.

Later, when Michelle's testimony was brought to the attention of Father Guy Merveille and other authorities experienced in these unusual areas, it was possible to deduce the design behind the seemingly chaotic events Michelle recounted that autumn—the eighty-one-day ceremony that lasted from September 7, 1955, until November 27, the final day of the Christian Church's liturgical year. Satan, they suggested, was beginning a Black Mass called the Feast of the Beast, a rite that takes place only once every twenty-seven years. It employs many of the same elements as the Christian Mass, but uses them in precise opposition to that service, and it obeys a strict plan.

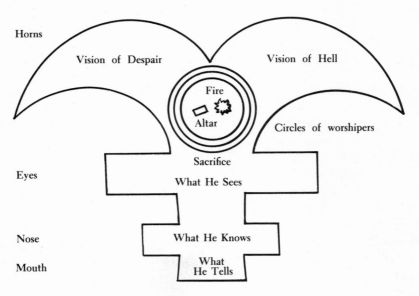

The plan is based on the Horns of Death, the Satanic emblem used on the altar cloths and the backs of cloaks. Just as the Christian Mass moves in the form of a cross, the Satanic worshipers trod the form of the Horns of Death, its shape that of the face of a horned pig. In abstract (see diagram), the emblem is a long, vertical triangle, point down, with curved "horns" veering off from the upper corners, and two bars drawn across the face.

The Black Mass starts at the altar, which is at the juncture of the horns in the forehead of the face. With files of high priests lining his way, Satan leads a procession up one horn and back again; en route he provides a Vision of Hell. Again from the altar, they proceed up the other horn—for a Vision of Despair. They return to the altar, and a human sacrifice takes place.

They proceed down the nose, and when they reach the first crossbar, which represents the eyes, Satan begins to recite what corresponds to the Gospel in the Christian Mass—his perception of the world at that time, his assessment of the current status of evil. Resuming the procession, he takes a large wooden crucifix and whittles it to nothing, from the bottom up, throwing the chips in the fire. As he does so, he reaches the second bar, the snout, and there he delivers his Master Plan, which corresponds to the Christian sermon. It is his design for what should happen in the world until he comes again.

At last the procession reaches the lower end of the face, the mouth. Satan instructs his priests and gives them fresh power through an elaborate ritual of counting and the arrangement of relic bones stolen from the sanctuaries of churches. New priests are initiated; they chop off the middle finger of one hand to signify their fealty and belonging. Finally comes Satan's parting words, his malediction. The Black Mass is over. Satan departs, and his minions go forth into the world to carry out his instructions.

Michelle felt there was something very wrong with her legs. They had been growing weaker and weaker, but now they would work hardly at all. She could barely stand. She wanted nothing so much as to collapse, to let the smudged, scabby little knees buckle as they yearned to do. But she forced herself to remain erect. If she collapsed, Satan would bellow, she was sure. More important, she would be failing in her promise to watch, to see everything.

Through heavy-lidded eyes she suddenly was aware that the awful circles were parting, peeling back and out. The high priests were forming two sets of converging lines leading away from the stone altar.

And now the Beast himself emerged from the fire! He was coming directly to Michelle! Coiling his tail around her waist, he paraded along on monstrous legs, dragging her up one of the paths defined by the rows of priests. Gasping, Michelle saw that, wherever he stepped, his footprints were burned into the ground.

"You see Hell!" he roared back at her over his shoulder. And as he spoke, the walls of the round room faded away, and it seemed to the child that she was in the middle of an enormous movie, with gigantic, soaring images. Satan now was bestriding the world, like Paul Bunyan in her storybook at home, and as he went, trailing Michelle behind him and leading a long procession of black-robed worshipers, there was a great rushing of wind, and the sky flashed and riled.

"You see Hell!" Satan thundered.

Below them, as if in some ultimate nightmare, Michelle could see masses of starving people, bodies on battlefields, a million acts of cruelty somehow made visual all at once.

> There's people with arms that are bleeding. . . . There's people with no eyes, and they're bleeding from their eyes. There's people that's got no noses! And there's people that got ears cut off. . . . An-n-n-n . . . and there's people with missing fing . . .

The nightmare changed abruptly, cutting off the dreadful vision.

"These are my armies of the living dead!" cried Satan, flinging his arms wide, and at that signal countless figures in black, with chalk-white faces, swept by and fanned out in every direction, as if Satan were pouring a sinister black oil over the planet, covering it.

And then the rushing stopped, the movie stopped, the walls closed in again. They were back in the round room, the Beast dragging her back down the path toward the altar.

Now Satan yanked the child out along the opposite path, between the rows of high priests. Again the walls blew away, and again she was plunged into the heart of a vast, macabre, imagined cinema.

"This is the future!" Satan exclaimed.

Looking down, Michelle saw a city, in minute detail. There was a man standing at a window high in a skyscraper. Behind him she saw a luxurious office. The man was looking out over the city, but his vision was turned inward. He was in despair. That was all she saw. A glimpse of a man, of an emotion.

The skyscraper and the man disappeared. Now she saw a nice-looking man, a good man who had made a mistake or come to the end of his rope. He was wearing a baggy sweater and he was shuffling along a street, oblivious to the autumn leaves and the glowing street lamps. The man went to a telephone booth on the corner, and dialed a number. The telephone rang and rang, but no one answered. He tried another number, and another. No answer there either. He leaned his head against the glass side of the booth for a moment, and then he walked away into the night. He had given up. It was too late.

Another scene was summoned up. A woman was sitting on a sofa in front of the fire. There was an empty glass in her hand. She was listening to a phonograph record. The music came to an end, but the record kept going around and around, wup, wup, wup. . . . The woman did not move. She sat there holding the glass, staring into loneliness. The child felt her despair.

People, people, people—sad, gray drudges, speckling every inch of the globe. *So many people,* thought Michelle, *they're running, but they don't seem to know what they're running after. They all look like they want to cry.*

And then they were back again, the vision over. They returned to the altar.

Once the explanations were arrived at, sometime later, it all was fairly intelligible—almost impossible to conceive of, to hold in the mind, but at least intelligible. But while Michelle was reliving it—bringing it up from her depths and pouring it out for Dr. Pazder while the video camera hummed, recording her gestures and expressions—it was confusing in the extreme. Just these two actions of the Black

Mass, the Vision of Hell and the Vision of Despair, took Michelle five weeks to convey—five weeks of painful extraction, five weeks of staring directly at bizarre, profoundly distressing images. Five weeks of patient integration by a frequently baffled, frequently overwhelmed Dr. Pazder.

Of all the memories, there was one that Michelle could not bring herself to divulge. He felt she must, or she would risk suffering the consequences of repressing a piece of disturbing knowledge.

"When you saw the people with the missing eyes and noses," he said one day, "you were talking about some others who had something else missing—and then you stopped short."

"I can't tell that."

"Michelle, it would be good to tell it, if you possibly can. You don't want to bottle things up, you want to get them out so they can't hurt you anymore."

"I'm not supposed to tell."

Dr. Pazder could see she was severely frightened. And then he realized that the Satanists had probably instructed Michelle never to tell—whatever it was. But finally she told.

"All the people that were around me," she said, her voice quivering.

"Yes. . . ."

"They've all got . . . missing fingers! Should I tell you?"

"Don't worry about that. It's okay. It's important that you tell me everything. They had all their fingers missing?"

"No," Michelle replied with asperity, "not all their fingers." She held up her left hand and curled down the middle finger. "This one."

"The middle finger of the left hand. They all had that same finger missing?"

"It's always the middle finger. I'm not sure if it's always the left hand. And it's just the people around me, the ones I could see in the inner circle. The ones we think are the high priests." She looked at Dr. Pazder in terror. "Oh, God, I said too much. Am I going to die?"

chapter 28

SATAN had gone back into the fire. Now he emerged, completely changed. For a moment he had a face, long-nosed, eyes wide apart. It was the face of a pig.

The worshipers had changed, too. They all were wearing white. They were ready for the first of the three required sacrifices.

From the dark tunnel came the noise of marching feet, and soon a force of attendants surrounded the outer circle. Each was carrying what appeared at first to Michelle to be a pole but then was identifiable as an up-pointed pitchfork. And under each arm they carried that object as necessary to the proper performance of the Black Mass as bread and wine are to the Catholic Mass—the body of a baby.

One by one the marchers approached Satan, with extreme defer-ence, and, kneeling before him, unloaded the little corpses in a pile at his feet. One by one he snatched them up and cut them apart, throwing the pieces to the worshipers. Eagerly they reached for the bloody fragments, sometimes fighting for them, and smeared their white robes with the gore, staining them red. White to red, purity to death—it was a basic liturgical dynamic.

And Satan addressed the worldwide representatives of his domin-ion:

> All the world tonight will hear,
> All the ears of yours are near.

My message spreads from mouth to man,
My message spreads from land to land.

Powers of darkness, powers of night . . .
Powers of darkness, powers of night . . .

The entire congregation was chanting now.

Strengthen our arrows for the fight.
Powers of darkness, powers of night,
Darken our shields against the light.
Prince of Darkness, Prince of Night,
Triumph wrong, full of right.
Bring your powers out of the night.
Make us strong for the fight.

A large red circle had been painted upon the floor, in front of the altar. Satan took his place by the altar, flames running up and down his back—and as he did so, a red cover miraculously appeared on the stone; a monstrous spider picked its way across the cloth. A vampire bat, with pointed, rumpled, squinting face and claw-tipped wings, perched on the altar's edge. And on the altar itself there appeared a shiny knife with its handle in the form of a snake. The fire on Satan's back flared up angrily, and his tail shot out at Michelle, wrapping around her legs tightly so that she was compelled to stand erect. It was just as well, in one way: She was on the verge of fainting.

The worshipers were chanting:

It's time to change from black to red.
It's time to change from alive to dead.

Prince of Darkness, prince of Night,
Burn your fire, burn it bright.
Call your powers here tonight.
Help us celebrate the feast.
Of the coming of the Beast.

The circles had re-formed, but now the worshipers were wearing the blood-stained garments from the baby sacrifice. They bowed, they knelt. The blazing image raised its arms on high.

> In the name of the great Evil One,
> The solemn mass has begun.
> And now to start, we must end.
> We must take up our sword and begin again.
> To my fire must go a human part.
> In death we live, in dying we start.
> Bring forth, bring forth the sacrifice.
>
> Bring me the one that's number twelve.

Attendants brought a large, wooden, X-shaped cross into the round room. On it was tied a pubescent girl. Her eyes were dazed. The cross was set upon the altar, and she lay there, legs spread, arms painfully extended.

Satan swaggered to the altar. He sprinkled the girl with a white power.

> Lay her down in front of me.
> Lay her down for all to see.
> Here is one as white as snow,
> Bound to beliefs that are bound to go.
> And with this point sharpened by a fire,
> I'll bring out the truth, I show who's the liar.

Seizing the knife, the Beast drove it into the girl's chest. With a few violent strokes he cut out the heart and, scooping it up, he heaved it into the fire.

> Twelve times two, and then add four.
> Cut it in half and then there's more!

With another strong stroke he cut the body in half. Michelle froze as the innards surged onto the floor. Working harder now with the knife, he cut the halves in half, then cut the segments in pieces and scattered them to the four directions. And then he called out:

> Bring to me the future to be.
> Bring them forth and let me see.
> Gather them round the altar of death.
> Gather them round to feel my breath.

Thirteen women dressed in black veils came into the room, walking strangely, as if sleepwalking. All carried little black bundles and, one by one, placed them on the altar. As they turned, the red Horns of Death symbol could be seen glowing on their backs.

> What have each of you to bring
> To me, your darkest king
> Out from under your veil of black?
> You have become my brides by giving death back.

The black bundles were in a circle on the altar. From the hand of the Beast, a flame leaped to the altar, setting the ring of bundles on fire. They burned fiercely and completely, leaving a circle of ashes. His twisted fingers raised a handful of ashes to his face and he blew mightily in one direction after another, breathing death out into the world, the wind of death.

Again, the dull, heavy voice resounded in the room:

> The sacrifice is done,
> The feast has begun.
> We begin by bringing death.

chapter 29

*L*IFE narrowed down somewhat. Dr. Pazder took patients only in the mornings. Michelle would leave her work on the new house and make the long drive to the office, arriving at two o'clock. And then there was the setting up of the cameras, the lights, and the recording equipment before each session, the agony of the remembering, and the difficult work of integrating afterward. The occasional trudge across the street for a bowl of soup at the end of a long day. The drive home. And back. In the middle of October, Dr. Pazder dictated a memorandum onto tape before they started work that day.

> We are in the EEG [electroencephalographic] lab at the Eric Martin Institute at the Royal Jubilee Hospital. The technician is doing a long series of electroencephalograms with electrodes in Michelle's scalp. I have set this up for several reasons. First of all, to rule out any organic pathology. Second, to attempt to understand the level of consciousness Michelle is working at. And third, as a record for further study in the future.

Dr. Pazder had always felt that there was a real need to study the neurophysiological parameters that accompanied depth therapy. He suspected that there were measurable changes when a person entered the depth where changes occur in psychotherapy. He had been following the results of the work in biofeedback with great interest. He guessed that there might be measurable changes in brain-wave activity

—alpha rhythms, for instance—that could be picked up when a person moved from cortical cognitive thoughts, which are shared back and forth between patient and psychiatrist, to the subcortical areas of recall. A change in the deeper areas, he thought, had to take place if a person was to make a permanent change in his or her way of living and being.

Most of the methods employed in psychotherapy—whether they were classic psychoanalysis, bioenergetics, primal therapy, Gestalt therapy, or any of the other accepted techniques and approaches—had a common goal: to help the patient move toward his depths and be able to touch his core. Dr. Pazder wanted to see if it was possible to identify at what level significant change took place and to validate this neurophysiologically.

He had explained all this to Michelle when he brought up the idea of conducting a session at the same time as a series of EEGs were being made. "Change comes from that movement in life that we all strive for in our endeavor to free ourselves and each other to live more lovingly. And it comes from the movement into our core. But before one can touch one's depths, risk that journey, an atmosphere, a contact, a relationship that is sufficiently trusting and safe is necessary.

"In a therapeutic setting," he said, "the task of the psychotherapist is to create such an atmosphere and relationship through the use of whatever tools and techniques he has acquired and is comfortable with. Only then is the patient able to touch his core, to re-experience the past. Then it is possible to make the journey forward in time and bring it back into higher levels of functioning, into cortical life, to integrate it. In my experience," he told her, "true changes come only from depth experiences, from re-experiencing and reintegration. I like to describe the process as core realization."

Michelle had been as interested as Dr. Pazder in finding out if there were any detectable neurophysiological changes when she entered her inner depths or during the remembering. With her agreement, Dr. Pazder had reserved the EEG lab for several hours that October afternoon.

It was the first time they had worked outside the office. He was concerned, just as he had been when they started working with the camera, that the unfamiliar surroundings would unsettle Michelle. The

EEG lab was a cold and forbidding place, full of strange apparatuses. Michelle was lying there with the electrodes taped to her. And the technician in the control room was watching her through the window. Dr. Pazder need not have worried. None of it made any difference to her, no more than Dr. Arnot's presence had when he had manned the cameras.

They accumulated a foot-high stack of recordings during their session that afternoon. When the neurologist, Dr. Charles Simpson, studied them later, he found no abnormalities. Dr. Pazder, however, felt there was an interesting correlation among Michelle's REM (rapid eye movements), her alpha rhythms, and the level of her remembering, one that should be studied further. A few days later he ordered a series of skull X rays done on Michelle, just to be safe. These also proved to be negative, showing no pathology of any kind.

"I haven't told you what the dermatologist said yet," Michelle reminded him after they had returned to the Fort Royal Medical Centre.

"That's right." He had sent her to a dermatologist a few days before to get a second opinion on her rashes.* "Let's get that on the record now."

"Well, he asked me all kinds of questions, like what have I handled and when did it first come. He kept asking, 'What kind of soap do you use?' And he asked me what I had put on it. I said I hadn't put anything on it. That surprised him. He said, 'Almost everybody treats a condition like this with something when they have it.' And I said, 'Well, I haven't.'

"He told me it had to be a contact irritation—a vegetation or some other sensitizing factor—and that I would have to watch everything that I came into contact with. That was the only way we'd find out what was irritating me. I asked him if it could be anything internal, and he said it wasn't a nervous kind of rash. 'It's contact rash,' he kept saying.

"And I asked what if it's not something I've touched. 'That's

*The X ray report and the dermatologist's report are in Appendices 4 and 5.

impossible,' he told me. 'It can't be anything internal, because it's not on both sides of your body. If it was anything internal it would be symmetrical.' And I told him that you would be interested to know that.' "

"Contact dermatitis, mmh? That's what he said?" Dr. Pazder asked. She nodded.

"Well, he's right, of course. It *is* a contact rash—but how could we ever make him understand that the contact was made twenty-two years ago?"

Michelle smiled. "Or," she said, "that it wasn't a plant I contacted but the tail of Satan."

chapter 30

*D*AY by day, as October drew to an end, Michelle kept returning to her memories and picking up from where she left off the day before.

It was time for the ceremony at the eyes of the Horns of Death, the ceremony in which Satan would say what he sees—the opportunities for evil.

The circles grew quiet. They knelt on the ground. Satan took a large book and opened it but did not read. Instead he began to recite:

> Listen with attentive ears.
> All the evil ones must hear,
> How to gather at this darkest hour;
> How to multiply our power.

Michelle had come to the point now where she felt she had no feelings. She was numb, completely anesthetized by the prolonged horror. She scarcely noticed now as a new vision began; she had grown used to the amazing fact that, whenever the Beast spoke, he also was able to project colossal three-dimensional images illustrating what he was saying, in the center of which were his listeners, and that his voice came from four directions at once. Earlier, she had been baffled as well as frightened by his facility for issuing four different messages in opposite directions simultaneously. She had learned that one must listen to one message or to the other, but never to all, or one would go mad trying to make sense of the gibberish. Now, however, stunned by terror and fatigue, these strange, disturbing manifestations had become the commonplace of her tormented little life.

The spaceless, foreboding images sprang up before them.

> These are the people lost in despair;
> These are the people that no longer care.
> These are the people who in their darkest hour;
> Can be easily turned to find my power.
>
> The ones that look for good,
> but then find me;
> They're the ones I like to see.
> There comes a point when everything's lost;
> And for peace of mind a soul's the cost.
>
> So I let them walk round and round.
> A little turn here, a little push there;
> A little less here, a little less there;
> Deeper and deeper in despair.
>
> Face yourself wrong, turn inside out;
> Start to fear, start to doubt;
> Start to look, try to find,
> Then it's easy to find my kind.
>
> No one can point a finger at me.
> If you're careful no one will see.
> The secret ways, the black art,
> A way to take and divide a heart.

The rhyming ceased, and then the circles parted to admit a new arrival. It was a woman dressed in white. She came and kneeled at Satan's feet. He spoke.

> Have you come of your own accord,
> To give up your soul, to take up sword?
> Have you looked everywhere to find

That what you want in life is mine?
I must see proof you'll do my will. . . .

The woman arose and approached the altar. She picked up the snake-handled knife. Looking over at the Beast, her gaze fastened upon him, she began to slash her clothing, cutting away at it until she stood naked.

She raised her arms and, holding her long black hair with one hand, sawed at it with the knife held in the other, sawing and hacking until the hair was gone. Then she lay on the ground—face down first and then on her back. She swung the knife over her head, around and around, and then, smiling lovingly, she began to slash her face, mutilating it at random. Satan called out to the attendants:

Make marks on her body so all who see
Will know that she belongs to me.

The marks will heal but not the heart;
It's been forever torn apart.

She's given up. She's given her face.
Mine will be put there in its place.

The burning tail uncoiled from Michelle's legs and writhed freely. It was a snake again now, a tail, a snake, a tail again. And then Michelle saw that it was not one tail but two. One of the tails began to slither into the circles, weaving along the ground among the feet of the worshipers. The figures would break rank and approach the tail, engaging it in an obscene, ritualistic dance. The Beast stood by the fire, watching his own tail perform with the celebrants. Now the fire shot up toward the ceiling; the dancing became more frenzied. Satan laughed. The tails merged to one again, and the one tail slid back across the room, withdrawn by its master. And then it lunged for Michelle.

I don't like his tail being around me! Ugh! It's wiggling. I don't want it to move. It's wrapped around my legs and starting to wiggle. I have to keep my legs really tight together. Oh, dear!

No! He thinks it's funny. I want to die. If that tail does anything, I'm going to die. I don't know what to do. I don't *want* his tail! I don't! I don't.

Michelle caught her breath. "What's happening?" She turned her head. There was a voice, a light. It announced its name, but in the din of the round room she could not quite make it out. She only knew that it sounded much like her own.

"Michelle, I can only stay a minute. Ma Mère sent me. She wants you to know that you are doing well. The Beast doesn't usually talk so much. And for once that's good. It will matter to the ears."

"Tell Ma Mère that I'm going to be all burned!" the child cried.

"She says there won't be any scars," the light told her. "She won't let your feelings be burned. She says you must be careful and keep your eyes open."

"Please, please," Michelle cried, "tell her I'm not going to make it!"

"You have to," the light replied, softly, calmly. "You have to. You will. But you must first stay—and then see and then find." And the light vanished.

The noise increased immensely—the NYUNG, NYUNGG, NNYUNGG below in conflict with the WHOOSSHH WHOOSSHH above. The forces of light had come to save Michelle from the forces of darkness. She had become a trophy of sorts in the cosmic strife. Victory would be determined by whether or not she could withstand.

Satan was furious. He roared so loud the sky seemed to crack, and he threw flame from his fingers.

"How dare you interrupt the Feast of the Beast! "

chapter 31

$\mathcal{F}$OR the followers of darkness, Satan's Master Plan was the high point of the feast, the long-awaited moment when he would reveal his intentions and his wishes for the next twenty-eight years.* The ceremony took place in the nose of the pig face, and its message was called "What Satan Knows."

Standing at the altar, Satan commenced the ritual.

> I write a Master Plan
> Of the destiny of man. . . .

Satan then picked up a large, wooden crucifix. During the course of the ceremony, he would whittle away at the carved statue of the crucified Christ until there was nothing left. Symbolically of the way he works in the world—undercutting—he would start his whittling at the foot of the cross and proceed upward.

> First, cut away the feet;
> Make a man feel incomplete.

*Michelle, in 1977, was remembering the Feast of the Beast that took place in 1955. The next Feast of the Beast, with its new Master Plan, is due—according to experts on Satanism—five years after Satan's return to earth in 1977, the event thought to have triggered Michelle's remembering. That is to say, in 1982, which would be twenty-eight years from the beginning of the year-long ceremonies in 1954, and twenty-seven years from Satan's actual appearance in 1955. Apparently, the Satanic method of counting is inclusive, so what commonly would be twenty-seven years is twenty-eight years by their reckoning.

Lose his footing, lose his ground;
Lose the way to walk around.

Pretty soon you have no knees;
Then you can't bend, can't say please.
Can't be humble, can't be small;
Have to stand up straight and be tall.
Taller than the rest;
Start to think that you're the best.

Then a hand might go away;
Without a hand it's hard to pray.
Where's the sign? Where's your cross?
Ha! It's getting very lost.

As he whittled, paring off countless slivers of wood, Satan flicked the fragments to the hungry fire.

He had reached the loins of the corpus.

Then I chip away at the part
They say should be connected to the heart.
But I can separate it with one cut,
And make it separate, make it smut.
Leave barren a fertile place,
Just a body, with no face.

As the grotesque hands approached the upper reaches of the body of Christ, Satan began to rail against the Christian Church.

You've grown so tall,
You can't be reached at all.
I'm the one that's accessible now;
I'm the one to show them how.

You're too far out to reach;
I'm right here, each to each.

My priests know which way to go;
The way I tell them, the way they know.

Some of yours have lost their way;
Some of yours don't know what to say.

Poor little sheep out in the cold;
Come with me, I'll mark you sold.
Some of it they cannot stomach;
So I cut it away.

If arms can no longer teach;
Then they can no longer reach.
Then the world is in my grasp;
And the breath, my breath, will be the last.

I always act, sometimes in haste;
But who cares if there's a little waste.
If I can reach a human heart,
I'll tear a human soul apart.

I just whittle away my time;
Cutting into the heart of the divine.
The Holy One, the One Most High;
Ha! Not for long, pretty soon it will be I.

He had reached the heart, the heart of Christ—and had splintered it
with his snake-gripped knife. And then he began on the head:

Thinking starts to be the first;
If they figure it out, they know my curse.
Get all caught up in their thought,
Forget about what they've been taught.

Think so much, no time to pray,
It's easier to listen to what I say.
In a world where there's only sense,
I'll make the most of my intents.

And finally, the eyes and the ears:

That's what's funny, funny to me,
They are losing their eyes to me.

They say they listen all around,
But they never hear a sound.

As he finished the whittling and tossed the last splinters into the fire,
he uttered his coda—

Slowly I whittle away.
That's one's gone, but another's been given.
Another's come along, so I'll start.
I'll start at the feet
Make a man feel incomplete.

—and then turned to his discussion of the political future.

I never leave anything to fate.
It's all set down, each has a date.

The sinister illusion was now a bottomless hole within a raging fire.
Falling into the hole, Michelle saw, were houses, cars, books, numbers,
paintings, animals, coffins—the whole world seemed to be tumbling
into the pit. For a moment Michelle thought she herself was beginning
to slide toward the edge.

Seventy-eight
Opens the gate.
On a day when twelve is black,
Everything will fall back.

Two times twelve and then add four;
Then there is an open door.

Pretty soon I'll have a chair.
No one will get to the Big House on time,
My gate will be open, the year will be mine.
That's the year of seventy-eight, that's the
year full of hate.

First division, that comes first;
Then it's followed by a hearse.
Then you multiply your dead;
It's easy to get a bodyless head.

Seventy-nine goes down to the fire;
It's the time when the flames grow higher.
Division and fight, death and hate;
Seventy-nine is an open gate.

If I turn them face to face;
Black against black, race against race,
If I can hold the legs straight so neither can bend;
Then it's a fight to the end.

When the year is seven and nine,
Most of the world will be mine.
They don't even know what I'm about;
By 1980 they won't even shout.

"O-o-o-k-i- Okinawa . . .
. . . Per . . . Per . . . Persia, Russia, Iran will mate;†
They will help open the gate.
No time to see light, worry about fate.

All countries round about
Will start to yell and scream and shout.
They think it means war,
But it's only a way inside the door.

All the countries around Rome;
The place they think is home.
All the countries you see, I set my traps,
Waiting for the boot to collapse.

Money and numbers and the power of hate;
These are the things on which I relate.

†The publisher first read these rhymes in 1978. They were then exactly as they are
above.

Numbers of people, so many, each one small;
Then so much money, the small are tall.

On and on went Satan, reeling off his seemingly absurd, twisted,
malign rhymes. Syllable by syllable he droned them out, until Michelle
thought her brain would explode and her heart would stop.

chapter 32

$\mathcal{M}$ICHELLE had been reliving for a week the period in which Satan was in the nose of the Horns of Death, whittling away the body of Christ as the Beast recited his Master Plan. She had listened as carefully as she could, day after day, while he ponderously declaimed and harangued, laying out a vast scheme of evil intention, concealed within the drivel of the rhymes.

On the last day of the time in the nose, soon after the Master Plan was done, Michelle noticed that Satan had suddenly shifted from the exhilaration of oratory to another of his rages. His eyes shot fire, his movements were hectic. He was snorting, sniffing. An odd thought came to her: *He is using his nose. He knows.* But what did he know? What mad knowledge was driving him to fury?

All the others soon were sniffing too—sniffing each other, like animals. There was someone who did not belong. There was someone in that room who was not one of Satan's own.

The high priests started rubbing against each other in a studied, formal sequence. They were watching for someone to make a mistake, someone who did not know the routine, the way to rub, the steps to take.

Someone has broken my circle of black!
If they have, put a knife in his back!

There was a great lowing in the Satanic congregation, a rising moan, and one of the high priests staggered out of the inner circle and slumped to the ground. A knife stuck out from his back. The attendants seized him and, lifting him above their heads, flung him into the fire. Michelle heard sighs of relief and pleasure as the body burst into flames.

She had thought she was numb, but this fresh horror deeply frightened her and, in panic, having nowhere else to go, she began to dig a hole in the soil of the floor, determined to dig her way to the other side of the world. But the dreaded Beast was there beside her, and as she dug he kicked the dirt back in the hole.

"Try, try to get out," he mocked, and the worshipers began to laugh and taunt.

She got up on her hands and knees and then pushed herself unsteadily onto her feet. She stood for a moment, and then she started to run. But everywhere she ran, the robed figures closed in. She threw herself on the ground and tried to crawl through their legs, but there was no squeezing through. She threw herself against the ranks of black, but there was no way out. There was no point in running.

The fire was growing bigger. As she watched, the flames parted around a blazing chasm. From deep within, she could hear childish voices, the crying of infants:

"Mommy! Mommy! Help!" a little voice called. There was the sound of running footsteps. A woman rushed up and pushed her way through to the center.

"Mommy! Mommy!" The small voice was full of fright.

"My baby!" the woman cried. "I've got to get my baby!" The fire grew higher and the black hole wider. Satan laughed.

The woman ran over to the black hole and reached down. As she fell, there was a scream, an undulating howl. It stopped abruptly. And that was all.

Satan laughed again.

> People will do anything for a child.
> They will kill and steal and run wild,
> Fall into my pit.

He slammed his tail on the ground. It was like a thunderclap. The hole closed up.

In his Master Plan, Satan had spoken of All Saints' Day:

> You'll know the day the march is begun.
> It's the day they say all saints are one.
> You'll know and feel it in the air.
> You'll know and feel the despair.

Later, they would conjecture that it was the day before, Halloween, when Satan's legions, marching from the four corners of the earth in still another colossal spectacle, brought bones to the round room. And Michelle, remembering it twenty-two years later, on Halloween of 1977, knew that at that very moment the marching legions were once again rallying to the call of Satan, newly arrived on earth for another five-year sojourn.

Into the round room came Satan's myrmidons carrying bones—some large and glistening white, others small and gray.* Watching the monstrous vision, Michelle saw people leaving their homes and families, children leaving home at night, empty houses, streams of haggard figures trudging the highways and byways—all of them coming to Satan, all of them bringing the bones they were required to provide.

The feast had moved now from the nose of the Horns of Death to the mouth, for the final phases of the rite. The people in the circles all had bones now, one large one in each hand, and they repeatedly raised them above their heads and clacked them together hard, making a sharp, hollow sound, then spun around and bent low and clacked them again just above the ground. They beat them in a crazy rhythm, a wild, insane dance of dead bones.

It was too much for Michelle, and to escape the terror and confusion, she again took refuge in one of her familiar fantasies—of being a puppy. She licked her paws, nudged an imaginary ball, snuffled, and

*It is believed that most of the bones were holy relics stolen from churches. Throughout Christian history, unto this day, reliquaries have been broken into frequently and their contents taken away. Newspapers refer to these incidents as "acts of vandalism," but some Church authorities understand otherwise.

yipped a little to herself. It felt so good, so comforting to be a puppy again.

But on the edges of the fantasy intruded a stern reality. She knew she should be watching, knew she was getting too deeply into dogginess, into make-believe. She began to fear that if she kept on pretending she was a dog, the fantasy would become too real. In the attempt to lose herself, she would in fact be lost.

The misgivings, the fear that she was playing too long, slowly receded. She became absorbed in counting the puppy hairs on her paws. There were so many hairs to count. . . .

"Not a dog," a familiar voice said. "That's not the way out."

"Where is Ma Mère?" Michelle cried. "She said she'd come and get me. I feel like I've been here forever. Is she mad at me for pretending I'm a dog?"

"No, not mad. But she was worried."

"Will you tell her my nose isn't working very good? I can't find my way home."

"You are not a dog," the voice repeated, and Michelle remembered his name. It was Michael.

"What am I, then? I have broken paws and my nose isn't working."

"No, you have hands, not paws. You must not forget where you are and where you are going. It is dangerous. You must be careful. If you play at being a puppy too long, you won't get out in time. Listen to what they say and remember that she is holding your hand." And he was gone.

The fire at Satan's back as he stood at the rough altar threw his shadow against the ceiling of the round room. Michelle stood next to him, held captive by his burning tail. The altar top was slightly tilted —away from the worshipers, toward the Beast—and so Michelle could see what he did upon its surface. On the altar was the large spider, black, with a red spot in the center of its back. It clambered across the altar cloth as Satan's long hands, covered with black hair and tipped with gnarled, black nails, moved rapidly in the performance of a rite. He was counting bones.

For ten days Michelle conveyed Satan's counting rhymes, word by word, line by line. At the end, she and Dr. Pazder and Father Guy analyzed the rhymes. They consulted scholarly works on the subject and telephoned certain churchmen with special knowledge. They discovered that, for Satan, numbers have power in themselves, and his counting is a way of controlling that power spiritually. And they arrived at tentative explanations for some of those rhymes.

> One and one equal two.
> These are bones that once were new.
> Add them up, you'll think it's right.
> Add them my way, it makes a fight!

The way "you'll think it's right" is the way people normally add— one plus one equal two. But done Satan's way, an X is used instead of a plus sign—since the plus sign is also the symbol he hates, the Christian cross. The X between the ones makes them "fight."

> One times three
> Equal me.

Three, for Satan, is the sign of the Trinity. He himself is the one. The times sign, an X, symbolizes his primal fight with the Trinity, a fight he expects to win.

> Twenty-eight
> Is the gate.
> Divide by four
> And you'll reach the core.

Twenty-eight is the "gate"—the opening to the Satanic future— because it is every twenty-eight years that Satan returns to earth, and because twenty-eight is traditionally Satan's number. He divides it by four because four has always been a spiritually powerful number: There are four seasons, four directions, four elements, four Gospels. The quotient is seven, which is the largest nondivisible integer. Written in

Roman numerals, seven is VII; Satan took the two Roman numeral ones and laid them across the Roman numeral five, like this: ⚔ The result was a schematic representation of the Horns of Death.

> There are numbers I despise,
> But I know them, and they make me wise.
> I know what numbers are all about;
> I count them carefully, I turn them about.
>
> Six upside down
> Helps me put on my crown.

The number Satan despises is three—because it stands for the Trinity but also because, doubled Satan's way, it is thirty-three, Christ's age at his death. Three doubled the conventional way is six, which Michelle saw Satan write in Roman numerals: VI. When he turned it upside down, he put the "I" under the inverted "V," like this:

⋀ It represented himself with a crown. There is also the implication that by taking three, doubling it, and turning it upside down, he had upset the Trinity—and won his battle.

> Then you take where I am equal . . .

This was just a fragment. Michelle was unable to convey the rest of this rhyme, perhaps because of an interruption or a failure to hear. "Where I am equal" is the doubling of Satan's number, seven. He writes Roman numeral seven by inverting the "V" and lining up the I's beneath it, like this: ⋀ This represents a spear. Two sevens is two spears, or double the power. Two sevens is also seventy-seven, for the year 1977—the year of Satan's return to earth.

At the end of the counting, which went on for days, Satan took twenty-seven small bones. Twenty-seven is traditionally God's number, and in Roman numerals, twenty-seven is especially powerful—two X's and a seven (VII)—and he arranged them on the altar like this:

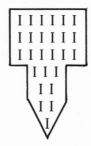

Building something upside down
So I can stomp it in the ground.

Outlining the resulting figure reveals it to have the shape of a church, upside down. The three rows of six bones each represent the apocalyptic number—666—the number of the Beast. The Book of Revelation states: "Let him that hath understanding count the number of the Beast: for it is the number of a man; and his number is Six hundred threescore and six." The construction symbolizes the power of evil pressing the Church—represented by the two rows of three (the Trinity), the row of two, and finally the one—into oblivion. He has turned the Church upside down—wrecked it.

Sweeping up the twenty-seven bones, Satan crushed them in his hand until they were dust. He took an ancient hourglass that stood on the altar and poured the bone dust into the upper funnel. Then he turned the glass upside down. Time ran out for the Church.

Michelle's attention was caught by the altar cloth. It was a white cloth with designs in it, but now that she looked closely she saw that the designs were not in the cloth itself. They had been created by bones, tiny bones that had been sewn on, looking almost like lace, forming a fringed border.

Satan was deeply absorbed in moving the bones about. It was like a solitary game of chess that he played as he spoke. Under cover of his hateful absorption Michelle had managed to move away from the altar. Now the black-clad figures began viciously prodding her back to her post. As they closed in on her, her head brushed the altar, and one of the bones was knocked to the ground. It fell at Michelle's feet. She quickly stooped and, unseen by anyone, picked it up and held it tight within her small fist.

The counting ended. It was time for the next phase of the final ceremony.

chapter 33

$\mathcal{T}$HE knife is ready. It is time to begin.
It has been poisoned and sharpened very thin.

Satan was announcing the initiation of new members into the high priesthood. Thirteen men left the second circle and, threading through the first, approached the altar. The thirteen men had removed their robes and now stood naked.

One stepped forward and prostrated himself before the fiery Beast, then arose and went to the altar.

> Cut it off on the stone.
> Cut through every bone.
> As a sign you give to me.
> You are mine for an eternity.

At this command, the man picked up the altar knife. He placed his hand along the rim of the altar, the middle finger lined up on the edge. Then he brought the knife down just above the main knuckle. Incredibly sharp, the knife cut through effortlessly, and the entire finger fell to the ground. From the other side of the altar, Satan handed him a white cloth to stanch the blood: The cloth turned instantly red.

> Turn what's white into red.
> You have the power of the living dead!

One by one, the other initiates came to the altar and severed the same finger. The pile of fingers grew on the ground below, and when the last was done, the others picked up the fingers, carefully, as if they were precious. Satan, counted them, and put them in a leather box.

Michelle suddenly realized that the Beast was looking at her intently, glaring at her from somewhere within his empty black hole of a face. He shouted at her with thunderous contempt.

> I want that bone!
> How dare you take my bone!

Michelle felt certain that Satan would kill her now. But something made her determined to hold onto the bone. It was all she had to protect her. She clenched her fist more tightly. She was as scared as she had ever been.

"Shhhh. Shhhh. Listen. . . ." It was just the thinnest thread of a whisper in her ear. "You must listen. You can't see me this time. But listen carefully." It was the voice she had come to associate with her friend Michael.

"He's going to hurt me," the child fretted. "I did what you said. I wasn't a dog anymore. But he's going to hurt me. Please tell Ma Mère I've got to get out of here quick."

"Au nom du Père et du Fils et du Saint Esprit," Michael said, blessing the bone in the child's hand. "Be very careful. There is a place where what you have heard can count. It must be before all the numbers are gone."

"I don't know where to go," she said frantically. "I don't think I can walk anywhere. My legs aren't working very good. How will I get out of here?"

"It may be hard for a while, but she is watching. Hang on tight. Hang on tight to what you know."

The circles of Satanists began to contract, to close in on Michelle. She took a breath and started running, to one side, then the other, back and forth, anywhere she could. In every direction were black robes, an all but impenetrable wall. But as they closed in, the circles began to jumble. Suddenly Michelle dropped to the ground. The worshipers, confused, encumbered by their long, heavy garments, were unable to see the small child crawling at their feet. She quickly dug a hole and buried the little bone. And then she was running again.

The black robes were everywhere now. She attempted to run by them—and saw Malachi. But they grabbed her and brought her forward. The Beast commanded her to open her hand. She did. It was empty.

Satan's rage was swelling with every moment.

> Give me back the bone that's mine!
> Then everything will be fine.
> Just go back and get the bone.
> I will let you go back home.

"I can't. I don't know where I put it," Michelle said to the creature. "You can have one of mine. You can take my bone."

Satan roared out a long, rambling curse, ending with:

> There will be no place for you to hide—
> No nook, no cranny, no rest.
> No place above, no place below.
> You'll always have no place to go.

No longer able to fight back, Michelle collapsed. *I'm not going to stand anymore,* she said to herself. *I'm not going to walk, I'm not going to crawl.* Through her numbness she realized that Satan was telling her that if she didn't produce the bone, he would hurt her mother.

> Don't you care if she gets hurt?

"She didn't care if I got hurt," Michelle said. "I don't believe you anyway!"

> Her days are numbered.
> She'll wander to and fro,
> Never know which way to go.

Across the room, Michelle saw her mother for the first time in a long while. She looked sick. She was staggering as she walked. She really did look as if she were going to die. And then the image of her mother disappeared.

The monster signaled his attendants, who came quickly forward and seized Michelle and stretched her out on the ground. They brought a bowl and dipped a brush into it and painted Michelle all black. It dried fast, and as it dried it pulled at her skin. Then they brought another bowl and in it dipped another brush. With it the attendants painted white lines on her body—a crude representation of a skeleton. The eyes were blacked out entirely. The mouth was a large white circle.

They made her stand. She had to force her eyes open. She saw herself in the shiny chalice on the altar and screamed.

chapter 34

"**I** don't feel like saying anything," Michelle announced when she came in on Friday, November 25.

"Perhaps you should just say something about how you've been feeling the past few days," Dr. Pazder suggested.

"I don't want to." She was not being stubborn. It simply seemed almost impossible to talk, more of an effort than she felt capable of making. She had been quiet and withdrawn all week.

"The weather hasn't been helping, has it?" Dr. Pazder asked sympathetically.

"Mm-mm," she shook her head.

"It's been the coldest November that I remember," he said. "All that snow. And a lot of rain."

"It makes your bones hurt," Michelle said almost under her breath.

"Your bones have really been hurting a lot, haven't they? You can hardly walk. And your rashes are back these past two days. It's been hard for you to work because they itch so much." He reached over and took her left hand. "Umm, they're coming back on this arm, especially on your elbow and your forearm."

She made no response, just sat quietly, looking unhappy. Then she burst out, "I can't talk anymore. I have nothing to say. It's like there's nowhere else. It's just"—she paused trying to find the words—"it's just a *dead end!*"

"Nothing else is happening?" he asked. "You're just lying on the floor, painted black and white—it just stops there? There's nothing else happening?"

"It's really a great way to get left, hmmm?" she said with a tinge of bitterness.

"You mean that's it?" he asked again. "It's finished?" Michelle made no reply. "I know one thing," he told her. "I know if you're left in that place, you are going to be left in that feeling. You're in a place of total exhaustion and aloneness. I can't hear what you're saying without hearing where you are in the past, too. I can't see us leaving everything where it is now. It wouldn't be good for you. Or for me or anyone, in fact. I can't accept that. It's too serious. It's too important. You've put too much into it."

He paused for a moment and then went on. "I know it's hard to go there, but I can't accept that there's nowhere left to go. I can't accept that you are stuck, finished, that there's no ending, no way out."

"I shouldn't have said anything." Michelle was almost sullen. "I was just trying to talk."

Eight hours later, Dr. Pazder dictated a memorandum into the tape recorder.

> It is seven-thirty now. We have been trying really, really hard all day to go back to the place. Michelle has not been able to. And we are feeling the pressure of time.

"You're frustrated with me," Michelle said when he finished, "and I'm frustrated with me."

"I didn't say I was frustrated with you," the doctor corrected her. "I said I was concerned. I am finding today very hard. Just as you are. It hasn't been an easy day for either of us."

"I don't feel that I can live with what I know," she said with some difficulty. "I can't stand living feeling like this."

"Whatever is there, it's really serious," he told her, "or it wouldn't be so hard to go there today." He suspected that her inability to talk was another sort of body memory. Perhaps something had happened to her back there, something that had made talking either difficult or impossible.

"I feel all clammed up," she said. "I'm so far away this time no one's ever going to find me." She was completely despondent. "They should have called me 'X,' " she said, making a languid sign in the air as if she were crossing out something. "I was all wrong from the beginning. You can never make wrongs right. Mistakes are forever. The best you can do is try to rub them out and write over them."

She stopped. Dr. Pazder waited for her to go on. The minutes passed. Finally she sighed, "I don't care if I get hurt. And nobody else does either. Should I tell you what happens, or should I just write it down?" she asked.

"I'd like you to tell me."

"I'm going to die backward," she said. Her voice was completely matter-of-fact. "It's got to do with the numbers. . . ." In the blink of an eye, she had taken that frightening plunge into the abyss. And then came Satan's grating words.

> If you say one word I say to you,
> You'll say it all until it's through.
> You'll run out of time, run out of space,
> Run out at the mouth all over the place.
> You can only go inside your head,
> And if you go there, then you're dead.
>
> So you see, I've turned it inside out;
> I've turned you around, turned you about,
> You always must come back to me,
> The only way out is to see through me.
>
> The more goes out, the more comes in,
> You'll start to end when you begin.

"I'm going to have a heart attack," the child cried. "I know I am."

First we have to blacken everything out.

"I don't know what he means," Michelle said. "Stay away from me. Ow! No!"

"What's he doing?" Dr. Pazder asked.

"They're covering up my eyes. I don't know. I can't see. Uhhh! They're tearing something . . . a paper. What's happening? Oh, I feel sick. They're . . . somebody's stuffed paper in my mouth. Mmm Mmmmm Mmmmm!"

Michelle's hands were clapped over her ears. "What are they doing to your ears?" Dr. Pazder asked.

"M-m-m-m-m-m-m-m . . ."

"Are they poking in your ears?"

"I can't hear," she cried. "I can't hear! I can't see! It hurts!"

"How are they hurting you?"

She could not answer. All she could do was moan.

"Have you got something in your eyes?"

"I can't be sick," she cried desperately. "I can't." She was silent, the only sound in the room her panting and the whir of the camera and tape recorders. "Got to be quiet," she whispered. "Just be quiet."

"Why do you have to stay quiet?"

"I don't feel good. I feel sick. I've got to get out! It hurts! I was staying really still. I was all curled up. I was really still, but my head started going inside. I've got to find my way out." The child was frantic. "Got to find my way out. Got to find my way out. Shhhh! Shhhh!" she told herself.

"Don't think about anything," she continued faintly. "Not about anything . . . there's nothing to think about . . . it's okay. . . . What's my name? Haven't got a name."

There was a long silence. And then the little girl spoke in obvious surprise. "I thought I was dead," she said. "I want to be dead." Her breathing was very shallow, very fast. "I want to go to sleep. When you're dead, it's supposed to be asleep here. Maybe that's all there is left of me. Just a head. I don't want them to look inside my head."

She began to scream at the top of her voice, as if she were being tortured. "I can't stand them touching me!" she screamed.

"Do you want to stop for a while?" Dr. Pazder whispered.

"I think so," she said tearfully. "I'm too scared. I can't stand it! I've really . . . I've gone crazy!"

"You haven't gone crazy. You'll be all right."

"I don't understand!" she cried. "Everything is all—it's all so separated! I don't understand. I feel like I've done everything wrong."

"You haven't done anything wrong. You've done well."

Michelle cried for a long time. When the sobs died away, they were both exhausted. It was well after midnight when they left the office.

The next day was just as difficult for Michelle. Dr. Pazder spoke into the tape recorder on Saturday, November 26, summing up their frustrations:

> It is now eight-thirty in the evening. We have been trying to work, but our efforts have only brought pain and terror to Michelle.

Every day had been an agony. The little girl in the round room was on the verge of death, and Michelle felt fragile, drained. She was fighting for her life, tenaciously hanging onto the present because she was afraid to go back to the past. But in the seconds that it had taken Dr. Pazder to speak those few sentences, she had returned to the remembering.

"I'm all messed up," she cried. "They took the things off me. Out of my mouth. Out of my ears. I didn't move. I didn't open my eyes. I just lay there for a long time." She was silent again.

"I don't understand!" she screamed suddenly. "I'm just . . . all a mess. I got blood all over! In my nose and my mouth . . . I'm all black and blue! I'm all a mess! I'm all broken up. . . . Oh, my hair! Some of my hair's come out! Where's my hair? I got no fingernail there . . . there. It's gone. And my baby toe! My baby toenail's gone! Where'd it go? I'm all the wrong color. I'm all broken. I'm just lying there. I'm lying. I don't want to move! . . ."

Dr. Pazder could see the child almost as clearly as if she were on the examining table in front of him. He had seen many abused children. Children who had been locked up in filthy, dark rooms with little or nothing to eat for days and weeks. Children who were black and blue and bleeding from beatings. He had seen children who'd been tortured in every way, but he had never seen a child as cruelly treated as this youngster who was suddenly seeing herself as she was.

"What is your name?" the Beast roared at the child who was lying on the ground weeping over her pain and the loss of her baby toenail. Weakly, she drew something in the dirt.

"I just go like that," she told Dr. Pazder and traced diagonal X's on his shirtfront with her finger. One X after another. "He doesn't mind that. It doesn't look like an X to me. I'm lying here and my eyes can see them straight because I made them. And it's *that,*" she said with a little surge of triumph in her voice. She traced a Christian cross with her finger. "But to him, it looks like . . . like his . . . like the way he adds. You know?" And she drew an X to make sure the doctor understood.

Where does she get the strength? Dr. Pazder asked himself. A minute ago she had been almost gone. Now she was enjoying her little victory over Satan.

Again came the sulfurous voice, gloating:

> It's taken you a long, long time,
> But now at last you know your crime.
> You never, never will belong.
> And this is simply because you're wrong!
> I cross you off and cross you out,
> So you'll forget what you're about.

"I've been crossed out," Michelle cried. "He's telling my mom she has to take me back."

> You have to live with this ugly little one!
> Until you can bring me a dutiful son.
> It's your mistake, you'll have to pay.
> I give her back. You can't give her away.

"I don't want to live at home!" Michelle said, wailing. "I don't want to." Dr. Pazder put her head on his shoulder and let her cry.

The strife between the evil forces and the forces of light was climbing to a higher intensity, and the round room was throbbing with the conflicting energies, the abrasion between the NYUNG NYUNG NYUNG below and the WHOOOSSSHH WHOOOSSSHH WHOOOSSSHH above. The child Michelle lay on the ground before the altar, her skin stained a macabre black and white. She was very close to oblivion. Her stomach was swollen from malnutrition, her flesh was flaccid, her eyes vacant and lifeless.

What is your name?

Satan demanded the intolerable answer, and she gave it: "I don't know," she said weakly. "I don't have a name."

Give me my bone!

"What bone?" the child murmured, mustering her last bit of resistance. "What bone?"

The Beast, enraged, plunged himself deeper into the fire, and issued a stream of sulfurous curses.

Across the chamber Michelle thought she saw her mother. As Michelle watched, her mother fell to the ground, and from the spot on which she fell there came a flash of light. Immediately Michelle realized that that was where she had hidden the bone.

Then she felt a hand on her head, and the touch was ineffably comforting.

"Look," said a voice. "Just look there." It was Ma Mère's Son. Lying on the ground, Michelle turned her head painfully and saw the crosses she had drawn in the dirt when Satan had asked her name. "Keep your eyes right there," said the voice, "and hang onto this."

There was something in her hand. She opened it. It was the fragment of bone. Very small, very old, very fragile. She closed her fist about it again and held it safe. *I've got the bone,* she whispered to herself.

The atmosphere in the round room changed instantly. The gnashing noise of the Satanists, the NYUNG NYUNG NYUNG, rose for a moment and then ebbed, finally disappearing, and above, a clear, warm light invaded the stygian black. The trophy had been taken, and the war was over—or, at least, the battle.

Now the fire began to die out, the grim atmosphere began to feel less intense. The heavy shadows were falling away. Then the sound of tramping began again, this time less martial, more like shuffling. The circles had broken; the high priests were moving into a loosely drawn line of march.

She looked over at the Beast. He was watching from the fire, supervising as his attendants packed the altar implements. Satan himself gathered the bones and wrapped them in the altar cloth. Then he turned. The ranks of high priests and worshipers filed toward him, and as each person approached he received a hissing shard of fire from Satan's hands. With that the hordes turned their backs to the altar and began to trudge away. The Satanic phantasmagoria had begun again, and through uncomprehending eyes Michelle saw the marchers pouring from the round room, some legions flowing out over the horizon like flocks of tattered vultures, others sinking into the earth itself. As they went, Satan rasped out to them his final charge:

> The time is ripe, the time is near,
> The time of the Beast, the time of year,
> The time to come, the time to begin,
> The time to spread, to thrive, to win.

chapter 35

*T*HEY were back at the office after a few hours' sleep. It was November 27, the first Sunday of Advent, the last movable feast of the liturgical year. And, as she had for the past week or so, Michelle was resisting going back to that place. In the early evening, Dr. Pazder dictated another progress report on the tape recorder:

We have been trying to work for over six hours now without success. The power has failed several times. The wind and rainstorm have come back stronger than ever. It makes it difficult to hear and to record clearly. Michelle is finding it very hard to go back into her memories. She is frustrated and irritable.

It was not that Michelle was not trying to work. She just could not seem to get herself to take that plunge. But, at ten forty-five, she shut her eyes and descended.

"All I have to hang onto is a bone," the child said, almost under her breath. Dr. Pazder could hardly hear her. "When things hurt you, you get grouchy. My bones have been hurting for a long time. I'm just not in a very good mood. I feel bad now," she whispered to him across the years, "because here comes a person I really care about and I'm grouchy. I don't like people seeing me grouchy. And I'm all a mess. She looks sad. I guess she's really disappointed with me. I'm scared. . . .

"Are you mad at me?" the child asked.

"No, *ma petite,*" came the soft voice.

"Well, I'm not very happy," the child grumbled. "I'm a mess. Where were you? Why didn't you come back sooner?"

"I wanted to, *ma petite,*" Ma Mère responded gently. "I came as soon as I could."

"Well, I don't understand!" The little girl was indignant. "I'm tired and I'm sick. And I hurt. I'm not going to look at anything anymore. Nothing matters," she shouted.

"If I had come any sooner," Ma Mère told her, "it would have hurt you more."

"How? How?" the child shouted. "I'm a mess! I'm never going to be the same again!"

"No, you probably won't," Ma Mère agreed sadly. She smiled at the child and asked, "Do you have something for me?"

"Uh-huh," came the grudging reply.

Dr. Pazder watched Michelle stretch out her hand and open it. "There," she said, "you better take good care of it. I haven't got anything else." She started crying, and so did Ma Mère.

"Why are you crying?" the little girl asked. "Please don't cry. I don't want you to cry. You're making me cry, and I don't want to cry." And then the tears came.

"Are you mad at me?" Ma Mère asked quietly.

The child struggled to master her voice. "I don't think I'm mad at you. I just feel mad. I'm grouchy."

"But you gave me the bone," Ma Mère said. "I know how you hung onto it."

"Was I supposed to? I didn't even know if I was supposed to. I didn't know."

"You did exactly the right thing."

"I thought you'd be mad at me! I wasn't supposed to be like a dog, but I buried the bone, just like a dog."

"That's where it should be," Ma Mère told her. "It is much better there."

"I saw," the child said. "Didn't I? Did I see right? Or did I do the wrong thing? I'm all mixed up."

"You did exactly the right thing."

"But now I'm a mess. I'm mixed up. I've got hair falling out. I'm all broken!"

"Hairs grow back," Ma Mère assured her. "And we can fix bones that hurt."

"But what about inside?" the distraught child cried. "I'm a mess inside. I know I am. I'm too scared!" The little girl was crying hard. "I'm too scared!"

Ma Mère looked at her tenderly. "The scars on the outside will help you when you can hear someone."

"Hear what?" She did not understand at all.

"Be careful when you start to listen. Always follow what you hear —here," and she touched her heart. "Everybody needs to cry, but not alone. Don't cry about this alone. Be careful. I don't want you to get lost."

"I don't understand."

"We'll put everything that you've seen and heard, we'll put it in a safe place. We'll keep it safe."

"How will the ears know where it is?"

"There is a special time and a special place when all the things you have seen and heard . . . you will remember them exactly."

"I don't want to. I want to forget about them!"

"Shhh. Shhh. I know you do. We would all like to forget about them."

"Does our Father know about what that bad man is doing with all the little bones and stuff?" the child asked.

"He knows."

"Then why did I have to?" she asked in bewilderment.

Ma Mère rocked her gently in her arms. "Children hear best from other children," she explained.

"How will I know what to do?"

"You will find a way. But you must be careful. The people here will not like it when you can speak. They will like it less when you walk. When you find a hand, hold on tight."

"Why can't you stay with me?" the child cried.

"Shhh. You are so afraid inside you are not hearing everything I am saying. If you start going too fast or too slow, you may not get where you need to be at the right time."

"But we've run out of time," the child worried.

"No," Ma Mère said confidently. "We have just enough time."

"Got time to talk about mouses?" Michelle was trying to stretch out the conversation so Ma Mère would not leave.

"Got time to talk about mouses," Ma Mère said lovingly.

"They got whiskers, you know," the little girl informed her. "They like to eat cheese. They all got funny little noses that go sniff, sniff," and Michelle wrinkled her nose and sniffed. "They got really big ears and they sleep in little holes."

Ma Mère smiled. "You don't have to sleep in a hole." She picked up a corner of the blue scarf that covered her head and touched it to her tongue and began cleaning Michelle off in the age-old way of mothers.

"I'm not a baby," Michelle protested.

"I know," Ma Mère smiled down at her. "But I'll clean you off a little. I like to hold you."

"If you want to, I guess it's all right." Michelle's crankiness was a thing of the past. She was delighting in Ma Mère's warmth and tenderness. Michelle sighed happily. "You smell good," she said. "Will I ever smell good again?"

Ma Mère held her a little closer. "You never smelled bad." The woman and the child were silent. Michelle was feeling better. The pain was ebbing. Her head felt clear again. She closed her eyes and pressed her cheek against Ma Mère's shoulder. Michelle felt safe at last.

"What will happen to my hair?" she asked sleepily.

"It will grow back."

"It doesn't feel like it will ever be the same," she worried. "I'm awful scared!"

"I know."

"Are you scared, too?"

"I get scared," Ma Mère said. "I get scared when it hurts."

"What will I do when I go home?"

"You will start to see and start to hear. You won't do make-believe. You will make a bed that's good and safe. You won't see much of your mother. There's a special place where everyone feels at home. Watch where you go, and keep track of the time. All of what has happened will count. You will not forget anything." Ma Mère was holding Michelle as she spoke. "Once you have told what you have seen and heard, they won't forget. And you will tell more ears that hear."

Ma Mère was solemn. "Don't forget what I told you before. You know who that one is. You know how he thinks. You know the way he works. If you forget, even if you don't want to, you can lose the way."

"I don't understand," Michelle whimpered. Then she took a deep breath and in a steadier voice said, "I have to stop saying that, don't I?"

"It's all right."

"What about the bone?" Michelle asked.

"I will put it back. I know where it belongs. If you had not taken the bone, things might have gotten much worse. You see, I could not come and pull you out. It is not the way things work. He denied that you exist. He had to put you out of his sight. He could not keep you in the darkness. But it also caught him a little off guard when you took the bone. He said many things that he does not usually say out loud. But now you've heard them."

"I don't like everything always being so serious," the little girl sighed.

"It is a serious time."

Michelle felt safe, and she felt quiet. The pain was going away. Ma Mère was loving and comforting her.

"You will feel as if you've been asleep. You will have time to heal," Ma Mère promised. "You will feel funny at first. It will be hard to think completely straight. But you will have help. I don't want you to be afraid. But I cannot say that it is going to be all right now. Not right away."

Michelle reverted to an earlier worry. "I don't want to go to live with my mom."

"You can live with her," Ma Mère said calmly. "You don't have to be what she is."

"I want your Son to come back. I didn't say thank you."

"He will," Ma Mère said. "And I'll be there. Remember: The years that the Evil One mentioned, and the numbers—they are important to understand. But be careful. He may be around when you remember me.

"I know you are frightened now. But you are going the right way. And in just the right time, you will see. As much as you have counted on me, I count on you."

"Will it get better?" the child sobbed.

"There's a much better chance now." She paused. "Michelle," she said, "your mother is coming to take you." Michelle looked up. Her mother was walking across the room. It was empty. All the people had gone.

"I don't want to go," Michelle cried. "I kept my promise."

"You kept it well."

"I'll keep it."

"I know you will."

Michelle felt calm. She was not frightened anymore.

Do you feel better? It was that soft, warm voice again.

"I don't feel as scared," she told him. "I tried as hard as I could. I'm sorry I ended up such a mess. How will I ever remember all this by myself?"

You will have help.

"You mean the ears?"

They will be much more than ears.

"What will the ears be like?" she wanted to know. "Like rabbits' ears?"

No, like my ears. He stroked her cheek. The feeling went way inside the child. Her breathing became deep and regular.

"You don't mind answering questions?" she asked.

I love to answer questions.

"I like to talk," she said happily. "But how will I know what to say?"

That is why you need two. It is easier to know what to say then. You have learned what's right. Don't quit talking. When you've got that, and he touched her heart, *you can knock on anyone's door and they will have to answer.*

"What if they don't?"

Sometimes you will knock again. Sometimes you will find a new door.

"I probably shouldn't say this, but you know something?" Michelle asked. "I know that you are her Son, because you keep saying 'you'll know' just like her. I don't mind," she said, "but it's really hard with so many 'you'll knows.' "

He chuckled.

"Thank you for the bone," she said. "I'm glad you came back so I could say thank you." She stopped, and her lips began to tremble. "Are you going to go? Can I talk to you again?"

You'll be safe in your bed now, and you definitely will feel good again.

"Promise?" the little girl cried.

Everything I say is a promise.

"I'm so tired," she said.

Close your eyes for a while. Think about the bunnies and grass and little lambs.

"I'd like to lie in the sunshine." Michelle sighed deeply, as if settling herself to sleep.

I know.

"Can I hold on tight?" she asked. He smiled and squeezed her hand.

"I don't have any more to say."

"Hmmm?" Dr. Pazder was startled.

"That is all there is." Michelle's voice was calm, her tone final.

And that was all.

The remembering was finished.

epilogue

*A*S this book goes to press, Michelle is thirty years old. When she thinks back upon the years following her ordeal, she does not draw upon her depths but upon her normal memory. And what she remembers is this:

She remembers that, at first, she was sick. She remembers being kept home, being told she had measles, being kept away from everyone in a darkened room. She recalls that she wouldn't eat, and that her mother—perhaps her father too; she can't remember if this was one of the times when he had returned to the family—seemed concerned. At least they gave her anything she actually wanted to eat. What Michelle wanted was rather limited—just salad, tomato soup, vegetables (especially cabbage), and ice cream. It was all she ate for a long time, maybe months.

Eventually she was allowed to start school. She knows she started school late. The other children were somewhat ahead of her, and for a while she felt left behind.

Had anyone noticed Michelle's absence from everyday life during her time in the round room? She does not know. Did anyone question her about it after her return? She cannot remember that anyone did. Did she ever again see any of the Satanists, at home or in the company of her mother? She has no idea. Since Michelle, as a child, had no memory of the horrible things that had been done to her in 1954 and 1955, she had no reason to be aware of such people.

Nor did she have any reason to resent her mother. In fact, she realized as an adult that she had actually idealized her mother, denied her shortcomings. Yet, as Dr. Gillespie recalled, her mother had found it difficult to cope. Michelle stepped in and took over much of the responsibility for running the household—the sewing, the cooking. She enjoyed it, and beyond that, she was pleased that she was helping to hold the family together. What was good in her life, she cherished. What was not, she endured.

Jessica Harding died in 1963. For Michelle it was a turning point. Her life was totally changed. Her father abandoned her forever, giving custody to grandparents, but within a year all her grandparents were dead. She was her on her own, dependent on her own resources.

In the early therapy, Michelle worked through the emotional turmoil resulting from her difficult family life. And then, in 1976, when the reliving began, she was obliged to confront the underlying, heartbreaking, reality. During her psychiatric sessions, she attempted to set down on paper her feelings about the past:

> I think I've figured out why I ache inside out so much. I *am* in mourning. Yes, a part of me is dying—really physically, nauseatingly, painfully dying. It's a part of "me inside," a part I had to have for years. It's the me who saw my mother as wonderful and loving me terribly, the part who worshiped my mom and saw me as the center of her world, the me who had a mom to play with, to tell my troubles to, the me who had hot chocolate with her on cold nights, who was tucked in and cared for. You see, for years it was all I let myself be, my pretend me, my me the way I wished and fantasized my life was.
>
> But now, my body memories have killed my make-believe, and I just can't get away from it. My body has told me the reality and never again will I have Michelle with only happy memories. I believe that in the end the Michelle I find will be happier and healthier even with her realities, but right now I don't know that. I just feel such a tremendous loss, I feel afraid and alone without my pretends to protect me. I feel so sad, it really hurts to let go, to bury my make-believe world and try to live with my life as it was. I don't want to but I know I have to. I have to be real no matter what the cost.

Michelle today is very real. She is not a dweller in some psychic limbo. The remembering is no longer with her. She is a busy and cheerful person. She has faced her past and resolved her feelings about it. It is hard for her to forgive her mother, but she hopes her mother will be forgiven. Michelle understands her and cares for her and prays for her.

When Michelle has to recall that bad time, as she did during the period in which this book was written, she feels fresh pain. But the pain is manageable, and it goes away. To Michelle, the truth is very important—worth the pain, worth the two years of her life she has spent on it. She has traveled to Rome to convey its message, and she has attended several psychiatric conventions with Dr. Padzer to talk about aspects of her extraordinary experience.

A friend asked her what means most to her today, and she replied, "The child," referring not to herself but to every forgotten or abused child. Later, thinking it over, she wrote an amplification:

> If we can no longer hear that child, then we have lost the meaning of life. We must never as adults abandon the child in all of us—the innocence, the trust, the wonderment, the unyielding hope and belief in good. We must keep it safely protected, close to the heart, where all children should be, to return to if we lose sight of who we are and where we began. This is the true part of us that was there, unblemished, before we started to grow, the part that no one can take away. It is that tiny, warm spot we all possess, which helps us move beyond the darkness to the sunshine, not because we see it but because we know it is there.

Michelle hopes the book will alert people to the horror of hurting children. The possibility that another child is now being prepared for the next Feast of the Beast—it is the time for it— is very much on her mind.

To both Michelle and Dr. Pazder, the friendship of Bishop De Roo has meant much. From their first meeting with him they have found him acute and compassionate. When Michelle's remembering was finished, he asked a priest and scholar, Father Amédée Dupas, to make a thorough investigation. Working eighteen hours a day for a week, starting at six each morning, Father Amédée questioned Michelle and listened to the tape recordings made of the key happenings. Bishop De Roo also listened at length to the tapes. When Michelle and Dr. Pazder went to Rome, in the company of Father Guy Merveille, and encountered a protocol problem, the bishop promptly got on a plane and flew halfway around the world to assist them.

The bishop's study of the case is proceeding. For it, Michelle and Dr. Pazder have organized the 3,000-page transcript of the audio tapes and placed it with the bishop for safekeeping. They are not impatient. They have every confidence that, in due course, Michelle's story will reach all those ears for which it was intended.

APPENDICES

appendix 1

FROM THE VICTORIAN,
FRIDAY, JANUARY 28, 1977
—BY PAUL JEUNE

'Witchcraft In City' Claim

Witches practicing black magic sound like something out of a medieval myth but they are right here—in Victoria.

Satanic witches—who summon the presence of the devil and make human and animal sacrifices for their beliefs—number almost 1,000 in the capital city, says a former Victoria resident who claims he and his wife barely escaped the witches with their lives.

Len Olsen, now living in Vancouver but formerly of Victoria, where he says he was a member of one of five local groups of witches belonging to the Church of Satan of Canada, says the witches could live next door to anyone—undetected.

Olsen said he and his wife got "caught up" in the underground church through a friend.

"Their meetings were held in a church behind a bookstore in Bastion Square. Another group had meetings in the home of the minister.

"Their meetings were miraculous, evil things—calling on the devil, chanting. And then a presence would enter the room, peoples' voices would change and personalities would become evil."

About four months after their initiation, the Olsens were told of a special meeting.

"At first I thought it was unusual. But at the meeting I became more scared than I've ever been before—they were holding a sacrifice service around us. They tried to kill us."

Olsen said he grabbed his wife and managed to fight his way out of the meeting.

The first place he stopped running was at the door of a church.

"I went to see the minister. After an hour with him I filed a report —complete with my membership number—with the Victoria police."

City police chief Jack Gregory told THE VICTORIAN Thursday that such a report had been filed but investigations turned up nothing.

"They're still in Victoria," said Olsen.

"Everytime I make a trip to Victoria I see at least a dozen of the witches. Many of them are prominent business people and a substantial number are newspaper people. During the daytime they can't be picked out from everyone else."

And they still work in Bastion Square, says Olsen.

"Their peddlar—or the man who tries to bring in new members— is a long-haired hippy-type character who carries a Bible under one arm.

"His method of enticing new members is to try and sell the white, or good, witch routine. There are no white witches—it's just a front. And, for the most part, they're after young girls."

Olsen said he hasn't been bothered by the witches since parting company with them but "knows he's being watched."

"It's scary—and for anyone who thinks they're going to play around with witchcraft they're playing with dynamite."

appendix 2

ANDREW E. GILLESPIE,
CONSULTANT PAEDIATRICS
Fort Royal Centre, Office No. 415
1900 Richmond Road, Victoria, B.C.

November 16, 1979

Dr. Larry Pazder,
225-1900 Richmond Rd.,
Victoria, B.C.

Dear Larry:

re: Michelle Smith

At your request I am trying to recall this patient. She seemed to
get into unusual episodes of poison ingestion. I recall seeing her on 2
or 3 occasions at the hospital emergencies, none of the poisonings
fortunately were serious. It was after the second or third episode however that I wondered about the mother's ability to cope. She was a
kindly but rather ineffectual woman, somewhat overweight, and when
I questioned her, realized that she was having difficulties with alcohol.
Her husband was away much of the time.

I do vaguely recall that Michelle was involved in an accident at
around 5 or 6 years of age for which she was admitted to hospital for
care. I believe this involved a car accident and that Michelle had some

difficulty with smoke inhalation from which she made a satisfactory recovery. I do not remember the details and am sorry that we do not have her old files. I suspect these were water-damaged during storage as I had to throw out a number of boxes of old files on earlier patients a few years ago. The present collection of files do not contain any records on the family.

With kind regards.

Yours most sincerely,

A.E. Gillespie, M.D., F.A.A.P., F.R.C.P.(C)

AEG/ld

appendix 3

DONALD L. POY, B.Sc., D.M.D.
1677 Poplar Street
Victoria, B.C.

November 19, 1979

Dear Dr. L. Pazder:

Re: Michelle Smith

On May, 13, 1978 I saw Michelle Smith presenting with extreme pain localized to the upper left central incisor. The radiograph did not show any periapical changes, however the root canal of the tooth appeared somewhat narrow indicating a degenerative change of the pulpal tissues, quite likely resulting from trauma to the tooth at an earlier age (6–10). On entering the pulp chamber necrotic tissue and odour was encountered. Root canal treatment was started on the tooth.

Yours truly,

Dr. Donald L. Poy

DP/kp

appendix 4

DR. HENRY JACKH, C.R.C.P. (C)
Consultant in Diagnostic Radiology
140 Fort Royal Medical Centre
1900 Richmond Avenue
Victoria, B.C.

Feb. 27, 1978

Patient: Smith, Mrs. Michelle
Referring doctor: Dr. L. Pazder

Report of X-Ray Examination:

Chest, pa and left lateral
The heart, great vessels and diaphragm appear normal.
The lung fields appear clear throughout.

Skull, 3 projections
No osseous abnormalities are demonstrated.
The pituitary fossae and clinoid processes are well calcified and
appear normal.
There is no evidence of any abnormal calcifications within the
cranium.

A. W. Taylor Lee, M.D.

[*305*]

appendix 5

KEMBLE GREENWOOD
645 Fort Street
Victoria, B.C.

September 26, 1977

Dr. L.H. Pazder,
225-1900 Richmond,
Victoria, B.C.

Dear Doctor Pazder:

Re: Mrs. Michelle Smith

Many thanks for referring this patient to me on September 22. This 27-year old woman has developed an acute but quite superficial contact dermatitis involving the back of the left hand and the left arm, and spreading onto the bends of both arms and onto the neck anteriorly in the past two weeks. The condition started on the left hand and left arm, and may well have been aggravated by the use of medicated soaps (Lifebuoy), and also an idiosyncrasy to some fraction of the steroid cream which was applied. However, the appearance was strongly suggestive of some type of vegetation contact initially, and there may also be a photosensitivity element. The right hand is entirely spared, and this is strongly against any form of toxic factor.

She should respond well to the treatment recommended, namely the following:

1. Allenbury's basic soap only for ordinary washing.
2. Savolitie soap flakes only for domestic washing jobs.
3. 1/2 strength Betnovate ointment as a topical application for sparing use when necessary.

I have asked Mrs. Smith to check with me again in ten days.

Yours Sincerely,

KEMBLE GREENWOOD, M.B., F.R.C.P. (C),
F.R.C.P. (ED.)

acknowledgements

*W*E are deeply grateful to the many people who have been so generous with their love and skill in helping us prepare this work. Their trust in us has been a precious gift.

First and foremost, we thank Cheetie Malouin, who has been our steadfast right hand and loyal friend. Cheetie is that rare kind of person who goes only where her heart takes her. We are thankful it led her to us.

We are indebted to those who gave so much of their time to the transcribing of the tape recordings made during the psychiatric sessions: Shirley Cole, Audrey Fraser, Colin Fraser, Peggy Little, Jim Mylord, Terri North, Eileen Ihara, Bea Sheard, Barbara McNulty, Mary Parson, and others.

For their spiritual care and understanding, we thank the Vatican officials who received us, Father Amédée Dupas, Father Leo Robert, Father Joe Jackson, and especially Father Guy Merveille.

We want to convey our appreciation to Dr. Rick Arnot, Dr. Jim Paterson, Dr. Hugh Bacon, and Dr. David Welch.

We thank Dr. Andrew Gillespie, Dr. Kemble Greenwood, Dr. John McCracken, Dr. Don Poy, Dr. Henry Jackh, and Paul Jeune.

The tremendous help and hospitality we have received from our publisher, Thomas Congdon, and his wife, Connie, have touched us deeply. And we are more than thankful to Gretchen Salisbury, a gifted editor and valued friend, for her extraordinary labors.

To an anonymous benefactor, who helped us begin, thank you for hearing.

And our fervent thanks:

to our friends who loved us without knowing anything, especially Ed and Roberta Piotrowitz, Donna Barber, Carol Huddart, Claire Gratton, and Jim and Julie Bowie;

to our families, with much love—Charyl, Archie, Ron, Lillian, Marylyn, Lawrence, Theresa, David, and John, and all those we cannot mention;

to Helen and Stan Pazder, devoted parents who have given so totally;

to Doug, particularly, for his strength and support, for not questioning but trying to understand;

and to Michelle's mother, whom she still loves, and to Ma Mère, for helping her to know that.